Our Magistracy
A Democratic Jewel Beyond Price

John Hosking CBE

WATERSIDE PRESS

Our Magistracy: A Democratic Jewel Beyond Price
John Hosking

ISBN 978-1-909976-75-7 (Hardback)
ISBN 978-1-909976-74-0 (Paperback)
ISBN 978-1-910979-91-4 (Epub E-book)
ISBN 978-1-910979-92-1 (Adobe E-book)

Cover design © 2020 Waterside Press by www.gibgob.com Front cover photograph by kind permission of the Magistrates Association. Photographer Philip Wolmuth: www.philipwolmuth.com

Main UK distributor Gardners Books, 1 Whittle Drive, Eastbourne, East Sussex, BN23 6QH Tel: +44 (0)1323 521777; sales@gardners.com; www.gardners.com

North American distribution Ingram Book Company, One Ingram Blvd, La Vergne, TN 37086, USA. Tel: (+1) 615 793 5000; inquiry@ingramcontent.com

Cataloguing-In-Publication Data A catalogue record for this book can be obtained from the British Library.

e-book *Our Magistracy* is available as an ebook and also to subscribers of Ebrary, Ebsco, Myilibrary and Dawsonera.

Published 2020 by
Waterside Press Ltd
Sherfield Gables
Sherfield on Loddon, Hook
Hampshire RG27 0JG.

Telephone +44(0)1256 882250
Online catalogue WatersidePress.co.uk
Email enquiries@watersidepress.co.uk

Table of Contents

About the author

John Hosking combined a lifetime in business with service as a justice of the peace. Chairman of the Magistrates Association[1] from 1987 to 1990, he is life vice-president of the Kent branch of the association (where he served on the Ashford bench). He has acted as a Deputy Lord Lieutenant and was awarded the CBE in 1990 for services to the magistracy.

Curriculum vitae magistratus

1962–99 Member: Ashford, Channel and East Kent Bench (Chairman 1975–84). 1964–99 Member: Executive Committee, Kent Magistrates Association (KMA) (Chairman 1973–78). 1970–74 Member: Kent Police Authority. 1971–90 Member: Council, Magistrates Association (MA) of England and Wales (Chairman 1987–90, Vice-president 1990–date). 1974–88 Member: Kent Magistrates' Courts Committee (KMCC) (Chairman 1984–88). 1977–89 Member: Lord Chancellor's Advisory Committee on Appointment of JPs. 1980–83 Member: Central Council of MCCs. 1982–88 Member: Home Office Committee on Recording of Police Interviews. 1983–86 Member: Senate of Inns of Court and Bar Disciplinary Tribunal, and of Bar Council's Professional Conduct Committee. 1989–92 Member: Council of Commonwealth Magistrates' and Judges' Association. 1989 Member: Lord Chief Justice's Working Party on Mode of Trial Guidelines. 1991–94 Member: Lord Chancellor's Advisory Committee on Legal Education and Conduct. 1999–2004 Kent Lieutenancy: Liaison with the magistracy. 2001–12 President KMA. 2012-date Life Vice-president KMA.

---

1. The opinions expressed in this book are entirely those of the author, and do not necessarily reflect those of the Magistrates Association.

This book is dedicated to the memory of

Joan Cecily Whitaker BSc (Hort) (1930–2017)

who gave me love, home, children, flowers, music
and companionship for 64 years.

Our Magistracy

Introduction

'The history of insidious encroachment of convenient centralisation shows how politicians and an attendant bureaucracy can enslave and devitalise a nation in the name of efficient administration. Rationalisation is not necessarily improvement. We must restore our national institutions, for it is they that have made us free; removing them leads to national decay'

Benjamin Disraeli (1804–81)

Because our democracy is built on widespread public participation, what happens to the magistracy of England and Wales — one of our greatest institutions — is of immense importance to our nation. In particular, if the lay magistracy's image and role are weakened, so is the structure of our whole democracy. Thus many far-reaching developments, and the manner of their introduction in recent years, should not only cause profound concern among those who cherish our way of life, our tradition of public service, and the institutions that have made us the envy of the civilised world, but should also provide useful lessons for policy-makers of the future.

In the light of subsequent upheavals, it can be said that most of the second half of the twentieth century was relatively a stable and prosperous period for the magistracy. Justices of the peace then controlled much of their own domain and were well-connected with ancillary organizations, such as the Probation Service; new courthouses were built, training and sentencing guidelines were introduced, the number of JPs increased, and a good working relationship existed between benches and their clerks; delays and adjournments were the exception, not the rule.

The wheels started to come off in the 1990s. Following publication of the Le Vay *Scrutiny of Magistrates' Courts*, the magistracy gradually lost powers and influence to civil servants and lawyers, budgets were cut, numerous courthouses closed and benches amalgamated, workloads decreased and JP numbers halved; the symbiosis between magistrates and clerks was broken, delays and adjournments increased, and the concept of local justice was destroyed.

It must be admitted that some of the reforms were justified or inevitable, but many were unnecessary, costly and damaging to the magistracy's status and confidence. As a result, not only has the institution been severely weakened but, unbelievably, its future is being called into question. If the magistracy is to survive as the preferred custodian of our summary jurisdiction, new and secure measures must be adopted to make it less vulnerable to the ravages of ambitious politicians, bonus-driven administrators and invasive lawyers. More must be done to raise the profile of JPs, not as servants of the state, but as free, respected and trusted members of the public; and to provide for more generous recognition and representation, vigorous recruitment, proofing and impact analysis, increased technical support, and extended powers.

The magistracy has proved itself to be a competent, flexible and loyal member of the judicial family, eminently capable of wider responsibilities within the justice system, and should be given the opportunity and encouragement to exercise these. There is evidence of goodwill towards the magistracy, and widespread agreement with many of the views expressed in this book, but government does not yet seem to recognise the urgency which now exists for its future to be given more attention.

This is not a plea for return to an out-dated past; it is an exhortation to safeguard the future of a priceless national asset under modern conditions. The nature of our democratic heritage suggests that it would be foolish to continue under-valuing an institution that has played, and must surely continue to play, a key role in 'making us who we are'. However, there are too many people trying to control the lay magistracy at the moment. It needs to be firmly strengthened and represented in its own right, not condemned to inferior status conditioned only by others.

What more appropriate time can there be for its revitalisation than now, when the nation is debating the abuses and changing nature of our democracy, the law is infiltrating every corner of our lives, control of the magistracy is at issue, and the Magistrates Association is celebrating its centenary?

CHAPTER 1

Winds of Change

'History is not what you thought; it is what you remember'

W C Sellar and R J Yeatman

- A torrent of new laws and reviews
- Illusions of progress
- Centralisation and diversion
- Transformation of courts and benches.

This book reviews some of the most significant changes within and around the criminal justice arena, draws attention to the consequences for the magistracy, and gives examples of inept bureaucracy and misguided policies which have contributed to its reduced status and usefulness. At the same time, the opportunity is taken to remind readers of the magistracy's under-stated qualities, its convenience and adaptability, its cost-effectiveness, the ignorance of its critics, and the importance of continuing popular participation in the justice system. Reference is also made to the ever-changing social and moral climate in which the modern judiciary has to work, the persistent failure to find more successful methods of crime prevention, punishment and treatment, the threat to the lay sector of increased replacement by expensive district judges, and the undeserved praise given to juries when compared with trained justices of the peace (JP)s.

While frequently expressing strong reservations about many of the changes in the summary justice system imposed on them, JPs have continued to maintain and improve their standards, meet training requirements, and keep up attendances — often against the odds. However, they have found themselves increasingly at the mercy of budget cuts, staff short-ages, reduced facilities and many other obstacles over which they no longer have meaningful influence. It has been a disruptive period for them, and much damage has been done to their status by ill-considered reforms. In general, they remain conscientious, adaptable and loyal, but there comes a point beyond which their patience and generosity should no longer be taken for granted. When too much is expected, it shows up in the number of early retirements, inadequate recruitment and loss of confidence.

A brief review of changes during the last 50 years or so may help to explain the decline in the lay magistracy's fortunes, and to suggest why and how the institution must be strengthened in keeping with its role as a key constituent of our democracy.

A torrent of new laws and reviews

None of our great institutions, including the magistracy, have been immune from the relentless changes of the post-war years. In Europe as a whole, this was a period of relative peace at home, interrupted by the 'Cold War' with Russia, the Northern Ireland Troubles, brief Bal-kan hostilities and the Iraq War. The European Economic Community became the European Union, and grew from six nations to nearly 30, some sharing the Euro currency, but all remaining as sovereign states with individual legal systems (at least, for the time being). Apart from the fluctuations of normal domestic politics, governments had to give increasing attention to global problems such as terrorism, climate change and population movements. However, subject to the (sometimes contro-versial) primacy of EU law, the UK legal code in regard to the magistrates' courts remained fundamentally intact; so it was British governments and their legislation that continued to define the principal changes affecting the magistracy, the courts service and the justice system.

Departmental reforms, new legislation and fresh 'initiatives', requir-ing extra work or additional training for clerks and justices, threatened to become particularly onerous during the Blair and Brown govern-ments (1997–2010), when more than 4,300 new laws or regulations were introduced, including: anti-smoking in public houses; anti-hunting of foxes; disturbing a pack of eggs when directed not to by an authorised officer; selling game birds shot on a Sunday; and, in Merchant Shipping Regulations, 'Reporting to the master or other officer in charge of the bridge a door to be closed and locked when it is not in fact closed and locked'. In the first nine years of New Labour, there were no less than 53 Bills connected with criminal justice; most of them contained fresh offences, some of which seemed designed to do no more than criminalise common behaviour. Unfortunately, every new government seems to feel that it must introduce and pass, among others, at least one all-embracing Criminal Justice Act, and this was no exception.

Many of the statutes bore the marks of inadequate forethought, were badly drafted, confusingly 'rolled out' in fragments, and burdened with instruments which allowed for delay, modification and complication of already enacted legislation. The magistracy and its clerks coped remark-ably well with all of these changes; but when the practical results turned out to be far from what Parliament had intended, the courts were criti-cised for unduly lenient decisions. Lack of preparation is bad enough for those who have to work with the immediate consequences, but when compounded by delayed implementation, the normal work of judges and magistrates becomes unnecessarily complicated.

The law and order debate continued to swing between toughness and leniency, which meant that the courts had to adjust to a plethora of new offences and sentencing options. The effects of burgeoning legislation were soon felt, not least in extra training. New laws are more than fine rhetoric; they require detailed conformity to rules and procedures, speci-fied forms and copious record-keeping, provision of information and monitoring of performance.

Government offices, over-staffed with placemen having to justify their existence, produced volumes of useless information about new schemes and re-organizations, without ever confirming whether or not any of them had actually been tested. An official announcement (consisting of 100 words, punctuated by only one full stop) issued in 2007 illustrates the inanity of this period. It referred proudly to 'a new government youth justice unit which merges the responsibilities of the former Ministry of

Justice Youth Justice and Children Unit with those of the Young Offender Education Team of the Offenders' Learning and Skills Unit of the former Department for Education and Skills. This joint approach', it continued, 'aims to contribute to the protection of the public by developing policy and law in relation to children and young people who offend and are at risk of offending and to ensure that children and young people in contact with the criminal justice system achieve all five outcomes of *Every Child Matters'*. It was obviously assumed that the reader was familiar with the Green Paper on this subject, published four years earlier.

One result of the legislative upheaval was a substantial reduction in magisterial powers, leaving a question mark over the concept of summary justice based solely on legally-advised unpaid lay magistrates. Meanwhile, the reforms appeared to have no noticeable effect on the volume of crime. If anything, it probably increased for a time the number of new cases coming before the courts, but it is difficult to be sure of the total result of introducing a large number of prohibitive laws over such a relatively short period. Any increase in the amount of work for the courts was unlikely to have been justified by a reduction in the crimes and behaviour for which the new rules were designed; it merely added to a sense of over-government by a 'nanny state'. The public will not usually support laws for which they cannot see the need, or in the enforcement of which they have no trust.

While government continued to be engaged in the struggle to reduce crime, prison numbers and costs, there was a growing taste for increasing control over lay influence in the courts, without apparently taking into account the effect this would have on the magistracy as a whole; and it is disturbing to realise that this omission caused so little concern in Whitehall. The reduction in magisterial responsibility inevitably led to a general loss of status, respect and localness of JPs. This was made worse by official insensibility, which virtually ignored local conditions, and left little room for concern about the long-term effects of re-organization, the Civil Service rule being that central government policy must be carried out—regardless. Magistrates found themselves more likely to be described in official jargon merely as 'sentencers serving the public by delivering justice to customers', than as 'lay judges administering local justice according to law'. In outward appearance, the basic form of summary jurisdiction may seem to have altered little but, beneath the surface, much was changing. Today, most of us reluctantly have to admit that 'local justice' no longer exists as we used to know it. It has lost much of its original meaning or been abandoned, thus removing one of the magistracy's strongest reasons for existence and success.

Illusions of progress

In the 50 years during which I was associated with the magistracy, we probably witnessed more changes in its courts and their management than during the whole of the previous two centuries. The evidence for this can be found in every branch of the judicial system today. Gradually, administration of the lower courts, the Probation Service and licensing were nationalised and centralised; presentation of cases passed from the police to an immature prosecution service; and justices' clerks, originally meant to be independent legal advisers, were required to become civil servants, with additional administrative responsibilities. At times during and after the Blair government, it appeared as if an indifferent MoJ had come to regard JPs as no more than small cogs in the grand machine of government—no longer independent judicial office holders, but unpaid servants of the state, enrolled in a crusade to 'make our country a safer place in which to live and work'.

Recollections of these years are dominated by a succession of governments and ministers seeking to capture and hold the law-and-order high ground, each promising to tackle crime and anti-social behaviour, and introducing one new initiative after another to toughen punishments while simultaneously trying to prevent courts from sending more people to prison. In general, it is a tale of failure, encouraging endless further attempts to find cheaper but more successful solutions through constant changes of policy. There is nothing new in this; political and official life has been thus for at least 2,000 years. Petronius Arbiter, a Roman Consul of the first century AD, reported that his government tended to meet any situation by re-organizing. 'A wonderful method it can be,' he said, 'for creating the illusion of progress, while producing confusion, inefficiency and demoralisation'.

The formation of the National Offender Management Service (NOMS) in 2004, and the establishment of the MoJ in 2007, are a case in point. After only three years and a cost of over £1bn, the former was merged with the latter, which itself had to be re-organized within a year of its birth. Heralded by the meaningless rhetoric of ministers struggling to restore confidence in a failed system, this grandiose department was created to provide 'joined-up management', 'a sharper focus on key priorities', 'essential savings', 'improved access to justice', 'effective administration' and 'improved relations with the judiciary'. Prisons, probation and community treatment programmes also came under the new ministry's giant umbrella, 'committed to public protection and closer working', with 'delivery responsibilities including courts and tribunals, legal aid, constitutional reform and devolution, democracy and human rights'. Empowered by such an array of hollow promises, the MoJ had assumed a large part of the Home Office's former responsibilities, in addition to those it inherited from the defunct Lord Chancellor's Department. Small wonder that by 2010, the Justice Secretary (Jack Straw MP) found it necessary to announce yet another re-organization, under the presumptuous motto 'Transforming Justice'.

In pursuance of greater efficiency between 1997 and 2010, the MoJ and its predecessors adopted a 'business management' ethos, giving rise to all manner of 'marketing' gimmicks, such as 'customisation' and 'branding', accompanied by slogans and logos. Management theory (widely believed to be inappropriate for much of the public sector, especially the courts service) was in vogue at the time. This was all part of the Labour government's laudable objective to create an 'image' of the national justice system as a 'partner' with the public in tackling the causes of crime as well as crime itself. In support of this 'mission', a stream of expensive glossy publications poured out of the MoJ, to herald the creation of 'a safe, just and democratic society'. However, society and, in particular, its criminal element remained unmoved. Violent crime continued to rise and Crown Courts to be over-worked, while the MoJ persisted in its relentless closure of courthouses and amalgamation of benches.

The MoJ was not the only government department that felt the need to boost its image by profligate spending on political branding and re-branding, glossy publications announcing staff appointments, and 'exciting' new projects using 'fresh skills to drive reform'. Catch-phrases were in fashion. The Home Office was 'Building a safe, just and tolerant society'; the Department for Constitutional Affairs proclaimed 'Justice, rights and democracy'; and the criminal justice system (CJS) itself asserted that it was 'Reducing crime and securing justice', 'Promoting confidence in the CJS', 'Working together for the public', and 'Working together to cut crime and deliver justice'. What a lot of nonsense! Every time a ministry or department changed its name, the whole costly process of re-branding had to be undertaken. Far from promoting confidence, these extravagant demonstrations of bureaucratic hubris made the justice system look like a market stall-holder selling worthless souvenirs. Norman Fairclough in his book *New Labour, New Language?* summed this up when he wrote, 'Government tends to act like a corporation treating the public as its customers rather than its citizens'.

At about the same time, John Humphrys in *Lost for Words* was describing the common use by officialdom of 'hurrah' and 'boo' words. He explained how modern governments, imitating commercial advertisers, use (and misuse) repetitive words and meaningless phrases to manipulate the public into believing that all good things are being fostered, and all bad are being vigorously confronted. 'Justice', 'democracy' and 'freedom', were scattered around so as to mean everything and nothing, while random use was made of phrases such as 'delivering justice', 'social justice' and 'social democracy'. Such labels are designed for image, not for meaning.

Claims were made by government that it was advancing the cause of justice, supporting the police or championing victims, but mottos and slogans were never likely to have the slightest effect on the work of the courts, the level of crime or the public's appreciation. If anything, society became more violent and less trustworthy, while a new tyranny—'political correctness'—entered the arena. How long will it be before someone in Whitehall dreams up a hollow campaign for 'modernising' our concept of justice? No-one can argue against the case for decency, honesty and fairness, but the nauseating thing is the way in which governments strive to give the impression that by 're-inventing the wheel' they have discovered a new and superior brand of justice.

A continuous increase in the volume of crime, especially in youth and motoring offences, accompanied by a mass of new legislation, led initially to an expansion of the courts estate and the services needed to support it. Later, the figures appeared to decline slightly, remaining nevertheless at an unacceptably high level. Much of this can be attributed to unprecedented increases in the use of the motor car, alcohol and drugs, violence, anti-social behaviour, the introduction of foreign cultures and the breakdown of family life. At the same time, the whole process of law, punishment and treatment has grown more complicated and costly. As a result, adjournments and delays have become endemic. In reaction to this, the government in 2006 introduced yet another initiative to speed up judicial process — CJSSS (Criminal Justice: Simple, Speedy, Summary).

New courthouses and procedural improvements, such as CJSSS and the removal of 'old-style' committals, were welcome. Improvements were made in such areas as the time taken from charge to trial, the level of guilty pleas received at first hearing, and the number of adjournments. But, taking the courts service as a whole, there is little to suggest that the billions of pounds spent on re-organization have yet produced the net gain in efficiency, cost-saving and justice that was claimed for them originally. No-one will stop to measure this, but any forecast savings on the one hand have almost certainly been more than wiped out on the other by increases in executive staff, consultants, red tape, extra travel and new causes of delay. Too many major changes have been proposed and undertaken without proper costings or assessment, and often for no better reason than superficial, short-term financial and administrative expediency.

Centralisation and diversion

By the turn of the century, it seemed that more offenders were having to be dealt with at greater length by more magistrates, travelling further to sit in fewer places. The cowardly response of government to the new problems it had created was to allow an enormous increase in diversion from the courts by encouraging the police, not only to use more cautions and fixed penalties, but also to allow the accreditation of bouncers, snoopers and other petty officials armed with quasi-judicial powers and the freedom to spy, fine, direct and punish on behalf of the police, without recourse to the courts — a boost for government-controlled officialdom, but a set-back for independent local adjudication. One of the disturbing consequences of this shift of power, away from the police and an impartial magistracy to a new, paid enforcement class, is to increase the risk of corruption and the number of cases going to the Crown Court.

Because governments have been known to manipulate crime statistics for political reasons, the public have little confidence in the figures they are given. Changes in classification or policing practice prevent fair comparisons, but there is no doubt that the decrease in arrests and charges have significantly reduced the need for formal courts. Contraction in the number of courts, sittings, magistrates and staff have followed, although business in the family courts may appear to have bucked this trend.

Diversion may be considered a preferable way of applying penalties for minor crimes or misdemeanours, but it is not unqualified 'justice'. It allows the police, and others untrained in judicial decision-making, to act unilaterally as prosecutor, judge and jury. Granting extra powers to car park and night club attendants inflates the authority of executives, while the impartial administration of the rule of law is diminished. There are obvious advantages, but these may be outweighed by more arbitrary and inconsistent decisions — not forgetting that many of the diverted offenders end up in the courts anyway. Although diversion may have a place in the system, it should not be allowed to subvert the law by regulation based on convenience.

Centralisation and diversion cut the heart out of local justice administration, affected all aspects of magisterial involvement, and caused much loss of morale among JPs. Part of the increased failure among newly-appointed magistrates to meet their basic obligations arose from this cause. In 2009, the Kent Magistrates' Area Training Committee reported that non-compliance with minimum attendance requirements by new JPs had reached a worrying 20 per cent in the county; but, absurdly, applicants could not be warned officially about the consequences of poor attendance until the centrally-published Directions were reprinted several years later. Even the wording of standard letters was dictated from London—not infrequently by civil servants, some of whom were apparently so poorly educated as to be unaware of the difference between 'principal' and 'principle' or 'licence' and 'license'.

Among the many consequences of central bureaucracy's triumph over local, voluntary administration is reduced magisterial independence, difficulties with recruitment and retention of JPs, and longer travelling distances for all concerned. Local managers—who could at one time make quick and effective decisions—are neutralised by delayed rulings made elsewhere and discouraged from doing anything that might endanger financial incentives. With 'bottom-up' having been replaced by 'top-down' administration, the former cohesion between magistrates, clerks, staff and local authorities has been broken. Today, many of the people with whom the magistracy is obliged to work (e.g. Courts and Tribunals Service and Criminal Justice Boards) seem to be 'on the other side', operating and saying things that are sometimes quite hostile to those whom they previously served.

Extensive re-organization was expensive and damaging, not only for the magistracy and local justice, but also for the nation and local government. Its cause was not proven magisterial incompetence (as was the case in the sixteenth and nineteenth centuries), but the lure of administrative convenience and the myth that centralised professional management is superior and cheaper. Experience from these years, however, now shows that dispersed—but monitored—power can be more efficient and is, on balance, preferable to concentrated authority. But when will government be prepared to acknowledge this, and to reconsider the advantages of devolution in the magistrates' courts?

Among schemes for simplifying and speeding-up the legal process was the introduction of 'virtual' courts ('virtual', according to the dictionary:

'almost or nearly the thing described'). These were aimed particularly, it was said, 'at improving the service given to victims and witnesses', by enabling them to remain in a local police station while 'attending' for the first hearing in a magistrates' court by video-link. Those who claim that courts are too intimidatory, and that witnesses are deterred from giving evidence in them, naturally welcomed this innovation. However, apart perhaps from the police and Prison Service, the idea seems not to have proved widely popular elsewhere so far. From the magistrates' point of view, this may be because the authority of the court is put at risk, especially if the offender at one end of the process chooses to commit acts of contempt to which the justices at a distance are powerless to give effective response. Pilot schemes have indicated that costs may be greater than savings and no time saved, but it would seem that there is a case to be made for their retention on a limited scale, particularly for first appearances and the avoidance of attendance for repeated remands.

Transformation of courts and benches

Quarter Sessions finally came to an end in 1972 and were replaced by the Crown Courts, allowing continued participation by JPs. By about 1995, 'cash limiting' had already become central government's chief weapon for controlling local management. The magistracy and its courts became just another item in the national budget. Everything from retiring-room coffee to the cost of training came under scrutiny. Almost nothing could happen without the approval of the Home Office (HO) or the Lord Chancellor's Department (LCD), both of which were subject ultimately to the dead hand of the Treasury.

Nationally, administration of the magistrates' courts had developed piecemeal and locally before World War II. After the war, the Roche Committee recommended the establishment of independent Magistrates' Courts Committees (MCCs) to manage them, based on county, borough and petty sessional divisions, overseen nationally by the HO on the penal and estate side, and the LCD on the judicial side. The 1949 Justices of the Peace Act implemented the Roche recommendations. MCCs, composed mostly of JPs representing the local benches plus a few *ex officio* members, were usually managed by a small number of local authority staff. Among the committees' most important responsibilities were the appointment of justices' clerks, the training of JPs and the provision of court facilities. Funding was split between the HO (80 per cent) and the local authority (20 per cent), giving the latter a major interest in the justice system. The 1949 Act deliberately intended that administration of the magistrates' courts should remain local and retain a large degree of autonomy, and they enjoyed this position for over 50 years. At this time, the magistracy also had considerable authority for the Probation Service in the counties, and numerous JPs were members of Boards of Prison Visitors and Police Authorities.

Dismantling of the old MCC system was accelerated after the 1989 Le Vay scrutiny, the 1994 Police and Magistrates' Courts Act and the 2001 Auld Report, with every major change making the next one more inevitable. By 1997, 105 MCCs had been reduced to 42; but even these were gradually starved to death by cash limiting, making it easier to claim legitimacy later on for central government control. The Courts Act 2003 finally abolished MCCs entirely, and created Her Majesty's Courts Service (HMCS) (later HM Courts and Tribunals Service) whose responsibility included the Crown Courts. Since then, dozens more courthouses have been closed and benches amalgamated.

The passing of the Courts Act in 2003 will go down in history as the point at which local justice (as we used to know it), and lay participation in its administration, were finally abandoned. Some prescient notes on the Act issued by the Magistrates Association give a taste of how this landmark was viewed at the time:

- Close local associations will be severed or substantially curtailed; local infrastructures will be destroyed
- Local involvement in court management is essential; proposed management bodies and consultative councils will be impotent and insufficiently representative of the lay magistracy
- There are no guarantees or safeguards against further centralisation

- Extended travelling distances due to court closures will undermine local justice and have a negative effect on recruitment and retention of magistrates
- It is proposed that the Supplemental List (i.e. of retired magistrates) be abolished; it should be retained
- It is important that not only are lay justices consulted before a district judge is appointed or assigned to a local area, but also that every effort should first be made to recruit more JPs
- Judicial powers must remain with magistrates, and not be transferred to justices' clerks or fines officers
- Serious concern that non-involvement of magistrates in the appointment of justices' clerks, and their new Civil Service status, will destroy the 'special relationship' and threaten the clerks' independence.

It is almost unnecessary to point out that, although all these statements proved well-founded, the majority went unheeded or were rendered worthless by those who were determined to drive through the changes. Nevertheless, several newspaper commentators expressed surprise at the magistracy's 'sleepy' reaction to it; one of them, referring to the huge implications of the proposals, asked, 'Why aren't the country's magistrates taking to the streets'?

The so-called 'police courts' of the past had become unpopular at a time when it was felt no longer appropriate for prosecution of offenders to be carried out by the same people as those responsible for apprehending them. So, in 1985, the Crown Prosecution Service (CPS) came into being. This effectively created an extra legal and administrative layer between the police and the courts, causing several years of bickering and misunderstanding between the police and CPS (at one time, it was said that in some areas they were barely talking to each other). One regrettable result of this — over which the magistracy had little or no control, but sometimes got the blame — was a further increase in the average time taken for cases to be completed.

When I joined the Ashford Bench in 1962, urban and rural areas were still divided into petty sessional divisions (PSDs) with their respective courthouses; in Kent, there were more than 20 county and borough benches at that time. In the boroughs, many courts were still being held in picturesque, but unsuitable, town halls, and small rural benches with less than a dozen magistrates were not uncommon. By 2012, only three benches, eight courthouses and one justices' clerk remained in Kent, a county of 1½ million people. The Ashford Bench and court have long since been amalgamated with others in the east of the county and, although only about 30 years old, its comparatively modern courthouse was closed in 2011.

The Ashford PSD embraced a medium-sized market and railway town, together with the small borough of Tenterden and a large rural hinterland. The courthouse, like many others in the country, was an integral part of a Victorian town-centre police station, where facilities (including cells) were fairly basic but functional. The workload was a typical mixture of urban and rural cases, comfortably managed by 15 to 18 magistrates, a local solicitor acting as a part-time justices' clerk, and two or three office staff. The usual court of seven JPs (reduced to three a few years later) sat once a week on Thursday mornings, starting at 10.30, and was usually over by lunch time. A juvenile (youth) court and a domestic (family) court met less frequently, and there was a divisional Licensing Committee and Probation (Case) Committee.

Cases rarely included drugs, but lonely middle-aged male 'regulars', charged with drunkenness, featured in most lists; they were a very different breed from the gangs of drink-fuelled, anti-social young men and women of today. In rural areas, the morning's agenda also included the occasional poacher or 'trespasser in pursuit of conies' (rabbits). Almost all the offenders were prosecuted by a police inspector, and a constable acted as both usher and gaoler. The inspector was later replaced by a police solicitor, and the constable by a civilian security person, so that uniformed officers became quite a rare sight in the courtroom. One result of this was that some magistrates feared for their safety when attending court, but it has to be admitted that there have actually been few notable security incidents since then.

At most hearings, representatives of the Probation Service and local newspaper attended, but these days such organizations cannot afford to have their staff sitting for hours in court without good reason. If police or reporters are seen in court now, it usually indicates the possibility of trouble, a good story for the press, or both.

About a third of the bench were women (without hats and gloves by then), but the ratio soon reached about 50:50, and has remained so. The chairman and deputy chairman of the bench were elected or re-elected annually by secret ballot, although there was no limit to the number of years during which they could hold office (today, it is restricted to three years). The chairman presided in the adult court almost every week; the remainder of the bench sat fortnightly. They were suitably 'diverse' (for those days), and included farmers, retired service officers, school teachers, housewives, council employees, railway staff, shop-keepers, postmen, and four local authority chairmen who were still *ex-officio* JPs at that time. The minimum sitting requirement was 26 half days per year or once a fortnight. Compulsory training for JPs was introduced in 1966.

Sentencing was comparatively simple. There were only five alternatives: fine, probation, prison, conditional discharge or absolute discharge. The fine was by far the most common punishment. The power to bind-over to 'keep the peace' was also found to be useful on quite a few occasions. In the juvenile court (if my memory serves me right), the choice was between fine, probation, attendance centre and borstal (which was then the prison for young offenders).

Courts cancelled due to absent defendants or witnesses, lack of staff or non-arrival of case papers were virtually unheard of, and adjournments used to be rare. Now, all these are quite common. The term 'cracked' (referring to a trial when time is wasted on the date allocated because the defendant pleads guilty at the last minute, or the prosecution offers no evidence) was not in the magisterial lexicon. 'Ineffective' trials (requiring adjournment, due to delayed action or inaction by one or other parties concerned) were also much less frequent than today. If such a colossal wastage of time could be avoided in the 1960s, it is difficult to comprehend why combined cracked and ineffective trials can amount to more than 50 per cent of those listed to take place in many magistrates' courts 60 years later.

The problem of delay between charge and completion, although lessened in recent years, remains a source of concern. One of the results is that magistrates now spend more time than ever in their retiring rooms, not making decisions, but waiting for others to organize themselves. This is not only wasteful but frustrating, particularly for busy magistrates who give up valuable time to sit in court. All too often such inefficiency leads to premature retirement from the bench of the best JPs—something the magistracy and the country can ill afford.

Recollections of my bench and others in Kent during the 1960s and 1970s, are probably typical of the circumstances in most English and Welsh counties at that time. Relatively, everything seemed so stable in those days, with JPs, a few stipendiaries and the clerks adequately controlling most parts of the system. There was little to suggest the extent of the transformation that would take place during the following 30 years.

Although it would be misleading to claim that the magistracy's former administration of its own affairs was ideal, politicians, lawyers and bureaucrats must take the lion's share of blame for the continuing problems in the courts service. Between them, they have done more than anyone to undermine the work and status of JPs and to destroy the concept of local justice. They have generated successive tides of change—many of them unwarranted—to which the magistracy has been unable to find effective response, even though it has probably been less deserving of criticism and less in need of wholesale re-organization than at any time in its long history. Moreover, when they could have done otherwise, the reformers have invariably chosen options for change that have weakened rather than strengthened the magistracy and its authority. Any gains from the growth of centralised bureaucracy or economies of scale are hard to identify, but the damage to the magistracy as a national and local institution is manifest.

CHAPTER 2

JPs in Recession

'Quem Juppiter vult perdere dementat prius'
(Those whom God wishes to destroy, he first drives mad)

James Duport (1606–79)

- Independence under threat
- Reduced power, influence and status
- Local justice abandoned

The status of the magistracy in England and Wales has been noticeably bruised by much of the legislation passed during the last 30 years or so, not least that which followed the 1989 *Scrutiny of the Magistrates Courts*, the 2000 Auld Report on the Criminal Courts, and the 2003 Licensing Act. In the process, it has also been subjected to a wave of centralising bureaucracy under which major decisions, including those affecting the quality of justice, were influenced by national targets, performance and budgets—certainly not by any consideration for the effects on local justice or the institution itself.

As early as the 1970s, the Law Society, the Justices' Clerks' Society (JCS), and even the Magistrates Association (MA), were beginning to talk about more integrated (as distinct from centralised) administration, but it is misleading to suggest that the MA had joined in proposing the wholesale centralisation of courts management. It was acknowledged that there was scope for further re-organization in the courts system, but the magistracy preferred to follow politician Edmund Burke (1729–97) in advocating that, when dealing with traditional institutions of state, change should take place gradually, rather than radically; it never visualised the extent to which the reforms were eventually taken, nor the negative effects they would have.

Independence under threat

It can now be seen that magisterial recession actually began when the JCS — representing in those days 300 lawyers on whom JPs relied for loyal support, administration and legal advice — 'broke ranks' in 1989. Without appearing to consult the magistracy, but with tacit encouragement from the Home Office, the clerks produced their own 'blueprint' for re-organization of the magistrates' courts. Publication of the document was quickly followed by an announcement from the Home Secretary (Douglas Hurd) that he had asked civil servant Julian Le Vay to conduct an 'efficiency scrutiny', the final consequences of which reflected many of the JCS views.

Naturally, the clerks declined to comment on the coincidence of timing, but their colleagues in the Law Society found their proposals 'disturbing'. The magistracy's public reaction was muted at first, the MA saying merely that it would not respond until full details of the government's plans were published; but privately, many JPs, while agreeing with some of the ideas, were quite taken aback by the perfidy of some of those on whose goodwill they had relied for so long. Lack of enthusiasm among magistrates was hardly surprising, for many of the proposals appeared to be based on the self-interest of the clerks themselves, rather than the wider benefit of the courts; they included a big increase in the number of stipendiary magistrates, the merger of more than 100 benches, new judicial powers for the clerks, an inspectorate, re-organization of court areas, better training and a more uniform career structure for assistant clerks and courts staff.

While Le Vay's principal recommendation was that the magistrates' courts should be run as a national service funded entirely by central government, he also added — significantly — that this should still 'allow maximum delegation of managerial responsibility and control of resources at the local level'. However, alarm bells began to ring when the Home Secretary later announced that he was studying proposals to bring administration of all courts under central control, prompting increased magisterial opposition to the apparent expansion of Le Vay's proposals. The government was persuaded to rethink for a while, and to consider three suggested alternatives; but of these, only one, in which the service would be run by a board that included magistrates, was remotely acceptable to the MA. Incredibly, this was eventually rejected on grounds of expense; but the damage had already been done, and the magistracy on its own was by then in no position to stop the combined force of reformers, centralisers and critics of amateurism from continuing to create some of the administrative blunders described elsewhere in this book.

Although the MA acknowledged that there was room for improvement, it always felt that the scrutiny proposals went too far—a fear which, with the benefit of hindsight, can be seen to have been fully justified. The main concern at the time was not so much the huge future cost, which was reason enough to raise serious objection, but the threat to the financial and judicial independence of the magistracy.

Following the MA's October 1989 Annual Meeting in the London Guildhall at which, as chairman, I voiced JPs' growing apprehension, the *Law Society Gazette* quoted me as saying:

> 'Unless far greater magisterial influence and statutory safeguards than envisaged are introduced, it would be impossible to convince magistrates that their independence is not being put at risk. Mr Le Vay is so concerned with questions of accountability, professional management and value for money that he seemed unwilling to give due weight to the expertise possessed by many magistrates, and failed to appreciate the uniqueness of the relationship between magistrates and clerks. The scrutiny is being used as an exit from a system beset with inter-agency problems, staff shortages, court closures, lack of money and chronic delay, over all of which the magistracy has little control'.

A motion, passed unanimously at the meeting, criticised the government's 'lack of commitment to providing proper resources to enable the lay magistracy to maintain its independent judicial role'. Headlines on the following day included: 'Magistrates fight radical reform for court funding' (*The Times*), 'We're facing crisis in court say magistrates' (*Daily Mail*), and 'Magistrates fear threat to their independence' (*Independent*).

The Lord Chancellor's assumption of responsibility for administration of the magistrates' courts in 1992 was followed two years later by the Police and Magistrates' Courts Act, which provided for amalgamation of Magistrates' Courts Committees (MCCs), the appointment of suitably qualified chief executives, the setting of performance standards and the creation of an inspectorate (which proved to be useless).

When the government eventually published the Le Vay *Scrutiny of the Magistrates' Courts,* the MA declared that, after centuries of managing its own affairs, it believed that the independence of the magistracy was threatened by the proposals. The county councils supported the MA in opposing them and, after more than 25 years of relentless mismanagement driven by 'efficiency and effectiveness', it now looks as if both of them were right to do so.

At first sight the scrutiny was mostly about funding, but it was much more than that. A series of subsequent disruptive measures finally ended magistrates' control of their own and other organizations at the heart of the justice system. MCCs, Prison Visitor Committees and Police Authorities (plus, later on, Licensing Committees) were eventually abolished, as were the magistracy's direct links with the Probation Service. New appointments to the bench was the only area in which positive magisterial influence was retained; but even there, the Lord Chancellor found opportunities increasingly to regulate the work of local advisory committees, of which a third of the membership became reserved for non-magistrates. The MA itself was also considerably affected by the changes, not least the loss of its leading role in training and, eventually, a 50 per cent fall in membership due to resignations from the bench and reduced work-load. Various ancillary duties formerly undertaken voluntarily and successfully by magistrates without remuneration were transferred, in one way or another, to salaried executives. Although there have been few signs of an increase in efficiency following these changes, the additional cost to the nation is now obvious. Yes, of course some aspects were changed for the better—but usually at substantial extra expense.

The arrival of a Labour government in 1997 revealed an arrogant disdain among some of its members for established institutions, and brought about a frenzied period of further reform of the courts service, driven by management theory. This included reduction of MCCs in compliance with the decision to make them, the Probation Service and the Crown Prosecution Service (CPS) co-terminous with the areas already fixed for the police by the 1972 Local Government Act. In announcing to the House of Lords his plans for re-organization of the magistrates' courts, Lord Chancellor Irvine said, 'We have no plans for a replacement of the lay magistracy with stipendiary magistrates ... I want to make it plain that this is not about losing local courts ... I am not planning mindlessly to sweep away tradition ... there is much that is good about our current arrangements, not least the involvement of intelligent, committed volunteers as magistrates ... I am committed to local justice'. Within eight years, and under the same government, these plans had resulted in a huge increase of district judges (formerly stipes), while dozens more courts, efficient working arrangements, dedicated volunteers and much local justice were swept away for good. Never rely on politicians who say they 'have no plans'.

In outward appearance, the operation of the magistrates' courts and estate may not seem to have changed much. Layouts and procedures, at least in the adult criminal courts, have remained more or less the same, although the dock in most courtrooms has had to be modified in response to the increase in violent criminals and lack of attendant police, and a few of the more tedious procedures have been abolished or refined. Three JPs became the normal complement of a magistrates' court by the end of the 1960s, and the use of permanent district judges (DJs) sitting alone was extended to all areas by 2010. The clerk or legal adviser has of course remained until now, as have ushers and probation officers, but police prosecutors were gradually replaced by CPS lawyers from 1986 onwards. Unless acting as witnesses, uniformed police officers disappeared from the court scene, and local newspaper reporters are now rarely present. Courthouses without secure cells of the required standard were among the closures; on the other hand, much was done in the newer buildings to improve facilities for witnesses and other members of the public.

Behind the scenes, a muted revolution and struggle for control of the courts took place, propelled by a combination of financial cuts, political pressure, target-driven bureaucracy and executive convenience. While the senior judiciary was able to retain some control over its courts, the magistracy ceded the remnants of its administrative power to the civil servants of HM Courts and Tribunals Service, and liquor licensing was finally surrendered to local authorities in 2005; even more courthouses were closed, dozens of benches amalgamated, and countless cases were diverted from the courts, while unpaid fines and alcohol-related crimes soared. Gone were the days of weekly courts, part-time clerks, set agendas and uninterrupted process. It was, and remains, an uncomfortable time for JPs; however, without their loyalty and adaptability, it would have been an even more disruptive period for the justice system.

It is interesting to recall that Lord Justice Auld, in his 2000 review of the criminal courts, recommended *inter alia* the creation of middle-tier district judge courts, which fortunately the government did not accept. It would almost certainly have reduced lay magistrates' powers even further and caused yet more resignations, unless such courts could have included JPs, and be used to take the most serious either-way cases at present confined to the over-burdened Crown Court (See page 90 and page 114).

Reduced power, influence and status

Magistrates have been aware for the last 20 years or so that official respect for their authority has been waning. They have continued to sound alarms (see, e.g. my letter to the *The Times* on *page 217*), but successive regimes have taken little heed. In 1997, the MA issued a briefing paper in which it expressed extreme anxiety that 'judicial functions are increasingly compromised for reasons of administrative expediency', and that 'the service is now close to the point where there are no more efficiency savings to be made without seriously harming its essential nature'. Nevertheless, retrenchment continued. More than 20 years later, the regrettable results of ignoring these concerns are all too evident. Administrative independence had been surrendered to an expensive centralised bureaucracy run by indifferent civil servants and, after the replacement of the Lord Chancellor's Department by the new MoJ in 2007, management of its judicial functions had largely been delegated to compliant presiding judges acting as spokesmen for the government justice minister.

The unique willingness and ability of JPs to provide an inexpensive, local service remains a neglected national asset. Having done everything asked of them—and more—some would say that JPs have deserved better than to discover that the foundations of their institution have been undermined by the actions of the very nation that pioneered lay participation in local justice; others will have noted how lukewarm has been the support of the senior judiciary for the magistracy in its 'hour of need'.

From being the principals in control of their own courts, training and licensing, along with their former substantial involvement in the Probation Service, prison boards and police authorities, JPs are now barely, or not at all, concerned with these responsibilities and duties. Only vestiges of their dominion, such as advisory committees on the appointment of JPs, remain—a situation not unlike that of doctors and surgeons in the NHS. This withdrawal had little or nothing to do with failure or inefficiency on their part, but everything to do with the ambitions of politicians and civil servants, bent on reducing the level of 'amateur' connection with administration, cutting costs and extending central government control and influence over all aspects of public life. In this transformation, the intrinsic value of the magistracy to the nation and democratic justice were disregarded, and JPs found themselves relegated to the side lines—both administratively and judicially. Today, police, CPS, social workers, victims, and even the criminals are more likely to receive sympathetic national attention and support than the magistracy.

In spite of a long and well-argued campaign against transfer, and for reasons which still remain unclear, the responsibility for liquor licensing was handed over to local authority committees in 2003, where decisions can be made once again out of public view. Although it is claimed that young people are now inclined to drink less, under-age drinking and alcohol-related crimes continue to flourish, and effective control of intoxicant sales is almost non-existent. A rarely-used appeal role for the magistracy is the only crumb left for those who had fought so hard to retain the licensing jurisdiction.

Retention of significant magisterial involvement may have been on the agenda at one time, but in the end political backing for this was not sustained or strong enough. Thus, within the space of a few years, the magistracy lost its formal association with the Probation Service (2001), liquor licensing (2003) and courts committees (2005). Continuing fears about loss of judicial independence and weakening of the relationship between JPs and their executives, forced the creation of new Justices' Issues Groups and Area Justice Forums, but these had a short life. Only in the JIGs did the magistrates retained a majority, and even that was at times inadequate to counter the combined power of area directors, justices' clerks and district judges, backed by co-operative members of the senior judiciary.

The loss of many of its former responsibilities has of course contributed to the magistracy's lowered status. This in turn has emboldened some of the ancillary agencies, bundled into ineffective new bodies such as the government-controlled Criminal Justice Boards, to criticise JPs unfairly at a time when the failings of their own organizations remain the cause of most of the ills, such as delays and cracked trials which, in spite of improvements, continue to beset the CJS.

Modern magistrates are better trained and equipped to perform efficient justice than ever before, yet the obstacles preventing them from fulfilling this have been allowed to grow. Indeed, the magistracy has been rendered generally impotent in attempting to arrest the constant removal of its traditional responsibilities. Today, it seems that as long as official and financial targets are met, it doesn't matter if it and the concept of tribunal justice are destroyed and replaced in the process. Compared with the substantial administrative responsibilities taken away in previous centuries, their removal in recent times may look insignificant; but there is not much now left from which to take more. The ascendancy of bureaucracy, professionalism and so-called business methods has been relentless. It is ironic that, at a time when so much is being done to encourage the greater involvement of people in their own governance, we now seem unsure about lay participation in the justice system. But it has to be remembered that—even if the result of change is less effi-ciency and more expense—politicians dislike surrendering power or providing money to those over whom they lack total control. They prefer that everyone should be elected and accountable to Parliament, where they can subject them to the increasingly harsh tone of public scrutiny, debate and accountability.

At the same time, a combination of default, carelessness and indif-ference have devalued lay justice as a whole. In the pursuit of fanciful efficiency, a priceless component of the country's judicial resource has been depleted, and a unique tradition of voluntary, summary justice has been needlessly abused by the cavalier demands of central govern-ment. Some of the changes were inevitable or necessary; but others were ill-conceived and needless. Many of them appear to have increased the overall cost of the CJS, without adding anything of value to the quality of justice or service to the public—in many instances, quite the reverse.

Following the removal of magistrates and their clerks from the main positions of authority in running the courts, not only have costs soared, but the gap between JPs and administrators has widened, with less than congenial results. Disrespectful civil servants have even had to be reminded occasionally that magistrates are still independent members of the judiciary, not junior staff answerable to the courts service direc-torate. The lack of understanding and regard for magistrates and their role, frequently shown by itinerant senior administrators, led one Kent JP in 2011 to go as far as to suggest that 'magistrates now fall somewhere between paperclips and toilet paper in the courts service's list of priori-ties'. Subtle dilutions in the status of JPs have also taken place elsewhere; for instance in the extended classes of people now permitted to witness signatures and statements. A bank officer—young or old—or 'person of similar standing' (whoever that may be) can countersign an application for a shot-gun certificate, but an experienced JP over 70 or on the Sup-plemental List is apparently no longer deemed to be of sufficient standing.

Waiting precedence is a further example. While it is in the nature of the court process that everyone cannot be fully engaged at the same time, it was accepted formerly that if anybody had to be kept waiting, JPs should be the last. Fifty years ago, courts were organized with the convenience of the magistrates—as busy people, giving their time for free—foremost in mind. Then it started to be said that the police service could not afford to have officers standing around waiting to give evidence, while magistrates were costing virtually nothing. So, the argument ran, if one or the other had to remain idle, at least it should not be the police; it did not seem to matter that many magistrates were giving up equally valuable time and income to serve on the bench. Meanwhile, several other agencies began to claim precedence or to excuse themselves from being ready on time, giving the impression that the court and the magistrates can wait on their convenience—and their inefficiency. JPs, it seems, are now expected to sit in frustration while duty solicitors plead for more time, prison vans arrived late, and barristers demand extra opportunity to speak to defendants. Magistrates can sit in their retiring rooms, sipping coffee while everyone else is allowed to hold up the system—a situation far less likely when the magistracy had more control over its own organization and proceedings. It has to be accepted that it is impossible to accommodate the preferences of all parties and, inevitably, someone has to wait some of the time. But there is no justification for assuming that magistrates' time and convenience are any less important or expensive than others'.

Today, it is sometimes difficult to avoid the impression that witnesses and victims are the ones to be least discomforted—perhaps because they cannot otherwise be persuaded to give the evidence on which the success of prosecutions so much depends—while the magistrates are expected to do the waiting (tempting us perhaps to amend a word of John Milton's poem on *His Blindness* to read 'They also serve who only *sit* and waite').

An illustration of this new 'order of precedence' may be found in a MoJ publication, in which a 'cracked' trial is defined as 'time allocated (that) has been wasted and witnesses unnecessarily inconvenienced'. Not a word about the cost or inconvenience to magistrates. It may not seem to matter if they are kept waiting, but today prolonged absence from their work may be expensive, if not ruinous, for themselves and their employers. The unpaid status of JPs should attract more respect, not less. Inevitably, the longer that busy justices spend waiting, the more frustrated they become and the more likely they are to resign from the bench prematurely. The magistracy can ill afford to lose some of its youngest, trained and most intelligent members in this unnecessary and wasteful way.

Time also became a factor in the discontinuance of regular sittings by magistrates in the Crown Court. As the workload in these increased, JPs found it more difficult to provide reliable attendance, especially for trials lasting more than a day; fewer and fewer of them were able to take advantage of the much valued experience of sitting with judges in a higher court, and the judges themselves were becoming less and less keen on the arrangement. Eventually, the practice was significantly curtailed by the Supreme Court Act 1981, which limited magistrates' involvement in the Crown Court to appeals and committals for sentence.

An additional sphere from which the magistracy has been forced to retreat is police authorities. Until they were abolished in 2012 to make way for single elected commissioners, these bodies were composed of nine county council members and eight independents, of whom three were JPs. The magistracy's connection with police administration goes back a great many years, but that remote relationship was becoming increasingly difficult to maintain in the face of a growing feeling that magisterial integrity could be compromised. In many areas, one of the JPs was the chairman of the authority—a neutral position for which they were well qualified—but it cannot be denied that this sometimes threatened to involve them in party political conflict.

Outside the adult criminal courts, only two important areas remain in which the magistracy has retained a significant role: the family court and the local advisory committees for the appointment of new JPs. At one time even these were seriously under threat from the reformers. A long tussle had to be fought against the claims of the county court for the retention of a substantial share in family jurisdiction, while the advisory committees had to resist numerous attempts by government departments to interfere in the selection process.

The modern magistracy has to work within a volatile culture, where the attraction of public service struggles to compete with the personal need of most JPs to earn a living, without the compensating status accorded in former times. Furthermore, respect for authority can no longer be taken for granted, due to the changed social climate in which discipline and decisions must all be challenged; in which leaders are expected to be compassionate at all times; in which elders defer to the young; in which the wise and experienced are derided as 'out of touch'; in which the law-abiding are subject to abuse and violence; in which criticism is rejected out of hand; and in which sound advice is ignored, while those who try to set a good example are vilified or ridiculed.

Formerly, JPs could regard themselves as independent members of the public appointed for the honourable purpose of 'keeping the peace' and deciding fairness on behalf of fellow citizens. Now, it seems that government direction and 'political correctness' are more likely to describe them as unpaid 'problem-solvers' and 'sentencers', dispensing treatment to recalcitrant 'clients'. This suggests a subtle transformation from magistrates administering justice under law to that of social services officers handing out means-tested 'benefits' under health and welfare to a range of so-called 'stakeholders'.

Local justice abandoned

The 1992 White Paper, *A New Framework for Local Justice,* and the Police and Magistrates' Court Act 1994 expressed the government's intention to provide 'clearer lines of accountability', a 'guarantee of judicial independence' for JPs and their legal advisers, and 'improvements in the efficiency and effectiveness of the courts service'; all apparently reasonable objectives to which JPs could not take exception. At that point, MCCs were still to be kept in being, although the Lord Chancellor wanted to be given substantially more control over their operation and composition. However, during debate on the Bill, many unforeseen objections arose and, although the government was forced to climb down on a number of its proposals, the centralising theme remained intact; the only real concession—albeit an important one—was in regard to judicial independence. In the event, the Act came to be regarded as an ominous piece of legislation which marked the beginning of the end of lay participation in the management of the magistrates' courts—and, actually, the demise of local justice as formerly understood.

Occasional reformation is necessary in any organization, but it is difficult now to identify a real net gain from most of the changes in the courts service during this period. What is certain is that 'they' virtually destroyed the reality and cherished concept of local justice, and have come as near as at any time in the last 150 years to eliminating the lay magistracy as well. It is a notable weakness of modern government that, in regulating state institutions, it rarely has the inclination, skill or time to examine fully what unintended consequences may ensue from its actions; policies are concentrated on change, 'modernisation' and short-term economy without proper consideration of the longer-term effects. Reformers who have no intention of heeding the advice of those whom they feel obliged to consult, frequently make changes which effectively remove the very things which they originally claimed to recognise as 'important'. The reality in this case demonstrates that, in the name of 'speed, efficiency and effectiveness', government can continue with impunity to do virtually anything it likes to the courts service and the magistracy, using JPs as expendable pawns. What also has been proved yet again is that, contrary to one of the most common reasons advanced for reform, net overall spending never seems to finish up lower at the end of the process than it was at the beginning.

Locally, magistrates continued to resist (mostly without success) unjustified closure of courts, reductions in the number of justices' clerks, and their dual appointment as both chief executive and clerk. All warnings of threats to the summary justice system were disregarded, as were the repeated requests to stop the unnecessary appointment of more DJs. An eminently sensible suggestion for strengthening the system and saving cost — i.e. removal of a defendant's right to choose expensive Crown Court trial by jury in either-way cases — repeatedly foundered on the obduracy of MPs, the legal profession and civil rights organizations.

To add insult to injury, successive governments have continued in the meantime to encourage the closure of courthouses, amalgamation of benches, appointment of more full-time DJs and diversion of cases from the summary courts. The result has not only been discouraging for JPs and their recruitment; it has also had a noticeably depressing effect on the morale of an institution that depends so much for its existence on the voluntary commitment of its members. Furthermore, for many citizens, their nearest court is probably now up to 50 miles away, served by magistrates no longer recognisable as members of the same community. Although advisory committees are among the few areas in which the magistracy has been allowed to retain influence, their freedom of action and right to be consulted have also suffered. Recruitment and retention have become increasingly difficult in some areas as economic conditions have led companies to be less charitable in allowing their employees to be absent from the workplace, and as central government has become less generous in supporting local recruitment drives. At the same time, appointment regulations have been modified, so as to encourage even greater diversity among those sitting on the bench; but such considerations do not seem to have been applied with the same zeal to the selection of DJs.

Foremost among changes requested for many years by the MA is that JPs' maximum prison sentencing powers for a single offence should be extended from six to 12 months. This would, at a stroke, do much to demonstrate support for the magistracy and restore confidence in its future, but ministers—with the tacit backing of the legal profession—continue to offer the insulting response that magistrates, if given extended powers, could not be trusted not to increase the prison population. A further indication of how hard it is for the magistracy to maintain its position is the ridiculous assertion of politicians and lawyers that lay magistrates could become too professional if allowed to sit more often. They prefer to see the laymen 'kept in their place', and appoint more district judges, rather than use willing lay justices to meet an increased workload or shortage of JPs. To many observers, such examples strengthen the belief that it is the undue influence of lawyers on government policy that continues to prevent such sensible changes from being introduced, especially at a time when so much emphasis is placed on the need for reduction in the huge expense of the CJS. If the legal profession could bring itself to be less selfish over retention of work in the Crown Courts, and less fearful about increasing the attendance of a few JPs, they might have more success in extracting money from the government for their legal aid fees.

JPs can perhaps be forgiven for believing sometimes that there is a master plan or 'hidden agenda' for their demise, endorsed by latent hostility in some quarters towards unpaid public occupations. Otherwise, it is difficult to understand why so little effort has been made to avoid sustained devaluation of their role. Major changes have increasingly borne the hallmarks of a deliberate policy unsympathetic to the voluntary magistracy, but this is of course always strongly denied. In this regard, all that Lord Phillips, as Lord Chief Justice and President of the MA, could offer JPs in 2005 was an assurance that, in spite of the constitutional changes being made at that time, 'the history and traditions of the magistracy will be retained and respected'. Not much comfort in that.

If a policy for deliberate abolition of the magistracy was to be confirmed, it is hard to imagine that its ingredients would be much different from the maddening changes imposed on it in the last 50 years. The combination of centralisation, financial restriction, removal of powers, court closures, amalgamations, work reduction, withdrawal of clerks, staff shortages, appointment of DJs and the absence of positive strengthening measures would be enough to enfeeble, if not ruin, any organization.

This is not the first time that the magistracy has been under threat. It would not have survived for more than 650 years without resilience, integrity and, above all, adaptability. On the way, it has suffered several periods of disgrace and bouts of criticism — the latter perhaps more frequent in recent times, due to the pervasive influence of the media, information technology and the speed of change. Nevertheless, it has continued to play a valuable part in the life of the nation during the last half century. In spite of numerous attacks on its status, scrutiny of its powers, and re-organization of its courts, the magistracy, numbering 25,000 to 30,000 at its peak during the period under review, remains in being. But it cannot be denied that it has been weakened by constant erosion of its work and increasing avoidance of formal court proceedings by the police and CPS, making extensive use of what has come to be known as 'diversion'.

We need to work harder to condition the public mind to regard the lay justice system with the same unquestioning reverence as is accorded to the jury system. Likewise, we must avoid allowing more and more judicial decisions — particularly for reasons of cost or convenience — to pass into the hands of unaccountable executives, operating outside the public arena, as is now allowed, for instance, to police officers, justices' clerks and other officials granted discretionary powers without having to observe the constraints under which the magistracy has to operate.

Recent governments have appeared to place small value on the magistracy's loyalty and public service ethos; they have preferred to listen to the lawyers and law school lecturers who continue to describe it as an anachronistic institution, one of the last bastions of amateurism. Equally, they have allowed themselves to be persuaded by various critics and reformists that — apart from juries — collective justice, however swift, is too expensive; they have been impressed by academics and so-called experts who argue — so far without proof — that there are cheaper and better ways of bringing crime and criminals under control. Hence the increase in fixed penalties and all manner of diversions from customary court procedure.

Looking back over the years, one can see a chain of government ministers hacking away at the foundations of the magistracy, repeatedly denying the obvious harm being done to it while continuing to declare their admiration and confidence in its future. Even the strongest building cannot withstand such persistent erosion of its foundations without eventually collapsing; yet almost no-one — least of all politicians — seems able or willing to pay attention to the warning signs, voice appropriate concern or take effective action to halt the process or repair the damage.

CHAPTER 3

Justice in a Moral Vacuum

'Men are qualified for civil liberty in exact proportion to their disposition to put moral chains upon their own appetites'

Edmund Burke

- Freedom, democracy and justice
- Changed attitudes and standards
- Reduced respect for law and honesty

I hesitate to tread the tortuous path of morals and human behaviour, but it is difficult to avoid doing so when considering the meaning and practice of justice in a democracy. It forms a major part of the abstract environment in which magistrates have to work; and historians in years to come may be interested to know something of the ethical and social climate in which we lived and worked in the second half of the twentieth century. This was a post-war period of revolution in standards and behaviour, coupled with a chronic national inability to find a lasting balance between civil liberty, regulation and fairness, that challenged the rule of law and left a vacuum in which the magistracy and traditional forms of summary justice were called into question. Above all, it is my enduring belief that a strong and independent judicial institution, such as that represented (among others) by the lay magistracy in Britain, is an essential part of the fabric of a truly free and democratic nation in which respect for the law is supreme.

There is no certainty and no complete answer to our law and order problem. A high level of offending seems inevitable among the free but selfish people of a nation that cannot rely on personal discipline, nor find the moral strength to create more effective ways of preventing crime and deterring criminals. The more we advance materially, the more difficult we seem to find it to be generous of spirit and compliant in behaviour. Two hundred years ago, philosopher Edmund Burke (1729–97) already knew the problem: 'Society cannot exist unless a controlling power upon will and appetite be placed somewhere', he said.

While we lose much as a result of the crimes we endure and the criminals we tolerate, we evidently believe that the freedoms we still enjoy outweigh the measures that would be necessary to ensure less crime and fewer criminals.

Freedom, democracy and justice

'The only liberty…is a liberty connected with order—not the French liberty (which is) nothing but the rein given to vice and confusion'

Edmund Burke (1791) An Appeal

The 'western' form of civilisation encourages us to live in society as free, virtuous and rational individuals, unencumbered by fear and coercion, governed by democracy, individual responsibility and tolerance. The rule of law and justice form a framework within which this can be maintained, but a well-ordered society ultimately relies on the attitudes and actions of law-abiding citizens who see it as in their own interest to behave towards others as they would like others to behave towards them.

Britain avoided such extreme proletarian uprisings as those experienced by France in 1789 and Russia in 1917, both of which were driven by powerful utopian theories which sought to change society and the entire system of government and law; although we flirted with revolution and republicanism for about ten years in the seventeenth century, we have since preferred to retain—and celebrate—the symbolic authority of hereditary monarchy, while handing law-making powers to elected government under the classic right of free citizens to be regulated only by their own representatives. Our freedom under the law is of different origin to the liberty gained on the Continent following the French

Revolution. Thus our legal systems have developed in contrasting ways. Our liberty is unconditional, i.e. legal until banned (although subject to 'human rights' since 1950); whereas the continental version is conditional, i.e. illegal unless specifically permitted. The guilty plea is, I believe, unknown in France.

Our system arises from the more gentle confrontation between King John and the nobles at Runnymede, resulting in the 1215 Magna Carta, the main effect of which was to secure the freedom of the church and the rights of the barons, in addition to restricting abuses of royal power. However, since the seventeenth century, it has been regarded somewhat inaccurately as the principal document of English liberties. It was described by Lord Denning as 'the greatest constitutional document of all times, the foundation of the freedom of the individual against the arbitrary authority of the despot'; it is also enshrined in the constitutions of major Commonwealth countries, and famously quoted in the US Declaration of Independence as a 'statement of principle': 'No freeman shall be taken or imprisoned, deprived of his freehold, liberties or privileges, or outlawed or exiled ... or deprived of his life, liberty or property, except by the lawful judgment of his peers or by the law of the land'. For more than 800 years, this 'bible of the English constitution' (as Pitt the Elder described the Magna Carta) has been a beacon of freedom under the law for the common individual, and provided a basis for the traditional British respect for fair play.

Such fine words have to be given meaning through democratic government and an impartial judiciary; otherwise the freedom — which we now take so much for granted — is too easily abused. To remain free, man must express himself within a framework of law and order that not only serves the needs of a civilised community but also has the respect and consent of the people. Moreover, for democracy to be of universal benefit, and for Lord Acton's 'delicate fruit of a mature civilisation' to be preserved for all, freedom of thought and belief must be unconditional, as must be the right to disagree; but freedom of speech and publication require control by laws against crimes of slander, libel, incitement or sedition (tools of restraint which appear to be impotent in preventing obscenely abusive remarks being posted anonymously in the social media); liberty must be moderated by responsibility, and licence by regulation.

Democracy and a free press are not by themselves a guarantee of freedom and liberty, nor even do they allow for people to govern themselves without first electing representatives and employing executives to act on their behalf. Even violent assembly can take place in the name of democracy, and a free press can generate its own brand of tyranny against innocent victims and legitimate minorities. Moreover, the advance of information technology, and the extra power this makes available to virtually every citizen, can encourage abuse of the freedom of speech through social media. Modern dissidents present a constant dilemma for government and courts dedicated to maintenance of the law and preservation of the fine balance between freedom and control. In that endeavour, we have to be careful not to encourage democracy to become so democratic that in the end we destroy it.

'Open judgment by a man's peers was the English rule', wrote historian Arthur Bryant, but today much nonsense is written and talked about 'peer justice' and the Magna Carta. Most people understand what was meant 800 years ago, when the nobles were demanding from King John the right of fair trial by their (noble) peers, but this has been misinterpreted over the centuries since 1215. The underlying principle in a wider sense has been strongly defended and kept alive in Britain by the existence of the lay magistracy and the jury system, but it is ridiculous to suggest, as some do, that the concept of 'peer justice' should be transformed to ensure that offenders are tried and sentenced only by those with whom they have some kind of affinity. Of far greater concern should be the fact that so many trials in our summary courts today are conducted, not by peers in the collective form of lay justices or jurors, but by single lawyers who most certainly cannot be described as the peers of those on whom they pass judgement.

The 'rights and liberties of the subject' were further strengthened in England and Wales through the 1679 Habeas Corpus Act and 1689 Bill of Rights—two legal landmarks which helped to distinguish the development of English-speaking civilisation. These statutes also formed the basis for the creation of the European Convention on Human Rights and Fundamental Freedoms, incorporated into United Kingdom law in 1950, which ironically has turned out in some cases to offend the British sense of what is right. One-sided application of human rights laws has produced some absurd results in this country, prompting the question: 'Why was the Convention's declaration not qualified by the attachment of corresponding duties?' Rights are a necessary part of democracy, freedom and justice, but they can only be taken seriously if balanced by obligations; any system that relies on the concept of rights presupposes that individuals will respect the rights of others out of enlightened self-interest, rather than to gain advantage. Today, we seem to spend so much time defending rights that we forget to mention, or choose to ignore, responsibilities.

There appear to be no bounds to modern interpretations of words like 'free' and 'freedom', but in every case they come at a price. Collective freedom, observed a former Chief Rabbi, 'means that my freedom cannot be bought at the price of yours'; he also said, 'a society in which the few prosper while the rest starve is not a place of liberty'. Somehow, government and society have to find and keep a balance between individual rights and the common good. A Grimsby resident was given a 30-day prison sentence by magistrates for refusing to pay his council tax, having claimed that he had no contractual obligation to do so under common law because he was a 'freeman' (a notion emanating from the United States in the 1970s). Such people, often adherents of so-called 'global democracy', believe that they are immune from normal jurisdiction, that the law only applies to them if they have contracted to be bound by it, and that 'true law' — like 'art' — is whatever they say it is.

Individual freedom was repressed in Britain for hundreds of years by the tyrannies of church, monarchy, landlords — even Parliament. Although each of these was eventually overcome, others have emerged — and will yet emerge. Democracy notwithstanding, industrialists and trade unions have acted oppressively in their turn — and let us not forget the many people who still suffer daily from fear of the mob, bullies, Twitter, criminal gangs and others who abuse concentrations of power and money. More recently, tabloid newspapers destroyed the careers of public figures and private individuals alike through illegal telephone tapping; and even the police were guilty of misusing their power, when they adopted a policy of automatic belief in the accuser's story when investigating spurious accusations against prominent, totally innocent, politicians and army officers. Many people are too scared to bear witness, give an opinion or exercise discretion for fear of vicious accusations of discrimination or racism. 'Political correctness', which started as a well-meaning way to avoid offending minorities, has itself also become repressive. The 'tyranny of the majority' (to use de Tocqueville's term), the 'intolerance of public opinion' (described by John Stuart Mill in *On Liberty*), 'group-think', the 'neoliberalism' of monopolies and international financiers, and the attractive dogma of 'equality' can all threaten individual freedom in one way or another. As is often recognised, power corrupts, especially when exercised without the consent of the people. Fortunately, in the western world we have become more aware and intolerant of power and privilege, but one person's freedom so easily becomes another's tyranny, and 'freedom fighters' in one country may be regarded as 'terrorists' in another.

Paradoxically, tyrannical regimes can sometimes provide a more comfortable feeling of security than may be enjoyed under the abused freedoms of democracy. For example, it used to be said that visitors to communist Moscow felt much safer walking the streets than visitors to capitalist New York, and there are all too many areas of urban Britain today where gangs of youths make it impossible for some people to live without fear, both in and outside their own homes. Imagine the alarm generated in 2008, when six men from different locations in our own country were stabbed to death within 24 hours, a horrific occurrence which prompted David Cameron (then leader of the Opposition in Parliament) to complain of the 'moral neutrality lying at the root of most of society's ills, leading to an erosion of social virtue and self-discipline, and of street violence which feeds off a morally neutral culture that tolerates welfare dependency and self-pity'. If peace and liberty are to remain permanent symbols of civilised society, democratic governments will have to find better ways of balancing the need for control of the few while preserving law-based freedom for the many. Successful democracy depends on the rule of law, administered by the police and the courts; every time the law is not enforced, for whatever reason, our democracy is weakened. It can only operate successfully in a safe and peaceful environment. Why otherwise are we called 'justices of the peace'? Only in this way can democracy play its full part in helping the world to become safe enough for liberty to thrive.

Churchill in 1947 said in the House of Commons, 'No-one pretends that democracy is perfect ... indeed it has been said that it is the worst form of government except all those other forms that have been tried from time-to-time'. For a while, the chaos which followed the 1917 Russian revolution was called 'democracy in action'. It should also be remembered that Athenian democracy invented the arrogance and hubris that led to tyranny, to its own inability to govern and, incidentally, to the murder of Socrates for challenging the empowerment of dissident minorities who had abused their freedom of speech and choice. So, while democracy may have a levelling influence on the actions of government, it may also encourage mob rule and anarchy. Unfortunately, the mob operates at the lowest common level and demands the right to unlimited protest, even if that is likely to cause violence and huge cost in trying to control it. As we have seen since World War II, it also encourages large sections of the populace to feel free to break the law or behave irresponsibly, having little or nothing to lose when arraigned for their crimes. Most of them have little money, no property, no employment, doubtful prospects, no respect for authority, no fear of harsh punishment, and no concern for others. They are virtually immune from fines, dispossession or deterrence of any kind, and the courts are often made to look impotent in trying to deal with them. The protection of 'human rights' merely enhances their apparently invulnerable status.

Britain's brand of liberty, justice and democracy — not to mention the benefits of work, socio-medical services and the English language — has attracted millions of the world's refugees, immigrants and their relatives to our shores since 1685, when 50,000 Huguenots arrived from France, following Louis XIV's revocation of the Edict of Nantes, under which they had enjoyed religious freedom for nearly 100 years. The influx of freedom-seeking and economic migrants from other nations and cultures has enriched our society in many ways (including some of our moral values), but in modern times it has also increased our exposure to unacceptable alternative values, violence, corruption and religious extremism, and has placed additional strain on our enforcement authorities and criminal justice system. The situation was not improved by an unduly charitable government policy which encouraged multi-lingualism and adapted local programmes to accommodate new cultures, instead of concentrating on the need to ensure that all immigrants could speak English and were fully absorbed into British society as quickly as possible. Even more serious, meanwhile, are widespread incidents of 'honour killings', enforced marriages and bodily mutilation arising from alien beliefs, and suggestions that imported religious codes should be allowed to take precedence over our national laws. Democracy breaks down under double standards. Without exception, all citizens must be subject to one and the same law; otherwise anarchy prevails. It is no more acceptable to allow the operation of separate Islamic courts in this country today than it was to allow separate Roman Catholic courts here in the 12th century.

One of the reasons today why Britain remains the envy of many in the world and so inviting to migrants is the simple attractiveness of good organization based on rules, and civilised behaviour based on law. With the powerful assistance of democracy, our society and customs have evolved, so that order and democratic regulation are found to be more tolerable than a free-for-all. There should therefore be no place in our society for those who abuse the privilege of British citizenship or flout the rules governing membership of our institutions. It is as unacceptable to indulge in selfish individualism by mocking formal dress codes as to claim immunity from trial under our national laws. It was understandable that many of the original immigrants found it difficult to adjust to a new set of moral principles. However, it is particularly regrettable that some of them and their descendants, now seek to exploit our liberal traditions by engaging in terrorism and subversion, challenging our concept of a virtuous society, and insisting on freedom to continue practices alien to our culture. Such abuse of the liberty and tolerance sought by their forefathers increases the likelihood of racial tension — and, most unfortunately, the need for new deterrent laws.

The cause of racial harmony was not helped by the 1999 Macpherson Enquiry's definition of a racist incident as 'any which is perceived to be racist by the victim or any other person' — a premise not unlike 'global democrats' claiming the law to be whatever they say it is, or members of the so-called 'creative' classes describing unmade beds as 'art' (*vide* Tracey Emin's 1999 Tate Gallery exhibit, later sold for over £2 million). How do these ideas fit with what we mean by democracy in a free and tolerant society? Perhaps this is a moment when we should remind ourselves that the Bolsheviks became tyrants in pursuing their idea of democracy, and the Spanish Inquisitors enforced their brand of Christianity by torturing those whom they regarded as heretics.

'Those who recognise the voice of their own conscience usually recognise also the voice of justice', said the Russian writer Alexander Solzhenitsyn (1918–08). But, like 'freedom' and 'democracy', 'justice' has become fragmented in our language. The dictionary description — fairness, rightness and reasonableness — today has to accommodate the many expectations of the public, including both victims and offenders, the innocent and the guilty; from those seeking revenge to those hoping for mercy, and from the maltreated to the wrongly accused. The meaning of tolerance has also become severely tested by the expansion of different cultures within our society.

Concepts of 'justice' change as our civilisation develops. So, it is perhaps not surprising that, even today, we appear to give it at least two meanings: that which is determined as ever by the courts under the law, and that, beloved by politicians and the disgruntled, sometimes known as 'social justice'. The latter is ill-defined, varies from one person to another, and is not easily subject to law; it sits uncomfortably at times with the preservation of individual freedom. It can embrace a spectrum of opinions, ranging from the politics of envy and social engineering, to poverty and the welfare of criminals, to discrimination, equality and the minimum wage, but it can never be fully satisfied. A practical illustration of this problem emerges from typical replies given by some shoplifters when asked to explain their actions, e.g.:

- 'Stealing from a shop doesn't matter, because you don't know them and they don't notice the loss … they can afford it; I don't steal from people I know, because you'd have to live with it'.

- 'I don't see anything wrong in theft from shops ... it's cheaper for them than having to pay for keeping my children in care ... my needs are greater than the shop owners'.
- 'Stealing from a shop is different from entering and stealing from other places'.
- 'I just felt it was something I had to do; I was so unhappy at home. I didn't think it dishonest, but I knew it was wrong ... I desperately didn't want to do it'.
- 'Modern prison holds no fears for me' ('professional' shoplifter).

In attempting, perhaps, to invoke 'the divine right of the state' to replace the church as the arbiter of behavioural standards, government likes to use words and phrases that have the ring of moral authority and the semblance of all-embracing vision. So, in attempting to appeal to the public conscience, politicians and the media have created multiple forms of 'justice', which now appear to include everything from recently-discovered 'climate justice' to the more mature 'social justice', 'community justice', 'neighbourhood justice', 'restorative justice' and, not least, 'the justice system' itself. These extensions assume that, in addition to (but not in substitution for) individual conscience, there is scope for a further brand — 'collective justice' — by which our society should now be devoted; this, however, begins to look like 'Facebook' or 'mob' justice, which is too awful to contemplate. Older and far more acceptable than all these new inventions is 'local justice', provided cheaply and successfully within the community for generations by JPs through the magistrates' courts.

Even Adolf Hitler embraced 'justice', when he claimed that 'as a Christian I have no duty to allow myself to be cheated, but I do have the duty to be a fighter for truth and justice'. The extended use of the word increasingly involves lawyers and the courts in the controversial area of 'human rights'. These, in turn, introduce all kinds of new-found concepts, such as 'the dignity of moral citizenship', described by a South African judge in a Scarman Lecture as 'a person's sense that he or she is a fully entitled member of society, undisqualified from enjoyment of its privileges and opportunities by any feature of his or her humanhood'.

Where does that fit, one wonders, with simple democracy and the need for clarity in the law?

Although liberty under authority implies the existence of regulations and a system to enforce them, this is accepted in a democracy as being vastly preferable to anarchy; it is also acknowledged that a free society cannot be built on legal authority alone. The role of the state is to provide a system, accessible and affordable to all, that offers the best guarantee of justice under the law. But this simple objective is impaired if, for instance, benches of three magistrates give way to single judges or the state exploits the courts as an avenue for the politics of social justice; it is also made to look ridiculous when the law is so deficient that citizens, defending themselves and their possessions against intruders, are prosecuted while burglars go free. The law, especially if conditioned by rights, is weakened and unacceptable when the criminal appears to win.

With the creation of the welfare state after World War II, equality before the law and the right to a fair trial became key ingredients of the 1949 Legal Aid and Advice Act, giving people of limited means free access to professional help. In principle, this was felt to be a great step forward, but a major unintended consequence was a mounting annual bill to the taxpayer, reaching more than £2 billion by 2009 — the highest per capita cost for legal aid of any country in the world, and estimated to be available to about 29 per cent of the adult population. For the lawyers involved in giving the aid this was a lucrative new field, but the cost was unsustainable, and the government had to find ways of reducing it, leading inevitably to confrontation with the legal profession. One positive result, welcomed by the magistracy and offering useful experience for students, is an increase in the number of university law schools offering free (*pro bono publico)* services. In the courts, it has to be said that legal aid is usually helpful, in that it not only ensures the defence case is clearly presented, but it also saves time. On the other hand, there is little doubt that, among hardcore criminals, legal aid encourages bogus 'not guilty' pleas, leading to unjustified time-consuming trials.

Benches of lay magistrates, independent judges and juries have a major part to play in the preservation of freedom against tyranny and the abuse of power; but it is difficult, if not impossible, to uphold the law through the courts if they do not feel that they have the whole-hearted moral support of the public. Without such safeguards, a vital component of our balanced culture and justice system is lost. We can continue to live in a free society only if we work constantly to keep it free under the law, and only if we give unequivocal backing to those who obey the rules and maintain high standards of behaviour.

Joining the clamour for a change in the law or the abolition of juries every time they come to a decision which we don't like is certainly not the way forward, and we achieve nothing when legislating for the benefit of the less fortunate if, in doing so, we create opportunities for the rest to take advantage through fraud; likewise, when we act to protect the law-abiding majority, but then — in the pursuit of economy or the satisfaction of 'human rights' — neglect to enforce them. Failure to punish offenders merely endorses the habit of law-breaking. Widespread tolerance of excuses and exceptions, and the limitless granting of yet one more opportunity to make good, weakens the power of the law until it becomes meaningless and unenforceable.

Magistrates should consider themselves to be among those who have a duty, both in and outside their courts, to promote the peaceful and responsible exercise of freedom and good order, liberty and democracy, for these great beliefs can only survive under firm laws, consistently, independently and fairly enforced. The most insidious threat to the maintenance of democratic values is apathy, a belief also expressed in 1995 by Mickey Kaus, American editor of the *New Republic*, when he wrote that 'the most serious threat to democracy in our time comes, not so much from the maldistribution of wealth, as from the decay or abandonment of public institutions in which citizens meet as equals'. It may be said that in our country the magistracy is one such institution, the current decline of which is undoubtedly adding to the impoverishment of our national democracy.

Changed attitudes and standards

'Over the centuries, Britain's supreme asset has often been the innate respect of her people for common sense and the unwritten moral law. Despite many shortcomings, neither they nor their leaders have been capable of substituting for the rule of individual conscience the monstrous abstractions of the collective mind. They have paid dear sometimes for complacency and laziness, but in the end have been saved by humility, wisdom and justice'.

This is a paraphrased extract from historian Arthur Bryant's *Years of Endurance 1793–1802* (written in 1942), in which he referred to a constant factor in our country's long fight against post-revolutionary France: our refusal to accept any new order that is not based on law.

Is this preference for the 'individual' sense of morality still indicative of our national character? Or has it been destroyed by the devaluation of authority, the transfer of power to the young, the weakening of Christian influences, the blurring of difference between right and wrong, the increase in self-gratification, *laissez-faire*, multi-culturalism, and the general decline in standards of conduct? After 1945, governments of all hues surrendered to the progressive wing of society; the new elite were more concerned with social engineering than Christian morals, and the 'liberal experiment' reduced respect for the law by encouraging indiscipline and tolerance of bad behaviour. As a result, the police, courts, prisons and social services have been engaged ever since in a ceaseless, and largely unsuccessful, flood-control exercise.

In our own generation, the beginning of the slide was probably the 1960s, which espoused indulgence, equality, relaxation of discipline and the disconnection of rights from duties. Challenges to convention and moderation were encouraged, but those who opened the sluices had no practical idea of how to arrest the resulting surge of crime, dishonesty and promiscuity. Seeds of excess were germinated, and the new-found freedom — unconstrained by responsibility — enabled radical reformers to shift blame from individuals to society, and to gain moral superiority over policy-makers and educationalists. The Longford Committee (1972) and the Williams Committee (1979) both accepted that 'degradation of public taste is progressive, and that yesterday's hard porn becomes today's soft porn'. Meanwhile, the tolerant 'good' majority became victims of the small 'bad' minority who cared nothing for anybody. We continue, 50 years later, to suffer from the consequent lowering of standards, victimisation and disrespect for authority.

In spite of Cicero's aphorism ('Nothing is more iniquitous than so-called equality') we, or at least some politicians, have also come to believe that, whatever it may mean and however non-achieveable, 'equality' is an objective to which we should all aspire. This may serve well for women demanding equal pay for equal work, but in the justice system 'fairness' is a more realistic aim. Contrary to the 1776 American Declaration of Independence, in which it is asserted that in life 'all men are created equal', modern knowledge of complex genetics suggests that this is not true; only in death do we become so. Meanwhile, 'equality of opportunity' remains our only realistic goal.

The universal concern with self-interest and self-fulfilment, largely emanating from America, makes it difficult to generate a sense of civic obligation and compliance with the law. Whatever the case, it is undeniable that there has been a significant change in the perception of justice, and in attitudes towards right and wrong, crime and punishment, during the last 50 years. While personal wealth remains admirable in America, it seems to have become more common in Britain to foster the politics of envy by venerating those with a poor and feckless background while despising the rich, however honestly they have acquired and generously used their wealth. 'Not guilty' is the automatic response of the habitual criminal among all classes, and is a natural consequence of the 'innocent until proved guilty' principle of British law which rightly places the onus on the accuser. However, it also encourages a denial, excuse and lying culture, requiring a confrontational process to sift truth from falsehood, costing the country dear and providing fame and fortune for generations of lawyers. Regrettably, members of almost every sector of our society — notably senior politicians, bankers, journalists, churchmen and TV celebrities — have demonstrated in recent times the same propensity for 'categorical denial' before being found guilty in a court of law.

The effects of the transformation in mood and attitudes have been particularly marked among the youth and in state schools where discipline has assembled a poor record. By the end of the 1980s, an education conference was being told that 'children as young as four are attacking teachers as the growing wave of classroom violence spreads to nursery schools'. A survey by the National Union of Head Teachers at that time reported more than 18,000 acts of school violence annually, and referred to 'the growing minority of selfish, miserably inarticulate children devoid of moral sense', who were reflecting the cheapened social and moral standards witnessed on television. By then, this wild behaviour was also being paraded regularly at night by drunken teenagers on urban streets. Max Hastings, a former editor of the *Daily Telegraph*, later referred to this ruinous period as: 'Years of liberal dogma (which) spawned a generation of amoral, uneducated, welfare-dependent, brutalised youngsters'.

Attitudes to crimes and penalties have also changed. Although remaining inconsistent, the public are generally more punitive than the courts; demands for 'justice' sometimes seem more like calls for 'revenge'. While there is still a substantial undercurrent of honesty, good behaviour and respect for the law, it has become less evident; if anything, the relationship between punishment, tolerance, compassion and forgiveness has grown more rigid. As a result, it seems now to have become rather laborious to charge and punish offenders — and even more difficult to forgive them when they are genuinely contrite and prepared to mend their ways. It can be said that, because law-breaking is now so commonplace, we regard serious crimes less seriously and punish them less harshly, but forgive less easily. This makes the work of police, magistrates, probation officers and social workers more difficult, because their authority is more likely to be challenged, more scope is left for criticism of their decisions, and there is always someone waiting to apportion blame when they think their particular views have not been respected.

Less than 100 years ago, severe punishments — such as hanging, hard labour and imprisonment — were given for crimes such as adultery, begging and petty theft; summary offences and punishments were fewer and simpler. Since then, many crimes have become more complicated and prone to dispute over detail and seriousness. New offences have been created for what used to be acceptable activities, e.g. child employment, smoking, collecting birds' eggs. Others have been varied by introducing degrees of severity, e.g. assault, driving behaviour, personal hardship.

Viewed from the bench, it is quite difficult at times not to see the result of changes in attitudes as a triumph of the wicked and feckless minority over the law-abiding and responsible majority. Misguided politicians, penal reformers and religious leaders, latterly spurred by human rights legislation, sometimes appear to be promoting the belief that crime is an illness or somebody else's fault, that it could be reduced by better understanding and treatment of criminals, that it is somehow not totally wrong in itself, and therefore that punishment may not only be unnecessary, but counter-productive. In such a climate, it is not always clear to JPs what their role is expected to be. Is it no longer to punish offenders, but merely to become compassionate mediators? Is it to buttress the social services? Surely not. The police and summary courts must remain the principal bulwark against lawlessness; but, as authority in general has become devalued, their influence on people's behaviour has become worryingly dependent on ever-changing political attitudes to prosecution, treatment and punishment.

The pendulum has now swung so far to the other side that people are sometimes more likely to be sent to prison for cruelty to animals than for serious acts of violence against fellow human beings; burglars may be punished with nothing more severe than a caution or short period of community service (certainly not hard labour), while their victims risk being charged with assault, even murder, if they try to obstruct them. We are so reluctant to enforce the law in some cases that we award compensation to criminals, allow easy access to drugs in prisons, and paint speed cameras bright yellow in the hope that motorists won't get caught; if anyone is so unobservant as to miss or ignore the warnings, it is the police and local authorities who are then accused of bullying and profiteering. If the police install CCTV cameras in places where they anticipate burglary or public unrest, they are said to be 'unethical' or acting like 'Big Brother'. While most of us these days are identified by, and accept the need for, bank cards and driving licences, as soon as someone suggests that national identity cards (widely used in other democracies) would greatly reduce crime and illegal entry, they are accused of infringing liberty and human rights. It seems at times that our sense of fairness has become so distorted that we would sooner be kind and encouraging to criminals than catch and punish them; sooner demand new laws than act to enforce those we have already. No wonder so many cases of crime and deliberate misdemeanour never reach the courts. Are these contradictory tendencies changing the face of English justice irreparably for the worse, or are they the dawn of an enlightened era of moral rectitude?

The replacement of sin by sickness, the absurd doctrine of 'creationism' (which, against volumes of evidence to the contrary, still insists that the world was forged in seven days), and the exposure of paedophiles among the clergy have combined to diminish the wisdom and influence of Christianity, and its convictions are increasingly challenged by scientific discovery, secularism, agnosticism, atheism and rival faiths. The church itself is now sometimes 'in the dock'. Therefore, it can unfortunately no longer be relied upon to act as the source of absolute truth and the scourge of the wicked, nor as the chief arbiter of moral values. Instead, it finds itself preoccupied with social welfare, semantics, clerical conduct, gender politics, and the ethics of wealth creation and distribution. Until around the end of the nineteenth century, the fear of God and damnation still acted as a brake on those tempted to misbehave. Today, that curb on individual conduct is weakened, leaving the police, the courts, social services and charities to fill the vacuum. As we exchange Christian rules of life for secular rules of law, we have to rely more and more on individual conscience and a passion for justice to keep the peace and protect us from chaos and anarchy.

While JPs are entrusted with deciding guilt, innocence and sentence, they have precious little opportunity to make decisions that seriously affect the amount of crime and number of criminals in our country today. The answer to that huge problem lies elsewhere—in the hearts and minds of us all. The rule of law is ours to trash or sustain. Unless and until we decide individually and collectively to be more honest, more disciplined, more law-abiding and less permissive, our country will continue to suffer the level of crime and dishonesty we seem at the moment to have chosen.

Reduced respect for law and honesty

'It is perfectly monstrous the way people go about nowadays saying things against one, behind one's back, that are absolutely and entirely true'

Oscar Wilde

The British still enjoy quite a good reputation for upholding the letter of the law, but it is questionable whether we really deserve it. Most of us privately deplore crime and dishonesty, but then go out and knowingly break speed limits and park illegally every day; we get angry when others steal from us, but we are quite happy to use the firm's time and equipment freely for our own purposes without permission, or to help ourselves to other people's apples, when it suits us. We repeatedly claim that we are respectable, law-abiding citizens until we are caught on the wrong side of the law; then we change, become abusive, accuse the police of being discriminatory or heavy-handed, and are unwilling to accept the consequences of our actions — or inactions. Honesty may pay in the end, but not enough to satisfy everybody. Even when we know we were wrong, we deny our offence and swear in the name of our god to tell the truth in the hope that the magistrates are patient and gullible enough to believe us — however much of the court's time is wasted in listening to our self-deception. Such common duplicity makes it that much harder to sustain respect for any kind of moral law.

The law should be regarded as a means, not an end; a safeguard, not a government weapon for the enforcement of ideology on a reluctant populace. The law should be something that individuals and the community can understand and accept as the best way of preserving a free and democratic society without constant fear of breaking the rules. Diverting serious re-offenders away from the enforcement process, 'chaining' the courts to curb their discretion and increase their 'understanding', and 'freeing' criminals before completion of their sentence merely to reduce the cost of punishment and treatment, are misguided policies which indicate that we are falling out of love with, and can no longer afford, justice. Inevitably, there comes a point beyond which its pursuit seems to become pointless and too expensive.

It is vital for the preservation of respect for justice in our country that no-one is allowed to be above the law, and that there should never be a semblance of one law for the rich and another for the poor, nor one for Christians, one for Muslims, and another for atheists. It is equally important that the law should be enforced. Even in a secular society, most people share a sense of what is right and wrong, and many of our laws reflect this. But if these are not applied as intended, their effect is diminished and the difference between right and wrong is obscured. Repeated leniency shown by the courts to re-offenders contributes to weakening the rule of law, so that breaking it then becomes more acceptable by default. Perhaps one of the most deplorable consequences of changed attitudes in our society is the apparent acceptance of dishonesty in ourselves and others, and a loss of faith in our own ability to curb it. In one prosperous part of London, shoplifting (theft from shops) became so commonplace that at least one supermarket stopped charging first-time offenders because there were so many of them. In the end, the weight of crime or corruption can become so great that the system designed to fight it is overwhelmed.

In 2007, a reader (who had exceeded the speed limit by more than 17 per cent) wrote to the editor of a respectable broadsheet motoring supplement: 'There are four road signs, the last of which is a 40 sign of which I was unaware', he said. 'I had slowed accordingly and was prepared to slow further when I was photographed by a mobile camera van at 47 mph. Using this area to trap motorists is highly immoral. I am pleading not guilty in court. Any advice?' To which the editor replied (with incredible irresponsibility and deceit), 'I totally agree with you ... what happens will depend on the mood of the magistrate'. With such encouragement, the self-righteous motorist no doubt 'had his day in court' — at his and the taxpayers' expense.

The huge cost of our criminal justice system is largely due to our propensity for denial, excuse and telling lies — even under oath — or for stoutly maintaining innocence until the last minute. Ingenuity is sometimes also a feature. The *Sun* newspaper's Honest Person Award was once offered the following response, given by a defendant answering a charge of dishonest possession brought under Section 2 of the 1968 Theft Act: 'It was my subjectively honest belief that the owner of the property could not be discovered by taking reasonable steps—so I kept it', he said.

Our 'innocent until proved guilty' principle encourages a refusal to admit wrongdoing when charged—even when we are advised that the penalty for a guilty plea is likely to be less. Much of the rest is the price we pay for the belief that the accused should be given the benefit of the doubt. It is quite disturbing to realise how much time and money is spent laboriously proving beyond reasonable doubt that so many of us are actually heedless liars, playing the system to the limit or naïvely hoping to deceive the court. But that is not all. Spurred on by the availability of legal aid and the eternal hope of 'getting off', it has become almost obligatory to extend the denial process even further by appealing against every unfavourable decision, come what may; moreover, if members of an ethnic minority are the recipients, they may still continue to reject the judgment, while accusing the magistrates or judge of being motivated, not by rational assessment of the evidence, but by racism or adverse discrimination. Is a willingness to prolong the judicial process part of our traditional respect for the law and the love of fair play, a lack of faith in benches and juries to make the 'right' decisions, a method of maintaining full employment for lawyers, or merely an example of typical British hypocrisy?

While many defence lawyers build formidable reputations on 'getting their clients off', magistrates have to remain dedicated to the skilful, often lengthy, process of filtering truth from lies and testing the relevance of 'reasonable doubt'—with little help from the use of the oath and a general reluctance to prosecute for perjury. As long ago as 1987, the Magistrates Association called attention to the common abuse of the oath and resolved to ask that it should be discontinued, as members found it was 'no longer suited to a multi-racial society', but strong religious opposition ensured its continuation to the present day.

In 1988, Prime Minister Margaret Thatcher, in a speech to Conservative Party members, referred to the change in moral standards. 'In the past, potential offenders were firmly told that they would be held to blame for any crime they may commit; but today, when someone assaults a passer-by, it is the attacker who becomes, by a perverse twist of logic, a victim of society', she said. 'Most people don't manufacture their own morality. They take it from the culture in which they live. But if a culture of excuses has been created for them, they can evade their own conscience and the bad opinion of others, and become more likely to rob and burgle as a result'. Later in the speech, she referred to her determination to change the climate of opinion surrounding wrongdoing, and to sweep away the 'fog of excuses' which she believed the liberal establishment had long employed to shelter criminals from the full consequences of their actions.

Improving the moral climate is more easily said than done, especially in a multi-cultural society in which concepts of truth and honesty may have various meanings. This is illustrated by an anecdote in which a judge asks a husband in a domestic case:

'Do you know what is meant by telling the truth?'

'Yes'.

'Do you know what happens to those who do not tell the truth?'

'Yes'.

'What?'

'They are after winning their case, my lord'.

Post-war immigration and the resulting multiplication of cultures in Britain has had an unhelpful influence on attitudes to, and respect for, the law. Achievement of a higher regard for the common good is made more difficult by the presence of significant numbers from ethnic minorities who reject British values and seek to replace them with the uncompromising demands of their own religion, thereby excusing themselves from subjection to the laws of their adopted country. Some Muslim extremist preachers have been heard saying to followers, 'Do not obey the law of the land; only obey the laws of Allah. It is what God has made lawful that matters, not what man has decreed. Islam is not compatible with democracy'. What should be the democrat's answer to the terrorist who tells you that he prefers to obey God rather than man, and that, by killing you, he is ensuring his place in heaven?

Religious tolerance is one thing, but this is quite another; it poses a major threat to the rule of law that most of us in this country have inherited and accept — at least in principle. Government recognised this as a serious problem in 2009 when allocating more than £80m towards building trust with British Muslims. Citizenship ceremonies were also introduced, to encourage stronger loyalty and bonding with their new country by immigrants, including the swearing of an oath requiring them to 'respect UK rights and freedoms, uphold its democratic values, observe its laws, and fulfil the duties and obligations of a British citizen'. Some ethnic minority members criticise and do not trust our courts and legal system (because some decisions do not accord with their alien expectations), but this does not mean that we should feel obliged to reform our laws in order to permit the rule of more than one system in this country. Those still attracted to foreign beliefs should accept—without complaint—the laws and procedures of the uncommonly fair and tolerant country in which they find themselves.

Fifty years ago and long before, much of the punishment for offending existed in the humiliation of a court appearance with subsequent press publicity, but today few cases are reported and manifestations of shame are rare. Maybe this arises from the absurd idea that remorse is feeble, or may leave young offenders exposed to a lifetime of guilt. It is now a common, and somewhat depressing, experience of JPs to be faced with cocky criminals in court who show no shame whatever, and who appear quite proud of what they have done to wreck other people's lives or property. Sentencing and attempting to rehabilitate such people, especially when they constantly re-offend, is difficult and frustrating; when faced with genuine remorse, magistrates would perhaps be more inclined to temper their decisions, for it is usually easier to be less punitive if the guilty are contrite rather than defiant. However, with more and more offenders not now appearing in court at all, it may be too late to plead for better behaviour and a stronger sense of shame in the public conscience—unless, of course, parents, schools and the media are prepared to do more than in the recent past to champion the cause among young people and to set a better example themselves.

All strata of our society, regardless of background or education, share in the expansion of criminal and dishonest behaviour, the worship of materialism and the decline of morals. Theft is no longer the prerogative of a poor underclass, 'low-level dishonesty' transcends social divisions, with greed as a common factor. It is disheartening to learn that members of the 'respectable' middle-classes are now more often among the guilty. According to a June 2007 report, this majority sector of the population is not as honest and law-abiding as traditionally thought. While the so-called working-class were said to be more likely to offend by theft, damage or violence, the law-breaking middle-classes use more subtle, but no less criminal, methods such as tax evasion, exaggerated expenses, and fraud of one kind or another. Quite well-to-do people confess to petty stealing and seem to have surprisingly few qualms about it. Even those who live comparatively peaceful lives, and who would normally be expected to 'know better', are not always innocent; the only difference is that they are more likely to resolve disputes and difficult situations in less public or violent ways. The decline in so-called 'middle-class values' of courtesy, honesty and the avoidance of physical reaction, accompanied by an injection of belligerent working-class mores into every level of society, has also contributed to a general rise in violence and anti-social behaviour. Aggressiveness begets aggression. This may account for the increase in swearing, punch-ups, road rage, and violence (including use of knives and firearms) to resolve disputes; it has also encouraged sportsmen to attack referees, patients to abuse nurses and passengers to assault bus conductors.

It is particularly damaging to the virtues of civic duty and maintenance of moral standards when those whom we expect to set a good example (from peers to politicians, priests to prison officers) betray our trust, break the law and then, worse still, deny having done so, just like the rest of us. Fraudulent solicitors were beginning to cause concern to the Law Society in the mid-1990s, at the same time as the chairman of the House of Commons public accounts committee was announcing that 'Public standards of probity and integrity have fallen to their lowest level since the creation of the modern Civil Service in the nineteenth century'. A Freedom of Information Act enquiry revealed that 34 Kent police officers, including four with the rank of inspector or higher, were dismissed or required to resign between 2005 and 2012 for disciplinary matters which included drink-driving, drug possession, assault and corruption; over 200 other officers were warned or reprimanded, the most frequent reason for action being related to lack of honesty and integrity. Even the judiciary has not been able to avoid the decline.

A bizarre contrast to the image of a peace-loving and tolerant society is the growth of uncompromising extremist groups such as those who flout the law in the single-minded pursuit of animal rights and environmental conservation. For them, it seems, the end justifies the means, even if that includes intimidation, personal violence and damage to private property. Their prejudiced and destructive activities against lawful research organizations and individuals is reminiscent of the worst religious intolerance and Luddite movements of past centuries.

It must have been much easier to be a JP before World War II, when the magistrates' courts had more authority, there were fewer choices of punishment, re-offending was not so prevalent, fine defaulters usually went to prison, there was little or no legal aid, and the standards used to judge offending and social behaviour were more straightforward. Today, the judiciary has to operate in a climate of moral laxity, variable standards, widespread tolerance of wrongdoing, controversial human rights, and tedious procedures designed to improve the perception of justice. However, basic legal and moral distinctions still exist, and magistrates should always be clear about their duty to uphold what is right in every case.

The fact that around 80 per cent of defendants are found guilty after trial is a sad reflection of the inherent dishonesty of the human character. It is also noticeable how more ready we are these days to deny or excuse offending than we are to praise those who lead exemplary lives; more inclined also to enjoy knocking down our elected leaders than to applaud those who champion honesty and high moral standards against the odds. If the majority do not show constant support for law, police and courts, the conflicting morality of the criminal fraternity and alien cultures gain ground. In a community so riddled with dishonesty and mistrust, it is not easy to sit in judgement without the support of moral authority and public confidence; but it would be virtually impossible if—as some critics of the magistracy insist—better 'understanding' of criminals was to become the principle by which justices and juries decide the difference between guilt and innocence.

CHAPTER 4

National Dilemma

'The wrong-doer cannot do wrong without the hidden will of you all'

Kahlil Gibran, 'The Prophet'

- Failure of prevention and deterrence
- Discordant public opinion
- Confinement versus freedom
- No perfect answers

Peter Hitchens, in his book *A Brief History of Crime*, published in 2003, pointed out the paradox that arises when tough measures, designed to curb criminal activity by the minority, interfere with the legitimate freedoms of the law-abiding majority. He wrote:

'The more harshly we treat wrongdoers and the greater the power of the state to punish and pursue them, the more we preserve liberty for the enormous majority who keep to the laws…(however) the more generously and considerately we create safeguards for transgressors, the fewer freedoms will remain for those who behave themselves. The more we treat crime as the symptom of a social and economic disease, requiring treatment rather than penalties, the more the state will need to become an apparatus of repression'.

A contradiction undoubtedly exists between the thirst for personal liberty and the need for regulation in a crowded country. One man's freedom often amounts to oppression for another; conflicts arise, for instance, over uncontrolled immigration and the use of identity cards, stop-and-search policy, the carrying of knives and random security checks.

Are these just a failure to accept that the benefits of control outweigh the fear of anarchy and vigilantism, or is liberty being restricted unreasonably by authority?

There is constant argument over the effectiveness of non-custodial punishments, and it is obvious that many of those wanting them to be used more often deliberately overrate their success — and underestimate their cost. There are therefore occasions when the Probation Service and others are unable to meet an increased demand from the courts because the resources are not adequate, the treatments on offer are not felt to be tough enough, or they are not available at all.

A notable shift in attitude has taken place in regard to victims. For many years, the liberal establishment patronised those who constantly suffered crime, while maintaining that offenders' rights were more important. Figures published in 2006 showed that 80 per cent of people thought the justice system was fair to the accused, but only 36 per cent felt that it satisfied the needs of victims. The persistent assertion that judges and magistrates are 'out of touch' is one of the general public's ways of expressing concern at the apparently favourable treatment given to criminals. In recent years, this has begun to change, as more is done to re-balance the scales and remove some of the measures which seemed to favour lawbreakers. However, obligatory compliance with European human rights legislation has thrown up some bizarre contradictions which do not help the victims' cause.

At present, our universal reputation as a just and open-minded nation appears to rank more importantly than that of being near the top of the European crime league. Thus we continue to attract and offer asylum to the world's victims of injustice and poverty, a disturbing number of whose children later abuse our culture and reject our laws; we allow bullies to prevail in some of our schools and streets, we compensate burglars for injury while making criminals out of householders who try to stop them, we idolise bad behaviour, and we permit individual human rights to take precedence over common sense and decisions of British courts.

Failure of prevention and deterrence

The rule of law depends—among many other things—on leaders and prominent people (including JPs) setting a good example of integrity in both their public and private lives. 'Ordinary hard-working people' (that phrase beloved of modern politicians) cannot be expected to keep to the law if titled people behave badly, businessmen falsify their expenses, politicians commit perjury, civil servants engage in corrupt practices, popular sportsmen threaten referees, priests abuse young children, and celebrities commit adultery. Contrary to what one might expect, it often seems that the more good fortune people have, the worse they behave, and the more greedy they become. It doesn't help that on top of absurdly high salaries, we continue to pay bonuses, and leave people with their jobs, titles and honours, even when they have failed or been convicted of crimes. All this laxity and tolerance contributes to the weakening of deterrence, and ensures that a high proportion of the prison population consists of undeterred recidivists.

Judging by the persistently high crime figures, the abysmal detection rates (less than eight per cent) and the unresolved arguments over the role of punishment and deterrence, we have little of which to be proud in our efforts to preserve law and order in twenty-first century society. Certainly, our efforts so far have proved insufficient to replace the deterrent factors on which our forefathers could rely; and we are apparently not prepared or able to make our alternative sentences effective enough to prevent constant re-offending. Fortunately, there is one important respect in which we still set a good example to the world: the relatively low incidence of corruption in our public services.

Although there have been substantial advances in the CJS during the last 50 years, too much government policy in this area has been driven by the media. Meanwhile, the national controversy over how best to deal with crime and criminals remains unresolved, which is disappointing to a magistracy that tries as hard as anyone to find acceptable answers to the problem. Sad to say that, while politicians and social reformers continue to cast about for new solutions, few lasting improvements have emerged; some of the most promising have foundered for no other reason than the perversity of human nature. Meanwhile, despite attempts to change it, members of the public continue to feel that the CJS tends to favour lawbreakers more than lawkeepers, and criminals more than victims. On the bench, having to make decisions many of which are circumscribed by the law and available options, it is sometimes difficult not to agree with them.

The journalist Max Hastings reflected the opinion of many, that the law does not work as well as it should, when he wrote, 'It is the first duty of a law-abiding society to protect the young and innocent. When prevention fails, as it sometimes does, our second responsibility is to ensure that the guilty pay the price. Every time (a criminal) goes uncaught or unpunished … the security of all our lives is diminished; the decency of our society is wounded. Until the late twentieth century, the middle-classes granted the police great latitude in protecting them. Today the wheel has spun', he said. 'The weight of the legal system, exploited by clever and handsomely-rewarded defence 'briefs' is at the disposal of every suspect … The range of legal devices for escaping conviction or imprisonment is awesome. There is a need for a new tilting of the balance … but the public must play its part'.

Discordant public opinion

In 1910, when he was Home Secretary, Winston Churchill said: 'The mood and temper of the public in regard to the treatment of crime and criminals is one of the most unfailing tests of the civilisation of any country'. More than 100 years later, it is still quite difficult to tell how Britain ranks in that test, because views on crime and what to do about it must be almost as numerous and varied as the number and variety of people who express them. Although huge resources have been thrown at the problem over many years, progress has been fragmentary. It is usually 'they', or the system, that are expected to provide all the answers; but society itself also has a big part to play in the solution. We come closest to knowing what this requires when each of us examines our own conscience, personal behaviour and the way we bring up and educate our children. Those who claim to have absolute remedies merely expose their naïvety or inexperience.

The public's attitude towards crime and punishment—although frequently conflicting—appears fairly constant; but fear of crime and anti-social behaviour have increased, as have signs of intolerance, 'road rage', and the violent conduct of single-issue minorities who prefer to force their views on the majority by taking the law into their own hands. Beneath all these concerns is the disheartening realisation that no modern form of punishment or treatment can be relied on to overcome crime and bad behaviour. Treatment methods which appear to have been successful in the United States are often seized upon as potential solutions for the UK, but many of them have proved to be less effective when tried in Britain. However, this does not seem to lessen the zeal for importation of American penal reform ideas, and the enthusiasm for replacement of punishment by therapy which usually attends them.

Magistrates are hindered in meeting society's expectations by the continuing contradictory attitude of both public and media to crime and punishment, and by widespread ignorance of the many constraints under which sentencers have to operate. Is it too much to hope that this will change, and that the courts will receive one day a more unanimous view of what the public expects and will accept? For instance, does the responsible, law-abiding majority wish the courts to treat more harshly, not only serious criminals, but also the numerous dishonest and irresponsible offenders who take unjust advantage of the state's compassion and generosity? Or would such a policy attract savage media and liberal condemnation? Having warned offenders, made allowances for their misfortunes, given them second and third chances, ordered expensive treatments to rid them of their criminal and anti-social habits, and finally sent them to prison, is it then fair to say to magistrates and judges 'you should never have sent them there in the first place, because prison doesn't do them any good'?

Alongside the steep rise in UK crime up to the end of the twentieth century—and, arguably, a modest fall in some respects since then—the last five decades have witnessed a running conflict over law and order, an endless dispute between supporters of hard and soft approaches to crime and punishment, between imprisonment and treatment in the community, and between zero tolerance and *laissez-faire*. Government and public opinion has vacillated in response to party political squabbling, economic 'boom and bust', and a noticeable shift in penal philosophy from punitive to reformative. Meanwhile, all manner of strategies have been introduced to bring down the number and cost of the prison population, including early release and judicial exhortation. Throughout this period of experiment, high sentiment and disappointing results, the courts have tried sensibly to reflect the many recurrent changes of mood.

Limited surveys of public opinion on the justice system conducted in both 1983 and 2012 produced similar results. In summary, they indicated:

- Ignorance of how the courts and penal system work
- Confidence in, but low awareness of, the magistracy
- Perception by some that judges and magistrates are (still) 'out of touch'
- Concern about difference between actual and reported crime; also about confusion due to frequent changes in recording methods
- Scepticism about fairness of the judicial system
- Exaggeration of the amount of violent crime, and of leniency by the courts
- Belief that too many are in prison for minor offences or on remand
- Substantial support for non-custodial sentences for non-violent offenders
- Call for more visible community service and offender reparations
- Disillusionment with effectiveness of out-of-court penalties
- Victim experience is rarely reflected in attitude to crime
- Support for more victim involvement; and
- A high proportion of victims think it not worth reporting minor crimes.

A man called Tony Martin, living alone in an isolated Norfolk farmhouse which had been entered illegally several times previously, sparked a national debate in 1999 on the right of individuals to defend themselves and their property against attack. He shot at two previously convicted burglars as they left his home, was found guilty of murdering one of them, and sent to prison for life. Public outcry followed. The charge was later reduced to manslaughter on appeal, and the sentence reduced considerably, but the wounded accomplice sued Martin for criminal injury. This was an important case because it raised no only the question of a householder's right to use reasonable or proportionate force to defend himself and his property, but added to the increasing impression that our justice system too often appears to treat the criminal as the victim. A subsequent attempt, reflecting public opinion, to 'restore popular faith in the rule of law' and to strengthen legislation in favour of innocent citizens, failed because the government maintained that 'it would create a licence to kill with impunity'.

From time-to-time, particular public concern arises from death or serious injury caused by careless driving. Until the coming of the 2006 Road Safety Act, courts were required to decide such cases on the degree of carelessness or inconsiderateness, regardless of the outcome, leaving death by dangerous driving as an unsatisfactory alternative. Relatively light sentences based solely on the poor quality of the driving led to invidious comparisons with the value of human life. While it is unlikely that the awful memory of causing a death ever leaves the accused, the family of the deceased or injured person can be outraged by the implication that one person's life is apparently worth no more than another's few years in prison. Such cases are made more traumatic for all parties when the press sensationalise the issues; it is cruel and extremely unhelpful of tabloid newspapers when they try to establish a link in people's minds between the level of a fine and the value of a human life. These unfortunate occasions are almost as heart-rending for members of the court as they are for the bereaved; they are a reminder of how imperfect the concept of justice for all can be, and of how impossible it is to remove totally the elements of chance and luck in life.

Dangerous driving, being a more serious charge, is likely to be heard in the Crown Court, where sentencing powers are greater, so the temptation to make comparisons between the scale of punishment and the value of a human life, although still pertinent, is likely to be rather less.

On the other hand, there always remains the possibility the court might not agree that the driving was dangerous, even though a death occurred. As the revised Act requires unintended consequences to be taken into account, it is now possible in theory that a driver who sneezes, and momentarily loses control, could find himself imprisoned for up to five years for causing death by careless driving.

The relative seriousness of crimes has become another source of controversy. In 1988, for some offences, opinion varied between the old and the young, male and female, victim and non-victim, manual and non-manual. In general, the old, female, non-victim and non-manual categories considered most crimes to be more serious than did other groups; the younger generation appeared to have a contrasting set of values, but there was little difference in seriousness rankings between social classes; incredibly, those who had experienced victimisation tended to regard most crimes less seriously. In 1955, a Gallup Poll had shown that 73 per cent of the population wanted corporal punishment brought back, and 70 per cent (more than ever before) favoured capital punishment — a view with which Parliament has consistently disagreed since the death penalty was abolished in 1969 (Northern Ireland 1973).

Research on offence seriousness published by Ken Pease in 1988 showed in summary that:

- Most crimes are regarded as trivial; victims may not report them, often because they think the police will not be interested or successful in solving them.
- Chief reasons for reporting crime were: insurance (20 per cent), hope of non-repetition (17 per cent) and hope of property recovery (12 per cent).
- Victimisation doesn't alter people's view of seriousness (except that assault victims often rate the crime against them to be more trivial than those not assaulted).
- Victim ratings alter total crime seriousness results significantly.
- Compared with older people, the young consider property crime less serious.

- There is little difference between social classes in rating seriousness.
- Degree of culpability should be added to seriousness before sentence.
- Offences against the person are considered the most serious by young and old.
- There is often a marked difference between young/old, male/ female, manual/non-manual and victim/non-victim; the old, female, non-manual and non-victim classes regarded crime more seriously.
- Most serious: Rape, mugging/robbery, sexual attacks, violence to persons.
- Least serious: Shop theft, soliciting/prostitution, [damage to] property.
- Victims prefer probation for offenders, rather than compensation for serious crimes.

The Sentencing Guidelines Council—now the Sentencing Council—will no doubt have taken research results into consideration when sorting out degrees of seriousness for the most common crimes, and all courts are now obliged to follow its recommendations closely. However, as crime affects people's lives in so many different ways, wide scope still remains for differing opinions. As a result of the council's work, sentencing in some ways may have become slightly easier than 50 years ago, but in others it has become more difficult; in keeping to the guidelines, magistrates and judges can still find themselves in some cases hammered by the press and public for failing to measure up to pre-conceived ideas of 'justice'. Even when the level of seriousness is beyond doubt, courts still have to determine how best to take it into account alongside individual culpability, the need for appropriate punishment and the competing aims of custody and treatment—and then give their reasons.

Penal reformers, politicians, police and the public are perplexed over what to do about anti-social behaviour and occasional outbreaks of rioting. The public usually wants violence and repeated crimes dealt with by custodial sentences and, in general, the courts agree; but, as prison numbers and costs climb higher, so government demands for more criminals to be punished or treated in the community grow—as do the numbers of police cautions and fixed penalties. There has been a limited response from the courts to each wave of pressure for alternatives to custody, but the plain fact is that for years magistrates and judges, especially the former, have been sending criminals to prison only as a last resort. Many of those who claim to have the answers to the problem clearly do not appreciate how difficult it is to punish or treat a criminal who has failed to respond to every type of sentence in the book, and who continues to offend—again and again.

Politicians always feel obliged to provide categorical answers to what they claim to be the failures of their predecessors. In recent times, their reactions to persistent crime and overcrowded prisons have concentrated on finding yet more ways of restricting custodial sentences while adding to the non-custodial alternatives, but the statistics and trends reflect the nation's continuing inability to find effective answers to drugs, alcohol, theft, property damage and violence of all kinds. Meanwhile magistrates, being neither the problem nor the solution, have little option but to continue conscientiously carrying out their judicial duties with the tools available, while the disputes between realism and reformism, custody and community, punishment and treatment, continue to rage outside.

Confinement versus freedom

Custodial versus non-custodial punishment is probably the biggest single penal issue of the last 50 years. As economic life and the study of human behaviour have become more complex, so has intensity of the argument between punishment by confinement and punishment by various other means. Beyond doubt, community sentences have their place as alternatives in the penal system, but justice is not served if they are regarded as 'a soft touch' by both offenders and public. There are no absolute answers; certain disposals are found to be essential or successful in some cases, alternatives are unsuccessful or are found to be of doubtful necessity in others. Courts are trained and competent to make decisions on verdict and punishment, but less well-equipped when it comes to treatment. How can sentencers know what fits each individual after only one or two court appearances and a single probation report? The Probation Service and others may be in a better position to provide part of the answer through longer contact with the offender, but even they cannot be expected to succeed in every case, especially if they are without sufficient resources to carry the extra burden of dealing with really hardened criminals and mentally unstable personalities in the community.

When the prison population remains obstinately high, government does little to discourage the police from using more cautions and fixed penalties — regardless of seriousness, inconsistency and offenders' means — as we have seen since 2007. Metropolitan Police Assistant Commissioner Tim Godwin, speaking to the Magistrates Association Council in 2008, gave some support to this view when he admitted that 'conditional cautions are all about cost and efficiency — nothing to do with justice', he said.

At one point, magistrates were being told by both government and judges that they should treat burglary as an imprisonable offence; a year or two later, when prison numbers were becoming a political embarrassment, they were advised that community service was the more appropriate sanction. When JPs responded to official urging that they should use punishment in the community in place of custody, the public continued (often with good reason) to regard the former as a 'soft option'. There are few occasions when the public can feel confident that the police, the courts and penal policy are really getting ahead of the upsurge in crime, but it is particularly disturbing for most people to hear that criminal invasion of the home can be treated with anything less than custodial punishment. Current statistics show some offences, such as burglary, falling; others, such as violent crimes, have risen. Even then, it sometimes emerges that positive trends are not due to successful government or police policies, but to changes in emphasis or the way the figures are collected and presented.

The latter part of the twentieth century was the period during which we learnt that on average those sentenced to life imprisonment spent 13.7 years in prison, and that a six-month sentence could mean that 'you may be out after only three months'; hardly surprising that some experienced criminals preferred to spend three months in prison than two years on probation. Legislators at that time were trying to face in two directions simultaneously; these days they are driven by economics as much as by other considerations. The legitimate wish of society to convict the guilty and acquit the innocent, while preserving the rights of those accused of crime, takes time and money. It costs the nation more than two million pounds to keep a 25-year-old killer behind bars for 60 years (the annual cost of prison being about the same as that for a year at Eton) — and rehabilitation is expensive, too.

The powerful post-war arguments of sociologists in favour of treatment rather than punishment, while failing to prove the superiority of the former, at least succeeded in persuading successive cash-strapped governments — if not the public — that the wider availability of non-custodial sentences can be taken as an excuse to avoid building more prisons. The tide of political opinion has been running for some time against custody and its high cost, but so has disillusionment with the alternatives; it also seems to be forgotten that community punishment schemes and treatments can be nearly as expensive if they are to be successful. For instance, in 2010 the National Audit Office estimated that a six-week stay in prison cost £4,500, but that a two-year community order — including intensive supervision, 80 hours unpaid work and participation in accredited programmes — cost almost the same: £4,200.

It would be comforting to know that the proliferation of alternatives to custody in recent years was due to the fact that, not only are they less expensive, but also that they have been successful in boosting rehabilitation of prisoners and reducing crime. It could yet happen, but there is little evidence so far that this is so, and the number of offenders sent to prison has tended to drift ever upwards. The chief driving force behind most post-war penal changes has been the need to curb the escalating cost to the Treasury of keeping people behind bars, but our permissive nation pays heavily in other ways for the criminals left free to continue offending. We still find it difficult to accept that keeping order and enforcing the law in a democratic country is expensive; and simply slashing the budget in the hope that 'savings will be found' is no answer. However, because we are not prepared to devote more resources or pay the full cost, we find ourselves in practice having to compromise and tolerate higher levels of dishonesty and crime than in theory are acceptable.

The courts — especially the magistrates' courts — have 'stood on their heads' to reduce the numbers sent to prison in the last 40 years, and governments have employed all kinds of early-release programmes and community schemes but, although these may have saved money in the short term, it cannot yet be claimed that they have played a major part in reducing the number of criminals or the overall amount of crime. The penal system, at least since World War II, has failed. The courts, the government, the police and many others are blamed but, although rarely acknowledged, the main cause is society itself — i.e. us (see quote above from Gibran's *The Prophet*). We indulge in and tolerate an increasingly higher level of crime and dishonesty, and refrain from contemplating the type and levels of deterrent punishment likely to be more successful. Punishment in the community may have a place in the sentencing spectrum, but it will never be the solution that many people hope or expect, because much of the rationale for it is driven, not by successful experience, but by political and financial imperatives.

Transportation worked while there was somewhere to send away criminals, but hanging has been proved to have little effect on murder rates. Neither prison nor community sentences are as universally successful in reducing crime as we always hope; at best, they contain it. What is there that can yet be found to work more effectively in a free democracy hedged around by the statutory rights of individual citizens? Is it a conscious change in attitude toward crime and criminals, so that they become even more unacceptable, or have we yet to discover how to make rehabilitation work more successfully? The modern answer currently preferred by a succession of desperate politicians, driven by bulging prison numbers and the need to find quick antidotes to the problem of recidivist criminals, is to cling pathetically to a new faith in various forms of 'restorative justice'. Their naïvety in thinking that the ingrained criminal habits of a lifetime can so easily be eradicated is astonishing, made worse by their habit of targeting reduction of the prison population, without first ensuring that there are sufficiently well-funded and effective alternatives available.

Spending enormous sums of public money in the well-meaning hope of reforming young adults whose habits from an early age have loaded them with indelible criminal instincts, often appears wasteful, unrealistic and disproportionate when compared with the poor chances of success. Bearing in mind the huge and unrelenting cost of probation, drugs and alcohol treatment, non-custodial punishments, supervision and prisons, ought we not to be asking ourselves whether less money and emphasis should be devoted to fruitless attempts at rehabilitation of hardened criminals, and more to the roots of the problem: the early stages of children's lives, parenting and primary schools, where inculcation of good and honest behaviour is easier and more rewarding, i.e. switching the emphasis from hopeless cure to hopeful prevention. The famous maxim, usually attributed to the Jesuits, recognises not only the importance and relative ease of inculcating good attitude and behaviour while children are very young, but also the relative difficulty and cost of trying to change damaged minds and criminal habits in later years: 'Give me the child until he is seven, and I will show you the man', they say.

Having initiated, in association with the Probation Service, a praiseworthy scheme in 2005 to teach gardening skills to about ten drug-taking recidivists, and thereby to help them reform their habits and lives, Monty Don, presenter of the BBC's *Gardeners' World* programme, found the addicts to be 'completely self-centred'. After seven months of 'frustration and very hard work by his heroic staff', he had to admit that he was able to claim only one 'success', which illustrates how difficult rehabilitation can be for all concerned.

Although research suggests that the public in theory wants less prison for minor offences, along with more community service and reparation, the general view still seems to favour some form of punishment, but with less leniency towards violent offenders and recidivists — a recipe which, if followed, appears to ensure that our prisons will remain overcrowded for some time to come. A tougher stance usually finds itself at odds with those who have undying faith in the virtues of human nature, and with a Home Office living in constant fear of rising prison numbers. Magistrates have the difficult task of treading pragmatically between the extremes, while at the same time trying to show that they are responsive to public opinion. But how should that opinion be assessed? Surely not through the expressions of emotional pundits or sensational headlines, for they are often the cause of public concern, not a reflection of it.

Demagogues can whip up prejudice against those whom they believe have innocently offended some unwritten rule of 'political correctness', and the media often feels obliged to justify its role in a free society by reporting only the wildest expressions of the mob, or by picking scapegoats before the courts have had an opportunity to identify the truth. In such circumstances, juries in particular need to be warned of the dangers inherent in knowledge obtained from pre-trial publicity. For magistrates, this is not such a problem, because of their training in impartial decision-making and the obligatory use of sentencing guidelines. In fact, JPs more often now find themselves trying to educate public opinion rather than react to it.

Nevertheless, the argument smoulders on; every now and again a government minister or penal reform group bursts into flame with a renewed expression of belief in the innate goodness of mankind and the ability of a reformed justice system to turn all criminals miraculously from sinners into saints, and sows' ears into silk purses, by offering criminals new opportunities for rehabilitation through relatively inexpensive treatment in place of endless punishment in costly prisons. Each wave of new ministers, penologists and 'experts' of all kinds condemns the 'failed policies' of their predecessors while claiming to have discovered new ways of stemming the perverse conduct of mankind. They occasionally have good, original ideas, but in the meantime the courts have to persist in their search for the sentence most likely to work for each individual criminal; they have little option but to continue using custodial methods for the most violent and persistent offenders—of whom there continues to be all too many—while state and public bear the huge cost and frustration of overflowing prisons and persistent recidivism.

Most post-war governments have been worried about the steady rise in prison numbers, unaccompanied by a corresponding fall in crime, which has occurred in spite of a parallel rise in community sentences. Solution of the problem is not made easier by the preponderance in Britain of high-profile lobbies that continually dispute the facts and deny the need for tougher responses to crime, more discipline in schools, and stricter control of TV violence, alcohol and drugs. Unfortunately, no groups with comparable influence seem to exist for long enough to challenge prevailing liberal views.

A dithering nation has failed to give the police and the courts a clear guide as to what is deemed acceptable socially, politically or financially. A substantial proportion of the public still demands more and longer prison sentences for many offenders, while impecunious governments, deluded penal reformers and unhelpful do-gooders clamour for more and cheaper non-custodial punishments. It is naïve and simply not good enough to maintain that 'prison doesn't work', and therefore to assume that any alternatives must be preferable. Among the liberals, there seems to exist an amazing ignorance of sentencing realities, compounded by blind faith in restorative justice. Shortage of money has allowed more support for this point of view than it deserves, with the result that current penal policy has emerged as a vague compromise between prison for the most serious criminals, punishment in the community for the rest and increased emphasis on rehabilitation for both.

No perfect answers

'We cannot improve the world faster than we improve ourselves'
Bishop Mandell Creighton (1843–1901)

It would be most gratifying if, after all the years of struggle with crime prevention, punishment and deterrence, we had found a justice system flexible and effective enough to fit all, or nearly all, cases. Probably my greatest disappointment as a JP was to discover how ineffective are punishments of all kinds—even the death penalty in countries where it still exists—in deterring people from committing crimes, and then in dissuading more than half of them from offending again—and again. If death and prison do not deter, and rehabilitation fails, the magistrates and judges of the civilised world are left today with no ultimate sanction—unless, of course, mankind can be persuaded to behave in a less violent and dishonest way in the first place. In my early days on the bench, I thought naïvely that most offenders would naturally respond to, and be deterred by, proportionate penalties and punishments. Human nature ensures that nothing is so simple.

Giving his 'thoughts' to the BBC *Today* programme, a Cumbrian priest who had visited a young offender institution said that he asked a prison officer what are the things most likely to save or change offenders. The officer, who was apparently unaware that he was talking to a priest, replied: 'Religion or the love of a good woman, but in any case the answer always involves people'. He should know. Even the welfare state does not provide women good enough to love and stick by inveterate criminals, but any religion that can make them think of other people instead of themselves is good news for the cause of restorative justice. I have known many occasions when the bench has preferred to give a non-custodial sentence, after having received persuasive evidence from a wife, partner, priest or other responsible individual who promised to help personally in preventing the offender from getting into further trouble.

We know that criminals are the takers from society; they are selfish, unrepentant and rarely volunteer to give back anything of benefit to the community; they are mostly unresponsive and ungrateful for the second chances and help that society constantly offers them. Yet we go on and on trying—at huge expense—to reform them and be kind and understanding to them. All we seem to get in return is more crime, more violence and more abuse. The restoration of persistent criminals to a permanently honest life has proved over and over again to be a thankless and costly task. Unfortunately for those who have to suffer them in the meantime, the reform of criminals often has as much to do with the moderating effects of increasing age as with the punishment or treatment they receive. It is small wonder that numerous well-intentioned rehabilitation schemes burn out, and the heroes who attempt to change the lives of inveterate criminals and drug addicts lose patience and give up. Why not re-direct their altruism towards helping parents and young children to avoid going off the road in the first place? Much easier, cheaper, and more likely to be successful. Basil Henriques, the British author and philanthropist, seemed to agree; after listening to a distinguished psychiatrist claiming how much more wicked and harmful it was to check young children than simply to pick them up each time they fell, said 'I still think there's more sense in having a fence at the top of the cliff than an ambulance at the bottom'.

While we have not yet found more effective remedies—or the will to use those that could be more effective—we must not forget the many admirable people who continue striving to uphold the law, prevent crime, reform criminals, live honest lives and set a good example; the people who are probably inspired by Burke's well-known assertion: 'All that is necessary for evil to triumph is that good men do nothing', or Haile Selassie's elaboration of the same theme: 'It has been the inaction of those who could have acted, the indifference of those who should have known better, the silence of the voice of justice when it mattered most, that has made it possible for evil to triumph', he said.

In terms of honesty, tolerance and observance of the law, we can still claim to be among the world's best, but it is most unfortunate that this positive side of our national character has to carry the disfigurement of a persistent criminal core that brings shame on the whole country, especially when this is manifest as violent and drunken behaviour on the streets of other countries. At worst, this rump consists chiefly of younger people responsible for most of the murders, rapes, damage and vandalism, burglary, theft, robbery, drugs and alcohol abuse; they tyrannise whole communities, intimidate witnesses, drive and behave in public without consideration for others, and threaten anyone who stands in their way. At best, they commit only one or two minor offences, learn their lesson, accept their punishment, co-operate with those who are ready to help them, and 'go straight' for the rest of their lives. At the end of each first offender's case in court, the natural hope of every JP is that the decisions of the bench will have done whatever was necessary to keep him or her from offending again, but all too often such ambitions are unrealised.

We have to keep trying. But it can be disheartening to find that criminal justice policy sometimes seems less concerned with observing the law than with keeping order, less with encouragement of good behaviour than with punishment for wrongdoing, less with long-term planning than short-term expediency—and, dare I say, less with the future of the magistracy than with the preservation of full employment in the Civil Service.

An example of the dilemma which faced magistrates doing their best to find an acceptable balance between a persistent offender, a punitive public, and the urgent need to reduce prison numbers, arose in 2008: A moped rider, who had previously been cautioned for carrying an offensive weapon, was found in possession of a carving knife; he was also in breach of a conditional discharge (for three counts of handling stolen goods), and had no licence, insurance or MOT certificate. The sentence, of two months' prison (suspended for 18 months), £100 fine for no insurance and six penalty points, caused a newspaper correspondent, outraged by the court's leniency, to write, 'Until we rid ourselves of the idiots that are magistrates, we won't rid ourselves of idiots on our roads'. After having been given several chances already, there is little doubt that this typical offender would have been sent straight to prison 50 years ago; but there are many today who would have said that, on the face of it, this was an appropriate occasion for no more than a community sentence. Others might have added that, until newspapers rid themselves of idiot correspondents, the magistracy and its work will continue to be misrepresented by the media.

Much of our current inability to deal more effectively with criminals has to do with conflicting attitudes to the causes of crime and the punishment or treatment of offenders. So, for a start, perhaps we should ask ourselves: If other civilised countries can apparently be more successful in reducing crime and dealing with criminals, why can't we? Singapore, for instance, which outwardly appears as, but may not actually be, a free and democratic country, succeeds in having relatively much less crime and fewer police per head than we do. There appear to be a number of reasons for this, most of which contrast strongly with our own situation. Firstly, they have managed through schooling and social pressure to establish an anti-crime culture, which leads to a healthy respect for the law and widespread commitment to the prevention of crime. Also, they jail a higher number per head than the UK; by our standards, their punishments are harsh and their prisons are awful, but they are apparently more successful in deterring re-offenders than we are. Criminals are scorned and attract no public sympathy there; and they have an effective rehabilitation scheme for first offenders.

A significant feature of what at times appears to be a rather one-sided argument is the combined power and influence of the liberal and reformist establishment in our country, represented by such bodies as the National Association for the Care and Resettlement of Offenders, the Prison Reform Trust, the Howard League for Penal Reform, Liberty (formerly the National Council for Civil Liberties), and others of like mind including, sometimes, the Probation Service. These organizations tend towards the 'understanding' ideology: 'if the courts would learn better to understand criminals, they would send many fewer of them to prison', they say. There is no organized equivalent line-up, lobbying for less leniency and tougher sentences. Meanwhile, no-one can honestly claim to have the perfect answer to the dilemma of human criminal behaviour. Prominence is given to isolated successes in the use of non-custodial remedies, and the authorities are quick to take credit whenever there is a slight fall in the number of certain crimes, but many of the supporting statistics lose value because of massaged figures, re-classified headings, changes in policing priorities, and other reasons which make useful comparisons almost impossible. The phrase 'lies, damned lies and statistics' comes to mind when even the police admit to skewing the crime figures to make their performance look better than reality.

Statistics attached to criminal behaviour may offer reasons and excuses but, after many years of dealing with criminals and offenders in court, I found it difficult to abandon the view that, to a large extent, society gets the crime it deserves; we can still reduce it substantially if we really mean to, but the primary responsibility for this lies within the community — not with government, not with the police, not with the courts. Crime is not just a matter for the CJS.

CHAPTER 5

Lawyers: Allies or Rivals?

'The one great principle of English law is to make business for itself'

Charles Dickens

- Justices' clerks and their successors
- Lawyer justice is not peer justice
- District judges are not lay justices
- Threat to the lay magistracy

Justices of the peace interact variously but significantly with members of the legal profession. First and foremost, with those who advise them on law, practice and procedure; then also with prosecution and defence lawyers in court, with judges in the Crown Court and with district judges (DJs) acting as fellow magistrates.

While the virtual abolition of the ancient office of justices' clerk (JC), and the infusion of more DJs into the summary courts, have done as much as anything in recent times to change the face of local justice and the traditional association between lawyers and JPs, it remains a fact that lay magistrates always need lawyers, but lawyers do not always need magistrates. Therefore, if future participation of the public in the justice system is to thrive as a primary feature of our democracy, it is essential that the two continue to enjoy a good relationship without detriment to the character and independence of the lay element.

Lawyers, in one way and another, have considerable power and opportunity to reduce the strength, influence and efficiency of the magistracy, especially when their livelihood is at stake. An example of this occurred in 2010, when the Law Commission (all or mostly lawyers) failed to support the abolition of committal proceedings in magistrates' courts—on the flimsy ground that it 'couldn't see sufficient benefits'—even though the 2003 Criminal Justice Act had already provided for it, and the MA had strongly urged that such an obvious 'cause of needless delay' should be removed to save both time and legal costs. Nevertheless, in 2013, committal proceedings were abandoned.

Lay magistrates and juries are now among the few legitimate obstacles to total dominance of the judicial system by lawyers who, it is sometimes necessary to point out, are not automatically entitled to monopoly of judgement. That lawyers are members of a most distinguished and talented profession is beyond doubt, but they can be as fallible, intolerable, inconsistent and illogical as the rest of us. Furthermore, it is in the national interest that our society is governed by the rule of law, not by the rule of lawyers.

Justices' clerks and their successors

The ancient, statutory office of JC was central to the local summary justice system. Now, under the provisions of the Courts and Tribunals Act 2018, it has—regrettably—been abolished, thus breaking the special clerk-bench bond on which the magistrates' courts had depended for hundreds of years. Unfortunately, those responsible for generating the breakdown of this relationship appear to have been careless of the damage they were doing to the foundations of the magistracy, thereby exposing it to fresh misgivings about its own ability to offer a reliable and efficient service in the future.

Many magistrates appear to have been slow to appreciate how thin the loyalty of some JCs had become by the 1990s. Until then, they had believed that most of their clerks were friends who could be relied upon to give full support to the lay justice system of which they were such an essential part; but, with the benefit of hindsight, it looks as if that assumption was misplaced in many cases. It could be said that the JCs brought the end of their role upon themselves. Some of them were showing signs of hunger for more powers and were actively lobbying the Home Office (the then responsible department) for radical change, others were seldom seen in court by their magistrates, and a few were suspected of spending working hours on private business. Increasing numbers were leaving the service to become district judges (DJs) or crown prosecutors. In the meantime, qualified court clerks (legal advisers), alongside experienced JPs, were finding it quite possible to manage without JCs. If the training of magistrates can be tuned so as to make them a shade more legally astute, there is no reason why this new partnership, using modern technology to the full, should not provide the basis for a stronger lay magistracy in the future.

For the system to operate at all, JPs have to continue relying on a symbiotic relationship between themselves and their clerks, founded on a tradition of public service and sensitive mutual esteem. Fundamentally, this collaboration recognises that advice may assist magisterial decision-making, but must never interfere with it. The most efficient and effective courts are those in which the chairman and the clerk work in complete harmony and understanding; a relationship described by a former president of the Justices' Clerks' Society (JCS) as akin to that in rugby football between the stand-off half and the scrum-half, in which the chairman should be able to 'pick up the ball' whenever the clerk throws it to him or her, and the clerk should always be ready and able to pick it up whenever the chairman drops it. Bad chairmen, who do not take the lead when their role requires it, and whose inadequacy creates a vacuum in procedure, should not be surprised if their clerk feels obliged to fill it.

Section 29 of the 2003 Courts Act is meant to guarantee the judicial independence of legal advisers, who were not subject to direction by the Lord Chancellor or any other person (and now only by the Lord Chief Justice or his designate). However, as civil servants since 2005, and now reporting in many areas straight to executive directors, it cannot be denied that they are influenced by government administrative policies, even when those policies are known to be unpalatable to the magistracy. All the while that clerks and their assistants are employed by central government through the Courts and Tribunals Service, the potential for conflict of interest and threat to the judicial independence of the magistracy remain.

Today's JPs may have cause for further concerns, such as increased vulnerability to the actions of those over whom they have no control, and decreased ability to ensure a reliable courts service in all circumstances. Court clerks have in the past shown that they are not above threatening 'industrial action' or 'working to rule', and lack of staff is not an infrequent excuse for delays. Shortage of clerks at any time poses an immediate threat to the operation of a service dependent on their advice and support, and renders it more exposed than ever to the importation of district judges.

It is a serious matter if courts have to be cancelled because absent staff are not replaced after budget cuts or resignations. Such a situation arose in March 1989, when 945 court sittings (equivalent to 5,500 cases) had to be cancelled because of a lack of clerks, and in 2008, when no less than five legal advisers in Surrey were on maternity leave at the same time. Staff shortage of a different kind caused concern among Manchester justices on more than one occasion, when their clerk found it necessary to act as both prosecutor and legal adviser.

Some have suggested that the answer to the problem of clerk shortages is for magistrates' courts to move towards mixed panels of lay and professional members, thus becoming less reliant on legal advisers. For reasons argued elsewhere in this book, and especially in this chapter, the magistracy would be likely to consider this an unacceptable solution, unless it could be used to pave the way for abolition of either-way offences. Such an arrangement would otherwise reduce JPs permanently to the same secondary role as they have in the Crown Court: supposedly equal decision-making partners on a lawyer-dominated bench. In no time at all, it would be found convenient and cheaper to dispense with the lay members altogether. However, as is suggested below, a more acceptable solution might exist if the most serious family and either-way cases could be transferred to a 'middle-tier' bench, consisting of two JPs sitting with a DJ as chairman—a reform which would save the country millions of pounds.

Lawyer justice is not peer justice

At a time when politicians and reformers demand more diversity and representativeness among JPs, it is ironic that it is not considered necessary to apply the same criteria to the selection of DJs; while excessive attention is given to the variety, ethnic background, age and gender of the former, equal concern does not seem to apply to the latter. If it is so important for JPs to be diverse (and even representative), why not even more so for DJs? It is also relevant to mention the large number of lawyers in Parliament (where barrister MPs are distinguished as 'learned', rather than 'honourable'). If any bench contained the same proportion of, say, farmers (however honourable) or school teachers (however learned), there would be an outcry. Why should unpaid JPs—always under oath 'to do right to all manner of people without fear or favour'—be the only body whose selection is so critically subject to personal characteristics, when they are these days the last people likely to fall victim to prejudice or bias in their decision-making?

The unique value of justice directed by locally-based lay men and women arises from the importance of 'community' in our lives, but justice conducted by single, unknown lawyers in remote courthouses destroys much of the inter-dependence on which communities rely for their wellbeing. The lay magisterial system and punishment or treatment of criminals in the community give the local populace an opportunity to share and direct some of the responsibilities and burdens of community life alongside its benefits, as used to be the case under the sixteenth century Poor Laws. In *The Judiciary in the Magistrates' Courts*, a government review published in 2000, it was found that 63 per cent of the public thought lay magistrates represent the views of the community, while only nine per cent thought DJs do so, and that JPs (41 per cent) were more likely to sympathise with offenders than DJs (12 per cent). The same review also found that three-quarters of the public felt that trials and prison sentences should be decided by a bench of JPs, rather than single DJs, and that the latter are more likely to use custody.

It is in the best interest of 'British justice' in general that a strong unpaid magistracy should be promoted as an effective antidote to the increasing hegemony of lawyers. Dominance by a relatively small group of professionals over the rest of the population is potentially harmful to the integrity of our democracy and encourages a monopoly of the right to judge. It is even less acceptable when members of such a distinguished profession behave like irresponsible trade unionists, prepared to 'withhold their services', take 'industrial action', or demean themselves by appearing as gowned and bewigged placard-carriers on the streets of London.

Although the relationship between lawyers and JPs has to be fairly close, the two vocations are not the same, nor should they be encouraged to become so. It is the essence of the magistracy that JPs are intended to be drawn widely from among 'ordinary' members of the community. They are trained as judges and decision-makers of both verdict and sentence, not as advocates who may have to take sides and win cases. Lawyers, in this context at least, cannot be described as ordinary; they are educated as professionals in the details of law and the art of advocacy, and many become highly skilled in drafting and interpreting legislation. Those among them who are members of Parliament also pass the laws that other lawyers have written — sometimes in language which only lawyers can understand. Even more power passes to this single class if — in addition to being the draftsmen, legislators, interpreters and judges — they are then permitted to assume the role of a single-member jury in the magistrates' courts. Although they can be relied upon to do an adequate job in that capacity, are likely to have a well-developed reasoning ability, and may have their verdicts taken to appeal in the Crown Court, this does not guarantee superior wisdom or a greater feel for justice. Lawyers are skilled and practised in deciding what is and is not legal, but it does not follow that they should be allowed in addition to possess a monopoly of decisions over truth and falsehood, right and wrong. Thus the magistracy, albeit with legal assistance, should remain 'ours', not theirs.

It is as much a mistake to assume that lawyers will automatically make good magistrates, as it is to imagine that good magistrates invariably result from more training. Furthermore, it does not follow that lawyers' law means justice for all, nor that those who are learned in law will be more fair; nor should they be permitted to keep the law to themselves. As one cynic, quoting Napolean, declared: 'Justice is too important to be left to lawyers'.

The strength and beneficial effects of popular justice lie in the clear separation of roles, enabling independent, unpaid laymen to hold a balance when necessary between competing lawyers. The magistracy must not appear to be an extension of the legal profession; it must be seen to be separate and independent. It is the people's jurisdiction and 'localism' that must prevail in the summary courts. This is the basis of the system described by historian Arthur Bryant in *Makers of the Realm* when he wrote about 'Local freeholders ... worthy and lawful men ... judges of fact and assessors of evidence, who know their neighbourhood and represent the interests of property and good sense of the local community ... deputed to take counsel of the neighbourhood'. The traditional links between law and people are severely weakened by the demise of local justice, the dominance of lawyers and the infusion of solo-sitting DJs. It is appalling to realise how the transfer of administrative power away from the lay magistracy so easily paved the way for cavalier politicians, lawyers and bonus-driven officials, in pursuit of arbitrary performance objectives, to destroy the concept of local justice by local people.

At least one senior, and much respected, metropolitan 'stipe' (Peter Badge) appeared to agree with this view in 1989, when he wrote in *The Magistrate*:

> 'Whenever asked if stipendiary magistrates will replace JPs, I invariably and sincerely reply that I do not believe it will ever happen, and I say emphatically that I would not wish it to happen. [I say this] because trial before a lay bench is trial by one's peers, and as such is priceless. Magistrates' courts are in every sense people's courts and the embodiment of democracy, and the system has proved itself over the past 700 years. But I fully understand the fear that if we [stipes] arrive in various court areas, the quality work will be given to us, and the dross left to the lay magistrates'.

Be that as it may, JPs naturally look up to and respect members of the senior judiciary; and most lawyers, by the time they become judges in the higher courts are, or appear to have become, supportive of the lay magistracy. However, among its nastiest critics in the past have been junior barristers and senior solicitors; it is probably also true to say that there has always been a simmering antagonism among some of those who, while gaining much of their living from the skilful practice of advocacy in front of untrained juries, have difficulty in avoiding a patronising attitude when it comes to less gullible magistrates. Why, for instance, have lawyers often been among those most eager to prevent JPs from sitting too often or becoming more competent in their work? It is also not unlikely that similar prejudice lurks in the minds of the 15 per cent of MPs who are lawyers, which may explain why JPs often appear to receive less than the passionate support accorded to juries and the legal profession itself whenever Parliament is considering matters affecting the lay magistracy.

Given the choice and self-serving human nature, lawyers are more likely to vote for measures that will provide lucrative opportunities for their professional colleagues than for those that will strengthen the powers of independent lay justices. Otherwise it is difficult to understand why, at a time when JPs cost significantly less and are probably more competent than ever, a greater number of cases are not diverted to the magistrates' courts from the over-loaded Crown Court, and why the number of DJs has been allowed to grow so needlessly to the current level. Furthermore, why was it considered proper — at least, up to now — for novice DJs to sit alone as sentencers on guilty plea cases, but not for experienced senior JPs to do so?

In a democratic country, there is something essentially right about a justice system in which the 'wisdom of the crowd' can be utilised and ordinary folk be widely involved — yes, trained for the job, but without membership of a profession or expectation of material reward. However, those who compiled the 1215 Magna Carta, establishing the 'liberty' and 'lawful judgment of fellow citizens' as standards of English law, and whoever it was who phrased 'defend our laws' in the National Anthem, would be horrified today to see how these key principles have been eroded by relentless centralisation and the substitution of non-peer lawyers on the justices' bench. It should be noted that the Magna Carta enshrined the right to trial by fellow 'peers' as nobles; not, as is so often misunderstood, by persons of the same age, status or ability — and certainly not by single professional lawyers.

In a 1967 *Times* interview, Lord Chancellor Gardiner, asked whether in an ideal world he would prefer professional magistrates, replied

'No, I would prefer lay justices. We have some fine stipendiary magistrates, but nobody who does nothing but crime day after day, year after year, is as good a court as a lot of men and women from different walks of life, all pooling their joint experience, and in effect representing the public'.

His successor, Lord Hailsham, said in 1971,

'I would regard the abolition of the lay magistracy as a sheer disaster. For getting through seventy cases or so in the course of a morning's work, there is of course nothing to touch stipendiary magistrates. But the public do not like their cases being disposed of summarily by a single man, however professional he may be. They do not like to feel that justice is administered like a factory production line. What JPs lose in professionalism they gain in local knowledge; what they lose in speed, they gain in the added humanity of having three quite differently constituted human beings putting their heads together. If you get rid of JPs, you will lose one of the most valuable and stabilising of your social institutions'.

Lord Chancellor Elwyn Jones, wrote in the 1974 handbook for newly-appointed JPs that

'our traditional practice has served us well, has proved itself, and should be continued. So long as lay magistrates are willing to accept the burden, and undergo the training which is necessary for them to discharge it, it would be the greatest of tragedies if we were to abandon the lay magistracy'.

Putting aside the obvious advantages of shared, as opposed to single, decisions on verdict and sentence, it is extraordinary that, during a period of prolonged national austerity, government, public services, courts administrators and senior members of the judiciary persist in supporting — often without justification or scruple — the appointment of so many DJs at a cost substantially higher than that of a lay bench, and that the accelerated infusion of DJs has been allowed to take place in spite of widespread concern about judges sitting alone, and repeated reassurances to anxious JPs from successive Lord Chancellors and Royal

Commissions. In such an irrational situation, it is difficult not to suspect the existence of prejudice, even corruption, somewhere in the system.

The deliberate increase of DJs, the apparent acceptance of single adjudication and luke-warm official support for the lay magistracy, have tarnished the acclaimed democratic image of British justice. Appointment of more and more DJs undermines one of the last strongholds of popular involvement, and replaces it with an inferior structure dominated by the legal profession. Opposition to DJs is not coming from JPs defending their own patch (certainly not their own jobs); it is from magistrates on the ground, in the best position to know the true value of the system, who are determined to save one of the nation's greatest institutions from further piecemeal destruction. They genuinely believe that a modern, diverse and suitably-trained magistracy, chosen to represent the most effective form of common peer justice, is an irreplaceable national asset which should be promoted, enhanced and maintained—not left to shrivel on the bough. Repeated expressions of faint-hearted praise and support are not enough to compensate for the collective loss of integrity and self-respect among JPs every time another inessential DJ is appointed.

The debate about the misuse of DJs—which must be allowed to continue, in spite of senior lawyers' attempts to close it down—should start from an unashamed belief in the supremacy of local lay justice, and from the premise that the full-hearted involvement of ordinary people is an indispensable component of our democracy. This also assumes that the employment of expensive DJs, for work which unpaid JPs are perfectly capable and willing to do, is a retrograde step—bad for justice, bad for the magistracy and bad for the voluntary public service tradition—and should be avoided by all reasonable means, especially when the motivation stems merely from pressure to satisfy short-term administrative convenience. It also accepts that, if potential or trained JPs are available, their appointment in preference to DJs must follow. This is not to deny that there are excellent DJs or that the stipendiary system can work satisfactorily; but it is to insist that, when there is a reasonably workable choice, there should always be a presumption in favour of lay JPs.

Ministers and senior judicial office holders should construct policies and speeches which clearly demonstrate how the lay magistracy can be entrusted with extended jurisdiction, greater sentencing powers and more administrative control, rather than be insulted by suggestions that JPs should become judicial social workers on 'neighbourhood resolution' panels, while leaving DJs with the bulk of the most interesting court work. Top of the agenda for Area Directors (ADs) in future should therefore be a combination of how to reinforce the role of the lay magistracy while reducing the number of DJs, not whether the former can be afforded or more opportunities be found for the latter. Rather than constant cheese-paring of the magistracy, the primary aim should be its preservation in tribunal form, using well-equipped and competent lay justices under an efficient, modern, devolved administration. Government should stop offering ADs the option of expensive DJ 'limos' when JP 'minis' are freely available.

District judges are not lay justices[1]

Maintaining law and order through county lieutenancies, justices of the peace and local militias worked well enough when England and Wales were predominantly rural but, from the beginning of the eighteenth century, it was clear that this system was no longer sustainable in the growing urban concentrations — later known as 'metropolitan areas' — notably London and Middlesex. The quality of so-called 'trading' justices in these areas deteriorated, and some of them were involved in scandals which aroused public indignation. At the same time, a rise in crime, coupled with the difficulty of finding suitable people for appointment to the bench, resulted in legislation which allowed a few dozen London magistrates (all of whom had to be barristers) to be paid. These were the first stipendiary magistrates (stipes). In 1936, a Royal Commission recommended that the stipes' courts and those of lay justices should be

---

1. Under this heading, and throughout the book, it is only district judges (magistrates' courts) sitting in the criminal and family proceedings courts of England and Wales to which reference is intended. Those sitting in the county court and other capacities are not included in the commentary. Criticism is not aimed at DJs as individuals — most of them do their job admirably and maintain good relations with their lay colleagues — but at the methods employed to bring about their unnecessary increase, the iniquity of solo justice, the reluctance to reduce their number in response to falling workload, and the lack of attention given to the consequences for the integrity of the lay magistracy.

amalgamated; another Commission ten years later noted that the stand-ard of lay justices had improved to such an extent that they could be entrusted with full jurisdiction.

A Royal Commission in 1948 said, 'Like that of trial by jury, (the mag-istrates' bench) gives the citizen a part to play in the administration of the law. Its continuance prevents the growth of a suspicion … that the law is a mystery which must be left to the professional caste, and has little in common with justice as the layman understands it'. The Com-missioners also agreed with the evidence of Lord Chancellor Jowitt in commending the lay system, and emphasised the inferiority of single adjudication when they added: 'Even a judge of the High Court is never asked to undertake the heavy responsibility of trying a criminal case except with the assistance of a jury of laymen, to whom alone is left the decision on the facts'. Years later, Lord Justice Thomas (who became Lord Chief Justice in 2013) said, 'There's great virtue in a tribunal of three'. It is therefore incredible that the increase of trial by single lawyer remains unchallenged, especially at a time when the meaning of justice is more under scrutiny than ever, and when most people would agree that a fair outcome is more likely to arise from the combined opinion of three judges than from only one.

Under the Administration of Justice Act 1973, the statutory maximum total of stipes was 60 metropolitan, plus 40 provincial—100 in all. Six-teen years later, the figures were 49 and 14 respectively, the policy having been strictly to appoint professionals only where it was absolutely nec-essary, or where temporary assignments could be used for a few months to relieve short-term problems. The agreed ceilings were not reached for about 20 years, but by 1999 the Lord Chancellor was proposing that the number of provincial stipes should be increased from 50 to 60, at which point an alarmed MA persuaded him to reduce the maximum to 56, and to agree that further appointments would be kept constantly under review and tight control. Meanwhile, this agreement became so totally ignored that by 2004 the figure had crept up to 104 full-time stipes and 100 deputies. So popular was the desire among lawyers to join the 'gravy train' that in 2009 there were 820 applications for 20 advertised posts.

By 2012, the number of appointments seemed to be out of control, the full-time figure having reached 143 (a surge of 38 per cent in eight years), plus more than 160 deputies; during the same period, the number of JPs fell by around 17 per cent from the 1990s peak. Although there has been a massive reduction in cases handled by the magistrates' courts since then, DJ numbers have changed little, while the lay justice figure has dropped a further 30 per cent to less than 15,000 in total. Why has the number of DJs not also been reduced in proportion to the smaller workload? Furthermore, less than a third of all district judges are women, making a mockery of demands for gender equality and diversity in the magistrates' courts, where there has been a rough balance between men and women on the lay bench for many years.

Until the explosion in DJ numbers during the early part of this century, it had been accepted by all concerned that they were essential in some metropolitan areas, and could be used on a peripatetic basis elsewhere if the work of the lay courts fell into serious arrears, or for potentially long or difficult cases. While it lasted, this understanding allowed a good relationship to exist between lay and stipe, and it could then be argued that the minority opinion of a 1948 Royal Commission member (Lord Merthyr)—that 'it is merely a question of time before lay justices disappear'—was unlikely to be fulfilled while the stipendiary system was there to relieve pressure on JPs without threatening to drive them out of existence.

After 1996, what became known as the 'Venne criteria' (not to be confused with references to Venne in a Protocol—agreed in 2012 by a working group convened by the Deputy Senior Presiding Judge, Lord Justice Gross—to support judicial deployment in the magistrates' courts) were accepted by lay justices as a reasonable basis for deciding which cases were more suitable for stipes than JPs; they included those likely to involve complex points of law or evidence, public health and safety, intimidation of witnesses, and extradition. Nevertheless, the greater number of DJs, and the need to keep them fully occupied, gave rise to numerous reports of justices being required to forego legitimate cases, and to concern over the increased number of trials being decided by a single judge. Previously, it was the stipes who were flexibly deployed to deal with the longest or most difficult cases, while JPs kept to their routine agendas. Now, it is the other way about; work for DJs has apparently to be guaranteed (even if that means taking ordinary cases), while JPs are expected to be more flexible and prepared to be laid off.

Meanwhile, changes—all detrimental to the lay magistracy—have moved things on. Several of the former, more acceptable, reasons for the appointment of DJs have become redundant under the weight of professional influence and administrative convenience; even the Venne yardstick has been softened to allow DJs to 'experience the full range of summary cases', thus enabling them more freely to take work from lay justices. There has also been a marked decline in the workload of the magistrates' courts, followed by severely restricted recruitment and a 50 per cent fall in the total number of JPs. It might therefore have been expected, especially at a time of national economic austerity, that an opportunity would be taken to cut back on the high cost of lawyer magistrates, and that their number would have been reduced accordingly. It is ominous that no such adjustment appears to have been made, which suggests that DJs must by now be taking relatively more cases from the lay bench—a probability supported by the fact that in 2011 they were hearing 30 per cent of 'either-way' cases, compared to only 18 per cent by lay justices (Ipsos MORI Report: *The Strengths and Skills of the Judiciary in the Magistrates' Courts*).

In spite of the cost argument having been firmly established in favour of the lay magistracy, those who have imposed unnecessary expansion in the number of DJs show no signs of readiness to change the policy. Of course, they never acknowledge the damage they have already done to the image and morale of JPs, and to the principle of popular involvement in the judicial system. Instead, having repeated the usual obligatory remarks about a great future for the lay magistracy, they adopt the time-honoured stubbornness of oppressors who, having won an ill-gotten advantage, refuse to part with their gain. Then, they loftily dismiss complainants as reactionary, and declare that the time has come for all to forget the past, accept that 'we are where we are', and 'move on'. Why should we remain silent and move on when maladministration and palpable injustice are allowed to continue, and the future of the lay magistracy is questioned?

In their pursuit of additional DJs and the invention of so-called business cases to support unjustified applications, HM Courts Service (HMCS) directors and others were among those prepared to dredge up every little imperfection and to set dubious targets, so as to denigrate the lay magistracy and place it at a comparative disadvantage. Unfair contrasts were made between the 'robustness' of DJs and JPs when conducting courts, and speed was emphasised *ad nauseam* (probably because, apart perhaps from case management, speed is the only respect in which DJs have a clear advantage). Shortages of staff and space were overlooked to make the need for DJ assistance appear stronger, and the justices' response look weaker. As workloads fell, sensitive advisory committees stopped recruiting JPs in many areas, but the Judicial Appointments Commission showed no corresponding willingness to reduce enlistment of DJs—a disgraceful omission. Retiring DJs continued to be replaced without provision for review of their role in changed circumstances. So, when fault-finding is added to a background of court closures, amalgamated benches, extra travelling and concerns over minimum sitting requirements, it can be seen how much easier it becomes to insert permanent DJs alongside a weakened magistracy, and why so many disenchanted JPs then resign from the bench before they are 70. Once again, we are reminded of Dupont's quotation: 'The gods first drive mad those whom they seek to destroy'.

It should never be forgotten that organizations such as HMCTS, wholly or partially financed by central government, can deliberately create situations designed to weaken those whom they plan to replace. Under the false excuse of saving taxpayers' money and increasing efficiency, they can throttle the funding of conditions and activities which enable JPs to function properly; they can set absurd targets, withdraw facilities, overload or starve them of work and, most infuriating of all, pretend to consult while having no intention of taking into account the advice they receive. The lay magistracy is particularly vulnerable to such manipulation when so much of its administration is in the hands of those whose future employment may depend on their achievement of unpopular changes. Although they may profess sometimes to favour devolution of power, governments instinctively revert to central control of public funding whenever possible, and they become suspicious of any local authority or national organization that dares to talk about independence. Centralised control of courts administration under HMCTS bureaucracy is a typical example of this syndrome. Overall, it has not proved more efficient, and certainly not cheaper; in fact it has shown itself susceptible to many of the same characteristic failings and crippling budget cuts as the national health and education sectors, where potential economies of scale remain illusory.

Area directors, faced with centrally-imposed performance targets and local organizational problems, many of which could be solved by other methods, find that the easiest way to meet them is to put in a request for a permanent DJ, paid out of central rather than local funds. They are not interested in what effect such changes may have on the magistracy, nor do they consider how its willing, unpaid volunteers could be used to do the same work just as well for much less cost. Without having to consider longer-term consequences, particularly for the justices involved, it is relatively simple to adopt the most convenient solution whenever responding to endemic problems in the courts service. Among those consequences, can any action be more irresponsible than to send home unpaid JPs, some of them having given up (often with much difficulty) a day's work to attend, and perhaps struggling to meet their sitting obligations, because not enough Venne-compliant cases can be found to keep surplus DJs fully employed?

Insult was added to injury for the lay magistracy in August 2000, when stipendiary magistrates became district judges, following the Access to Justice Act of 1999. For many years, London stipes had voiced a dislike of the word 'stipendiary', and had apparently been petitioning the Lord Chancellor to be called 'judges', a proposal which was seen by outsiders to be more about securing better personal pensions. However, a senior London stipe admitted (to me) in 1990 that he and his colleagues considered themselves to be part of the professional judiciary, and did not like appearing to be an 'appendage of the magistracy'. The chief stipendiary magistrate at the time also mentioned that 'stipes want to distance themselves'. At first sight, these claims may seem unreasonable, but it is interesting to recall that the magistracy itself had lobbied successfully after World War II for its courts to be distanced from the police, in order to avoid appearing to be an appendage of the local constabulary.

For more than ten years, the Lord Chancellor was left in no doubt by the MA that JPs would be offended by any suggestion that the stipes' title might be changed; it was particularly opposed to 'district judge', on the grounds that it implied inferior status and lesser powers for JPs. Many magistrates at the time felt insulted by this suggestion. 'The title should reflect the fact that they are meant to be doing the same job', said the MA; if there had to be any change at all, it preferred 'district magistrate'. The MA's views on this issue at that time were as rational as any but, after at least eight other titles (including, would you believe it, 'commissioner of law') had been considered, Parliament ignored the association and sided with the professional wing of the judiciary by deciding to change the title, the primary objective of which was, of course, never admitted. Inevitably, as soon as the alteration had been made, the government directed—and the MA meekly accepted—that the word 'lay' be dropped from the magistracy so that an appearance of equality could be preserved, and the new judges could still be called 'magistrates' (by the same token, perhaps magistrates should equally then have become 'lay judges'?); it was also emphasised that DJs when sitting as magistrates had no extra powers, and that JPs were still members of the judiciary.

Whatever government and political correctness may dictate, it is important that a distinction is preserved between salaried professional DJs and unpaid lay JPs, and thus that the 'lay' title is retained and used. Whatever smoothing-out these manoeuvres were designed to achieve, the lay magistracy remains a distinct part of the judiciary—and should continue to be so. At the time, it probably did not occur to anyone that JPs might have good grounds in the future for wishing to distance themselves from DJs, in order to avoid appearing to be an appendage of the legal profession.

The MA was astonished to hear in 1997 that the Home Secretary believed 'trials of young offenders should be heard before a single stipendiary magistrate'; and, in keeping with its long-held view that 'a one-person court is intrinsically less satisfactory than a bench of three', the AGM of the MA in 2007 unanimously passed the following resolution: 'This meeting believes that trials in magistrates' courts should normally take place before a bench of three. Only in exceptional circumstances should a trial take place before a district judge sitting alone'. This motion was not intended as an attack on DJs, but as a genuine defence of a fundamental principle: that justice is more likely to be achieved when decisions of guilt or innocence are made by a jury or bench of three magistrates. The MA returned to the point in response to a 2009 government Green Paper on *Rights and Responsibilities*, covering the relationship between citizen and state, when it said, 'a decision on guilt or innocence should always be decided by more than one person'.

Solo decision-making is an inferior form of judgement and a retrograde form of justice. It is used, often unnecessarily and unjustifiably, as a costly alternative to a bench of three JPs; it is contrary to democratic ideals, and susceptible to bias and corruption; combined with lack of diversity, it represents a capitulation to administrative expediency and abolishes the participation of ordinary citizens in the administration of the law. The tribunal form of the normal magistrates' court is symbolic of 'good justice' which, by comparison, the unrepresentative solo DJ is clearly not. Furthermore, surveys suggest that the majority of defendants prefer to be tried by JPs. Lay justices are said to show more courtesy towards defendants and other court users, more concern for distressed victims, and to use more simple language. There is also research evidence that opinion-formation through group discussion, based on different viewpoints, is more accurate in detecting lies of all kinds than that formed by an individual. Paradoxically, from this it might also be concluded that liars are less likely to be convicted by a district judge than by a bench of three magistrates — good news perhaps for mendacious criminals, bad news for those expecting to find the best form of justice in the magistrates' court on every occasion.

DJs are normally the only instance in the CJS where both guilt and sentence are decided by a single person. It is incredible that, at a time when participation and collective decision-making are said to be so vital for the health of our democracy, a significant proportion of the public apparently remains content to be judged by single lawyers. It is also surprising that, although many defendants opt for trial by jury in the Crown

Court — presumably because they believe (or are advised) that 12 of their so-called peers makes acquittal more likely — few of them object when faced with trial by a court consisting of only one person. This may be due to the fact that they are not given the option, or that they want to get through the ordeal more quickly, although some have been known to complain after their trial by a DJ that they had been cheated of real justice. Others have benefitted from a degree of leniency unlikely to be matched by a bench of three JPs. An example of this occurred in 2005, when a DJ was reported to have 'cleared on all charges' (described erroneously by another newspaper as 'an absolute discharge') a police officer who drove dangerously in an unmarked car, at speeds of more than 90 in 30 mph zones, more than 100 on A-roads, and up to 159 mph on the M54, on the grounds that he had 'suffered enough punishment' during the two-and-a half years of proceedings against him.

When DJs are felt to have become 'invasive', their presence has clearly gone too far; and any boasting about the inherent quality of British justice is made to sound hollow every time a DJ conducts a trial alone. It is a self-evident strength of a full bench that it is more likely to reach balanced conclusions, and that it is more difficult to deceive three judges than one. Decisions made by a bench of three depend on at least a two-thirds majority (juries need five-sixths), but DJs can only be 100 per cent right or 100 per cent wrong; the risk of injustice thus appears to be greater with the latter. In contrast to ever-changing benches of three, individual DJs may not only be subject to moods, and reputations for softness or toughness, but they are also more likely to develop a closet mentality, be inclined to make decisions 'on the hoof', be unaware of their own prejudices, or become case-hardened, autocratic and even eccentric. The fact that JPs are not lawyers is a strength, not a weakness, of the summary justice system.

The only true advantage that single DJs have over three JPs is speed — even then, only when dealing with guilty pleas. Research commissioned by the Lord Chancellor's Department in 1997 concluded that, although stipes worked slightly faster in general than lay justices, it was only by a factor of 5:4. When it comes to trials, there is little difference in the time taken. Are we prepared therefore to risk damaging the magistracy (perhaps irrevocably) merely for the sake of speed and the blind pursuit of performance targets? In *The Magistracy at the Cross-roads* (2012), Professor Andrew Ashworth wrote, 'Despite the pressures of time, the appearance of haste quickly becomes the appearance of unfairness, and of summary justice at its worst'; and he asked, 'Would I be entirely wrong to suggest that the lay magistracy should promote themselves more as a fair way of dealing with cases than as an economical way?' The nation has shown precious little concern over lay magisterial decline in recent years; so perhaps government may in future be more easily persuaded to support and strengthen the lay magistracy as much for its unique fairness as for its economy.

The 2011 Ipsos MORI report, *The Strengths and Skills of the Judiciary in the Magistrates' Courts,* commissioned by the MoJ, relied on the flawed and out-dated Morgan and Russell calculations to arrive at the relative cost of DJs and lay magistrates; it showed a 2.85:1 ratio in favour of the latter, but again had unfairly included 'volunteer costs' against JPs to reduce their advantage; it produced little information that was not well-known already about the relative merits of magistrates and DJs. While many of the differences were not significant, the advantages attaching to JPs, mentioned in the report, were overwhelming. They included closer connection with, and specific knowledge of, the local community; greater fairness (particularly in a trial situation) and more balanced decisions; more experience of life, more 'in touch', more democratic, more open-minded, and less 'case-hardened'; much less expensive, less likely to impose custodial sentences, and more representative of the national working population in terms of gender and ethnicity. As usual, professional court users, whose self-interest rarely allows them to be complimentary about 'amateur' magistrates, nor to acknowledge the benefits of public participation in the justice system, were less appreciative of lay justices.

Following the MORI report, the MA's Judicial Policy Committee commented, 'The conclusions seem to say that, while magistrates are fairer, less case-hardened, more diverse, more democratic, cost less, send fewer people to custody, and are actually more efficient than may be thought, district judges are quicker. This is the only perceived advantage of district judges, and there are two clear reasons for this: they are legal professionals, and they sit on their own'. If speed is all that really matters, it could be argued quite logically that (fast) single DJs should replace (slow) Crown Court juries. Why not?

Detailed research by the Kent MA found that the actual daily cost of a DJ (magistrates' courts) was about £640 in 2010, while that for a bench of JPs (including one member claiming maximum loss of earnings, and each claiming lunch and travelling allowances) totalled only £165. On this basis, the single DJ cost nearly four times as much per day as the three lay justices at their most expensive, and this balance in favour of JPs is unlikely to have changed significantly since then. Training costs in both cases were ignored; but even if these were added, the total JP figure was only slightly increased. No doubt DJs also have additional costs; likewise, it is true to say that, when courthouses are closed and JPs have to travel longer and further, their private as well as public costs rise accordingly—but nothing like enough to make a significant difference to the balance in their favour. It seems that money can always be found to finance the appointment of expensive DJs, but not for any increase in the use of relatively inexpensive JPs.

These researches also discovered that, in the one Kent bench where a DJ was permanently attached, the number of JPs failing to achieve their annual minimum of 26 sittings rose by 112.5 per cent in the first full year, indicating that the DJ was carrying out much of the work which would otherwise have been done by lay members who had been deprived of over 800 sittings. This is outrageous. The clerk to the justices confirmed that, during the same period, there were no cases anywhere in Kent which could not lawfully have been heard by JPs. So much for the claims that it is more economical to employ DJs, and the denials that they take work from magistrates.

It is also worth mentioning that, when comparisons were made on a cost per session or per case basis, but without taking into account their 'lifetime' or superannuation costs, DJs were found to be at least seven times more expensive than a tribunal of three magistrates; and a DJ sitting with two JPs would of course make both the cost and speed of cases appear even worse. Inexplicably, DJs were (and probably still are) paid from central funds; so HMCTS Area Directors could apply for additional judges with financial impunity—knowing that they would not be required by presiding judges or the Lord Chancellor to provide costings—and thus avoid solutions using JPs charged solely to local funds.

The Courts Act 2003 introduced a protocol to govern the appointment of DJs. This code is narrow in scope, and constructed so as to leave as little room as possible for flexibility or judicial review; it restricts discussion to 'business' aspects relating to 'efficiency', 'effectiveness' and the assumed benefits of creating DJ posts; and, above all, it makes consideration of wider issues, such as the effect on the lay magistracy, appear irrelevant. Incredibly, it does not require or make provision for the direct views of the MA or justices' clerks (these can only be made collectively through bodies such as the former Justices Issues Groups), nor for consultation with, or receipt of written opinions from, any concerned individuals or organizations other than local advisory committees; it does (or did) not allow for appeal at any stage, nor does it require the final decision-makers to publish their reasons for endorsing the application and business case; there is still no sign, after more than ten years, of provision for the discontinuance of DJ posts if the circumstances which were held to justify their original appointment no longer exist; and there is no mention of a periodic review of the protocol itself. It is an unpalatable fact that, while lay magistrate numbers have fallen by more than a half since the 1990s, DJ numbers have trebled.

The protocol was drafted after consultation and agreement with the MA, and has been slightly amended once or twice in response to criticism, including the re-filling of posts without full local discussion; but, while it may have been thought acceptable initially, it has since proved divisive in operation, harmful to the lay magistracy and too easily abused by HMCTS. This is partly due to the fundamental bias in favour of appointing DJs, giving the impression of a foregone conclusion, and partly to reliance on the production of a business case which is anything but businesslike, in that it requires neither cost nor impact assessment. For the future, more detailed guidance needs to be available on what criteria must be met if a business case is to succeed beyond reasonable doubt, greater attention must be given to alternative solutions that are less damaging to the lay magistracy, and provision must be made for annual review (including possible discontinuance) of every DJ post.

It appears that the motivation for a DJ application does not have to be about money or the future of the magistracy—two considerations which, one would have thought, should be paramount. It arises simply from the Lord Chancellor's 'duty to ensure that there is an efficient and effective system … to support the business of the magistrates' courts', which means that those to whom the duty is delegated can—and do—place whatever interpretation they like on the meaning of 'efficient' and 'effective'. Thus it becomes quite easy for area and regional directors to convince themselves, presiding judges and the Lord Chancellor that, without the need for a budget forecast or inclusion of alternative options, appointment of a DJ is justified—even when the cost may be up to seven times greater than that for a bench of three JPs. The deficiency of the protocol therefore encourages arbitrary applications and ill-considered business cases. Some of them, lacking the inclusion of genuine facts, should never succeed; but they still do—leaving the magistracy desolate. Would any business executive worth his salary ever try to convince his directors of the need for radical change without first providing a detailed cost analysis and a survey of possible alternatives? Highly unlikely.

With the benefit of hindsight, it is disturbing to realise that most of those responsible for DJ expansion were so busy chasing targets or finding minor faults with JPs, that they omitted to take into account the inevitable consequences of injecting so many professional lawyers into the heart of the lay-based summary justice system. Worse still, they failed to appreciate the wisdom of maintaining a strong popular component in the judicial sector of a mature democracy. They did not see, or chose to ignore, that there were (and still are) serious flaws in the 'business case' method of assessing the need for DJs, that it could be, and is, manipulated for dubious reasons, and that the lay magistracy might just as well not have existed, for all the notice that was taken of its opinions by those making the final decisions.

Threat to the lay magistracy

As long ago as 1986, in response to a joint Home Office and Lord Chancellor's Department paper, which included a statement on criteria for the appointment of stipes, the MA commented,

'If there is a trend to appoint stipendiary magistrates, the eventual and logical conclusion must be the demise of the lay magistracy. This would take the lay element away from the majority of criminal jurisdiction, and could logically lead to the eventual demise of the jury. The importance of the lay element in a democratic society cannot be overstated and should not be weakened in any way'.

Although the Lord Chancellor in 1988 said that he 'would not seek to impose the appointment of a stipendiary magistrate in an area where the justices were opposed to such an appointment', this sentiment and numerous protests since then have been almost totally ignored, to such an extent that the persistent infusion of professional lawyers has come to represent one of the most serious threats to the lay magistracy in its 650-year history, casting doubt on the whole concept of lay justice. Expressions of concern by JPs are routinely deprecated by the powers-that-be, but to anyone with knowledge of how the New Zealand lay magistracy (originally modelled on ours) has been degraded and displaced in the last 40 years, the signs here in England and Wales are ominous. If we continue to ignore them, JPs could find themselves with little more to do than witness documents — as is virtually the case in NZ, where there was no formal end to their judicial duties; just gradual replacement by lawyers. However — significantly — a recent report suggests that higher costs and a shortage of judicial officers in NZ have encouraged a minor revival in the use of lay magistrates there.

Members of the legal profession have benefitted from the creation of hundreds more DJ posts in the last 50 years, but have refused to acknowledge the lay magistracy's concern. This was obvious in 2011, when a senior presiding judge with responsibility for JPs told simmering members of the MA that he was not minded to support their request for a moratorium on DJ appointments; he gave no reasons, which made him sound like an impatient parent trying to quell a peevish child with a final 'because I said so'. Understandably, this did not go down well with members, and it still rankles. Although other attempts have been made to play down the creeping increase in DJs, and to deny that suitable work for JPs is taken by them, there have otherwise been few signs of official recognition that the problem remains. For instance, the huge fall in cases destined for the magistrates' courts could have been taken as an opportunity to reduce the number of DJs substantially, in line with the decrease in JPs—but it was not.

JPs regularly receive and accept legal and procedural guidance from lawyers—that is an essential part of the relationship—but there are times when their advice is not so welcome. For instance, senior judges with delegated responsibility for the magistracy have been known to make haughty reference to the 'sterile animosity' that sometimes arises between JPs and DJs, insisting that the spotlight ought instead to be on 'the administration of justice and service to the public'. In defending the practice of DJs sitting alone on trials, all that the senior presiding judge could say to the MA Council in 2012 was: 'Certain professional judges do sit on their own, and it is wishful thinking that this will change. You should focus not on what DJs are doing, but on what you are doing'. Such dismissive statements reveal, if not bias, a lack of understanding about the depth of feeling among JPs. When they wave through unjustified DJ appointments without question, and tell magistrates to stop whinging about the consequences, senior judges should be challenged to say why they themselves are not focussed instead on reducing the need to appoint so many DJs, and why they are so unconcerned about the damage that this does to the lay sector.

So far, the MA has been unable to find an effective way of persuading government to reverse the trend without running the risk of appearing irresponsible or self-serving. The magistracy as a whole, with self-esteem and duty to the nation in mind, continues to ask itself: What more can it do, or could have done, to avoid or resist this further erosion of its powers and status? Of course, it also has to ask: How much of the situation was created by its own avoidable shortcomings, and do they still persist? In how many areas of the country could a combined and successful effort yet be made by government, judiciary and magistracy to achieve a reduction in the number of DJ posts and an increase in the strength of lay participation? Where there is a will, a way can usually be found; but is there a will?

Of course JPs and DJs, being civilised and realistic people, will always respond sensitively to calls for co-operation, and will try to work in harmony once the die has been cast. They have a service to provide and a job to do, and must get on with it. There are numerous examples of amicable working relationships between the two, but this should not be taken as a reason for meek acceptance of yet more professional appointments; nor to suggest that senior JPs are being unreasonably obstructive if they continue to express discontent. The magistracy must never be observed in public to be at odds with the senior judiciary or DJs; it must always be ready to work closely with both, but this should not prevent continuance behind the scenes of a robust private defence of the principle that all summary courts should be conducted by lay justices, unless there are agreed exceptional reasons such as those listed under the Venne criteria.

It is surely more in 'the interest of the administration of justice and service to the public' that the lay sector should be extended, than that the grip of the legal profession on the courts system should be tightened. Wherever there is any reasonable possibility that the magistracy can be used and maintained at full lay strength, its continuance should be non-negotiable, and strenuous efforts should be made to remove any doubts about its future. Bearing in mind that many DJ appointments were (and are) superfluous, were pushed through on the back of specious business cases, were opposed by local benches, and were made irreversible, it ill-behoves presiding judges to persist in advising lay magistrates that they should meekly accept the *status quo*. Nor is it reassuring when other senior members of the judiciary, in routine attempts to mollify suspicious JPs, plead ignorance of any policy to rationalise the magistracy, while their senior colleagues are routinely approving additional DJ appointments. There may not be a 'policy' as such, but it happens nevertheless.

In theory, DJs should never be allocated trials which are considered suitable for JPs by the Venne yardstick, yet the 2011 report on the distribution of work in the magistrates' courts contained evidence from some areas that DJs are more likely to be given either-way and 'more interesting' cases. Other information, arising from the report and passed to the MA, included accounts of work taken from JPs who were known already to be struggling to meet their sitting requirements and competence levels. At the 2006 annual general meeting of the national MA in Coventry, the Lord Chief Justice said 'there is no intention that DJs should take over the work of JPs'; yet, within a year, it was being proposed that an unwanted and unnecessary DJ should be appointed in Kent, a move which could not easily be achieved without later taking a substantial chunk of work away from the lay justices in the county. In 2008, it was reported to the MA Council that in at least one Essex court 'the sentencing function belonged to the district judge'; elsewhere, there was talk of DJs who considered themselves unaffected by the same rules as JPs, e.g. in completing sentencing forms. Some Kent JPs were told that, if their cases were cancelled in favour of a DJ, they could sit with him—but 'not as equals'!

The Magistracy at the Crossroads, written for the MA in 2012, was an excellent initiative and produced much material for discussion and ideas for the future, but the one major subject it seemed to avoid was the threat to the lay magistracy, and the collective system of justice it represents, posed by the relentless expansion in the number of district judges. Is this because it is now considered 'bad form' and disloyal to mention such a sensitive subject? The MA has, perhaps understandably, never wished to appear irresponsible or hostile in the dispute, and preferred to give general advice to its branches, rather than side with them openly against the wishes of government or the advice of local clerks and the senior judiciary. This made it easier for courts service directors to ignore and overcome local opposition. However, the basic issue remains: that, on all too many occasions, the appointment of a DJ should not have been contemplated in the first place. Inappropriate assignments are made worse by the lack of provision to relocate DJs or discontinue posts; but it remains a fact that, when workloads fall, it is much easier to sacrifice part-time, unpaid JPs, and reduce the size of their benches, than to lay off full-time, highly-paid DJs and upset their established appointment structure.

It is small wonder that some magistrates believe there is 'a cuckoo in the magisterial nest'. A few others see the situation in a different light; they deny the existence of any threat, preferring to regard the roles as complementary. For instance, Jack Straw MP (lawyer, and no friend of the magistracy) when addressing the MA as Lord Chancellor in 2007, declared that the summary justice system works to best effect when there is a mix of lay JPs and professional DJs. His goal was to have 'a stipe on every bench', thus enabling a 40 per cent reduction in JPs. From the viewpoint of a courts service administrator seeking promotion, or an influential lawyer viewing lay magistrates as a bunch of meddlesome amateurs, it can, for a fleeting moment, be understood why the magistracy appears at times to be so vulnerable to the ambitions of zealous reformers.

It would be invidious to suggest that JPs in general should be chaired by lawyers; but if such an unwelcome idea was ever to become a reality, absurd logic would suggest that the foreman of the jury should also be a lawyer. Fortunately, a number of ways remain open for the improvement of the JP:DJ relationship. These could include abolition of the right to choose Crown Court trial, reserving the more serious either-way offences for hearing only by a DJ sitting with two justices as equals, and leaving the remaining lesser offences to be heard exclusively by lay magistrates. This idea was suggested as early as 1937 by the Maxwell Committee, but not pursued because of the war, and the Auld review also recommended a middle-level court in 2001. By this means, probably more than 70,000 cases could be taken out of the Crown Court and millions of pounds saved. Moreover, a mutually beneficial opportunity for JPs and DJs to work together would be created, the DJ threat removed, the independent lay magistracy strengthened, the justice system simplified, and the whole judicial process speeded up.

A DJ sitting with two JPs—creating a new intermediate tier—could be welcomed by the lay magistracy, especially also in complicated family cases, as a way of accepting without bitterness the usefulness of hitherto unnecessary DJs, and increasing the amount of interesting work done by lay justices. Under the present system, the expensive Crown Courts are grossly overloaded, while the work declines in the far less costly magistrates' courts—a ridiculous situation.

CHAPTER 6

Fallible Juries

'Trial by jury is more than an instrument of justice, more than a wheel of the constitution; it is the lamp that shows that freedom lives'

Lord Devlin (1956).

- Them and us
- Weaknesses of jury system
- Miscarriages of justice

Them and us

It may seem odd to include this chapter in a book about the magistracy, but the jury is the other great manifestation of democracy in our justice system; furthermore, JPs act as 'professional' jurors when deciding verdicts. However, in our inimitable British way, we criticise the magistracy for being amateur, while praising the jury for being even more so. This is probably because in the public mind JPs, like it or not, have always been 'them'—representatives of authority—while the jury are unquestionably 'us', the people who, some would claim, instinctively 'know best'.

Even though a bench of JPs is in a sense a surrogate jury, this is not enough to satisfy those who assert—ridiculously—that trial by magistrates is a denial of the 'basic human right' of trial by jury. The irony is that, the more 'professional' JPs become (and, incidentally, the more cases that are heard by single district judges), the less they seem like the peers of those whom they try. So-called pro-jury 'activists' regard magistrates as 'part of the establishment' and therefore assume that they are biased against offenders; even though JPs are trained and experienced observers, skilled enough to handle more than 90 per cent of criminal cases, with less than 0.1 per cent successful appeals against their decisions, critics nevertheless maintain that they 'do not have the same critical eye as juries', are 'unqualified' and 'get matters out of proportion'. To those more supportive of the magistracy, and those more inclined to take victims into account, the jury's persistently higher acquittal rate suggests there could be something amiss with the system; juries being twice as likely to acquit could indicate that their judgement might be wrong twice as often. It must be remembered, too, that anyone convicted by magistrates (or district judges) has a right of appeal to the Crown Court. A cynic's solution to the problems arising from the differences might suggest that we should stop training JPs, or allowing them to gain experience, so that they could look and behave more like a small, inexpensive bench of regular jurors.

Although the jury is an even older establishment than the magistracy, both institutions have centuries of history behind them. Each relies on recruitment from among the general public for their composition, and is charged with the supremely important responsibility of deciding verdicts. Otherwise they have little in common, which can make comparisons between them unreasonable. Over the years, there has been relatively little development in the jury system; the magistracy, on the other hand, has changed significantly. It has become more meritocratic, more diverse and certainly more competent. When cost is the issue, trial by jury is at least five times more expensive than trial by magistrates. Jurors are not volunteers; they have no training and sit only a few times in their lives, if at all. They are an amorphous body of independent citizens, chosen at random. They sit 12 at a time, and somehow elect from among their number at each trial a temporary chairman, of whom they know nothing and have probably never met before, and who may or may not be up to the task, much depending on how helpful or unhelpful the other jurors are. Unlike justices, juries take no part in sentencing, and give no reasons for their decisions. Even these days, there are few, if any, comparable public activities in which experience is not needed or regarded as an asset; it also places jurors alongside politicians and parents among those for whom training is deemed unnecessary.

Both the magistracy and the jury are tokens of a free society, and arise from our consequent belief in the benefit of wide public involvement in the CJS, which is not to argue that one is better than the other, but at least to recognise that they are different. Perhaps the most significant contrast is that, although now more often criticised than in the past, the jury still appears to be relatively immune from the imperfections of which lay justices are habitually accused, and it may be helpful to examine why this is.

For a start, the magistracy has no guaranteed allies on whom it can depend for the same degree of support as that given routinely to the jury by the legal profession, many of whose members rely on its existence—and its vulnerability—for their livelihood. Politicians praise the magistracy when it suits them, but rarely show genuine concern about its future; administrators tend to regard JPs as a nuisance, lawyers often find them irritating, and reformers find it useful to blame them for many of the deficiencies in the justice system. Being both judges and sentencers, JPs present a sitting target for critics by comparison with transitory juries whose failings are obscured by their sanctity and amorphousness. Whenever any form of criticism is raised against the jury, there is a howl of protest, usually led—not surprisingly—by its constantly uncritical champions: members of the Bar. The magistracy deserves, and should receive, an equally loud expression of universal support but, despite its acknowledged proficiency, it is rarely accorded anything like the devotion given to the relatively inefficient and expensive jury. However hard the magistracy may try to convince the public, the media and the lawyers that it is cheaper, more efficient, less prejudiced and likely to be more fair; however often the jury is associated with perverse decisions, major miscarriages of justice and costly trials, the irrational distinction between the two is unlikely to disappear any time soon.

Much of the rhetoric surrounding the right to choose a jury trial arises from a romantic and somewhat out-dated image of it as 'the foundation of English liberty'—the 13th century Magna Carta and all that—a favourite prop used by the legal profession, emphasising the principles of judgement by 'peers' and innocence until proved guilty; a view which sometimes leads to the manifestly false conclusion that trial by a trained and proficient magistracy is somehow unfair and inferior to that by a disparate, untrained jury, and that the latter's incredibly high acquittal rate in some areas indicates a superior standard of justice. By contrast, none other than the former Master of the Rolls, Sir Frederick Lawton, agreed that the jury system is flawed, and that references to Magna Carta are 'historical nonsense'.

Modern juries are not as representative as we think, because the so-called 'random' method of selection used these days allows so many of the most active and intelligent people to find ways of avoiding service altogether. However, since the abolition of peremptory challenge in 1988, selection has become less farcical here than, for instance, is still the case in the USA, where so many challenges are permitted that the composition of the jury can appear to influence the trial outcome more than the evidence (*vide* O J Simpson).

In 1993, the Royal Commission on Criminal Justice (the Runciman Commission) was set up in response to unease about a series of miscarriages of justice—all of which, incidentally, arose from jury convictions. Among other matters, it agreed with the then Director of Public Prosecutions—who was supported by many others, including the Treasury and several prominent judges, such as Lord Justice Auld—that the right to jury trial in either-way cases should cease to be automatic; and, in doing so, the commission expressed its confidence in the magistracy. Predictably, this was met by a barrage of protest from the legal 'unions' (i.e. the Bar and Law Society), whose members benefit most from the present system, and civil liberties groups claiming, among all manner of unconvincing reasons, that juries have a 'collective wisdom' (apparently denied to magistrates), that they are 'a constitutional safeguard against miscarriages of justice', and that 'the rights of the citizen were being whittled away in favour of the state'—a wholly exaggerated and disproportionate reaction, the vehemence of which could only have been justified if the commission had recommended the total abolition of jury trials.

The law in regard to either-way offences has not changed for 30 years, although the number of such cases tried in the Crown Court, rather than magistrates' court, has fallen considerably. In spite of many brave attempts to alter it (especially in the 1997 Narey Review on delays in the criminal justice system), the defendant's right to choose jury trial—even for the most trivial offences in this category—remains as a classic case of irrational obstinacy. However, even such a sensible change will always be difficult to achieve while juries acquit such a high proportion (up to 50 per cent in London) of those who plead 'not guilty' in the Crown Court, and while lawyers can (truthfully) advise their clients that they are more likely to 'get off' if they choose jury trial, or (untruthfully) warn them that 'magistrates will automatically find them guilty'. In the meantime, we must not forget that the magistracy possesses its own collective wisdom, and is itself a constitutional safeguard against injustice, an area in which it has an infinitely better record than juries. Moreover, those who refuse to contemplate any reduction in the use of expensive Crown Court trials, for even the smallest theft, are guilty of hypocrisy if they do not also raise objection to much more serious cases being tried summarily, without defendants having a choice, by a single district judge (DJ) in the magistrates' court.

Whatever the reasons, further signs of criticism of the jury system emerged with the publication in 2001 of Lord Justice Auld's *Review of the Criminal Courts*, in which he challenged the existence of a right to jury trial and insisted that magistrates, not defendants, should decide where 'either-way' cases should be tried. At the same time he suggested that jurors should be more widely representative, that entitlement to entry on the electoral role should determine their right to sit, and that legislation should be introduced to ensure that juries cannot acquit defendants in defiance of the law or disregard of the evidence. Such proposals should mitigate in favour of an increased role for the magistracy in the future, but the perversity of the influences still existing against changes in the hallowed jury system will ensure that no such sensible decisions are made in the near future.

What makes the right to demand jury trial even more ridiculous is that those who, for instance, assault police officers, take expensive cars without consent or fraudulently claim benefit, do not share the same right as petty thieves, and can be tried only in the magistrates' court. Some lawyers believe that the right to jury trial is merited for all offences, however small, which carry an element of 'dishonesty'; this is, according to a 1989 letter to *The Times* from a member of Lincoln's Inn, because 'all allegations involving dishonesty are necessarily serious' and may lead to unique stigma and career damage—a point of view which implies that either-way crimes to which no dishonesty is attached are not so serious or so likely to attract disgrace and suffering, and can therefore be confined to the magistrates' court where JPs, being less prone to emotional reaction and having more experience in weighing evidence, may be less likely to acquit culpable offenders. This belief also seems to imply that in some incomprehensible way juries can be relied upon to arrive at the lawyers' interpretation of what is the 'right' decision, while magistrates cannot. The answer is to make all 'serious' offences indictable, and the rest 'summary'. 'Either-way' offences should be abolished.

Meanwhile, the expensive resources of the Crown Court are also abused by the fact that, of the 30,000 either-way offenders who are enabled to claim the right to elect jury trial each year, 80 per cent change their plea to guilty on arrival. Another 70,000 or so are sent up by magistrates who feel that their powers are not adequate; 20,000 of these need not have been referred—because the Crown Court eventually gave them no stiffer sentences than the justices could themselves have given—creating extra costs of more than £40m a year. Others were disappointed to discover that, having elected to go to the Crown Court, they were three times more likely to receive a custodial sentence than if they had remained in the magistrates' court; furthermore, a 1993 Home Office study found that a third of those who chose jury trial said that in retrospect they would have preferred to be dealt with by JPs. In spite of these statistics, the pressure (for obvious reasons, some would say) from lawyers, to reduce the risk of an 'adverse' decision in the magistrates' court, continues.

Following the government's Spending Review in 2010, the Victims and Witnesses Commissioner, Dame Louise Casey, in her report *Ending the Justice Waiting Game: A Plea for Common Sense*, called for 'an end to the right to trial by jury in petty crime cases which clog up the court system', and for 'the prevention of late guilty pleas which allow criminals to string out their cases at the expense of the public'. She also referred to the 50,000 defendants each year who changed their plea to guilty on the day of the trial, costing around £15 million in wasted Crown Prosecution

Service (CPS) preparation costs, and to the 40 per cent of Crown Court business which is taken up with cases that could just as well be heard for millions of pounds less in magistrates' courts. Lady Casey is not a lawyer. At the time of writing, more than ten years after her report, her plea for common sense remains virtually ignored.

The magistracy—with as much claim to sanctity as the jury, but from whom so much more commitment and experience is demanded—is a constant victim of cuts in public spending; yet, the nation—obsessed as ever with the spectre of innocent people being convicted—appears unwilling to consider any reduction in the high cost of the jury system, even though there are obvious ways in which it could be pruned with little effect on the cherished principles of peer justice. For instance, the number of jurors could be reduced from twelve to seven; and huge financial and other savings could be made if all persistent minor offenders were deprived of the right to jury trial by abolishing the either-way category of offences At present, each time one of them opts to go for half a day in the Crown Court and plead 'not guilty' to stealing a can of lager, it costs the taxpayer thousands, rather than hundreds, of pounds; yet, because it is deemed to challenge one of our basic rights, government bows to defence lawyers and refuses to reform it. If the nation stopped believing in collectively-decided verdicts as the most reliable form of justice, and concluded that it cannot afford lay magistrates, it certainly cannot afford juries; and, if it is acceptable to have single DJs replacing a bench of magistrates, one may be justified in asking why single lawyers should not also replace juries in the higher courts as well?

Weaknesses of the jury system

When the value of JPs to the nation and to the overall quality of justice is in question, and while the jury system remains relatively unimpeachable, it is right that attention should be drawn to the inherent weaknesses of the latter. Gullible juries are sometimes more easily persuaded to have doubts, and therefore to require a higher burden of proof, than JPs. If the untrained mind of a juror is subjected to a wide range of possible doubts and 'political' excuses, it is more likely that he or she may lean towards acquittal, particularly in cases where the criminal's intent has to be proved. Lawyers are well versed in the art of challenging the veracity of evidence or making it sound unreliable, and they may use varying degrees of pressure, from bullying to more subtle approaches, to persuade witnesses to change from being 'sure' to 'not absolutely sure', a technique more likely to raise a 'reasonable doubt' in the minds of a jury than of a magistrates' bench. Former Lord Chancellor Hailsham, during a House of Lords debate on the Courts and Legal Services Bill in 1990, spoke of proceedings in the magistrates' court being very different from jury advocacy. 'It is far easier to pervert the jury', he said.

Lawyers can make a big name for themselves by skilful use of this fact, which may help to explain why juries convict fewer offenders than magistrates whose experience enables them to work with a lower standard of proof, while still adhering strictly to a judicial oath which is far more demanding than that sworn or affirmed by a jury. To victims and the law-abiding public, this can mean that a jury, unaccustomed to the discipline of total impartiality, is less likely to arrive at a fair decision, or be more likely to acquit, than a bench of trained magistrates, a view which is certainly not shared by those who perversely equate high acquittal rates with higher quality justice. While rightly maintaining that defendants should benefit whenever serious doubt remains in the minds of the bench or the jury, there is often sneaking admiration for the lawyer who can gain for his client a 'not guilty' verdict against all the odds. In these cases, the jury is praised for its innate sense of justice, while JPs in the same situation are criticised for being 'case hardened' and 'too ready to convict'.

In 1977, following the James Report on the distribution of business between the magistrates' courts and Crown Courts, there was much debate about the difference between JPs and juries. Contrary to what many had supposed, figures published at the time by the government showed that on average magistrates acquitted a slightly higher proportion of defendants pleading 'not guilty' than juries — 57 per cent to 48 per cent. However, a Cardiff Law School study of cases involving bailed defendants in 62 English and Welsh Crown Courts between 1987 and 1990 found a wide variation between 'hard' and 'soft' areas in which judges and juries took consistently harsh (20 per cent average acquittal rate) and lenient (40 per cent) attitudes towards offenders; the number of cases thrown out by judges also varied—from five per cent to 50 per cent—and the study identified a group of towns (e.g. Birmingham and Southampton) where juries seemed to find it particularly difficult to reach a verdict at all. Official statistics for England and Wales between 1990 and 2000 also indicated that acquittals rose to well over a third of contested trials, which must have left behind a substantial number of aggrieved victims, discouraged police officers—and, maybe, of unpunished criminals.

When figures from magistrates' courts reveal far lower levels of inconsistency, they are condemned by the media and calls are made for abolition of the lay magistracy, but when it is juries who are at fault, inconsistency is apparently acceptable. At any event, justice has to be done, if at all possible, as much for the victim and the public, as for the defendant. It should therefore be a matter, not of satisfaction, but of concern for the entire law-abiding society when juries show a tendency to return fewer guilty verdicts.

It is difficult to know for certain what are the causes of the high jury rates; it could be a combination of the removal of the property qualification for jury selection in 1974, greater reluctance to believe the police, a more demanding standard of proof, younger and more suspicious juries, human rights influences and poor presentation of prosecution cases. Some would add the possibility, as yet not officially acknowledged, that there has been a noteworthy increase in jury and witness intimidation. Researchers at the Kingston Law School in 2001 found that individual jurors are more likely to empathise with those of similar age, race and sex as themselves, and that ethnic minority jurors are more likely to acquit ethnic minority defendants.

A legal researcher (Green, 1968) who studied the incidence of stereotyping among juries, described their presumed impartiality as 'legal fiction'. On another occasion, a juror was heard to say, 'You've got to be emotional, sympathetic and caring if you're going to do the job properly', i.e. the antithesis of the qualities needed for dispassionate judgement. Research made available to the 1991 Runciman Commission, in which more than 8,000 jurors were questioned, found that 27 per cent did not think they were told enough about their duties beforehand, only 56 per cent said they sat on juries where all members understood the evidence, and nine per cent admitted finding it difficult to understand or remember the evidence. In 2005, Lord Woolf said, 'The variety of prejudices that jurors can have are almost unlimited ... [such as] the accused's class, accent, habits, occupation, physical characteristics ... and prejudice fostered by pre-trial publicity'. There is always a greater risk among juries than JPs that they may be swayed by the pervasive influence of mass hysteria, false news, the social media (anonymous *Twitter* particularly) and mob psychology, especially in cases such as paedophilia and rape; also they are more likely to be influenced by witnesses who give misleading testimony or use the ability of their minds to construct false memories (especially if 'encouraged' by an unscrupulous lawyer). This is why witness statements made immediately after an event are often more accurate and valuable as evidence than those made later on, after the witness has had time to 're-construct' their memory.

Results published in a Ministry of Justice Research Series Report (February, 2010) *Are Juries Fair?*, based on studies by the University College London (UCL) Jury Project, indicated that two out of three jurors do not understand the legal directions given to them by the judge. However, at the same time, the UCL research found that: (a) there was no evidence that all-white juries discriminate against black and minority ethnic (BME) defendants, (b) they almost always reach a verdict, (c) they convict two-thirds, and (d) there were no courts where they acquit more than they convict. It also found that they want more written information on how to do their job, and some admitted to finding it difficult to ignore media reports of their case. In view of (a), the authors of the survey concluded that there is no need for 'racially-balanced' juries in BME cases. Similar findings were made many years before in regard to magistrates' courts. Some reformers continue to argue for wider representation in the selection of both JPs and jurors, in the misguided belief that this would advance the cause of justice. However, it must be said that, in trials where criminal intent is an issue, it may be an advantage if a jury contains some members of the same cultural background as the accused; but this is less likely to be practicable on a magistrates' bench of three, and impossible if the court consists only of a single district judge.

There is a dearth of information on what happens in the jury room; anecdotal evidence varies from the horrific to the impressive. The BBC's 2007 controversial programme *Verdict*, in which 12 celebrities acted as the jury in a fictional rape case, was an attempt to lift the lid. Whatever else might be said of such a programme, it illustrated (apart from the general thoughtfulness it encouraged) how many irrelevancies the members wanted to introduce to their discussion, how few of them had experience of rational, structured debate, and how critical it is that a good foreman emerges right from the beginning. One of them said afterwards, 'We shouldn't have to go in cold, without a clue how to do it'. Another said, 'It's all about bringing in 12 people's biases ... there was a risk of being swayed in the wrong direction by a persistent, strong juror ...' It was also interesting to hear how their views changed during the course of the trial, as new witnesses gave their evidence. (Note: Before the introduction of 10:2 majority verdicts as recently as 1967, it was possible for a determined single juror to veto the decision of the other eleven).

A good example of how emotion may be more likely to feature in jury decisions occurred in the aftermath of the Jeremy Thorpe conspiracy-to-murder trial in 1979 when, surprisingly, the *New Statesman* was allowed to interview several of the jurors about their deliberations. The published account quoted the forewoman as admitting that she and other jurors were influenced by the view (planted by Mr Thorpe's barrister) that Jeremy and his wife 'had suffered enough'. This could possibly have been an acceptable reason for mitigation of sentence, but surely not acquittal.

Miscarriages of justice

'A jury is a number of persons appointed to assist the judge in preventing the law from degenerating into justice'

G K Chesterton

Lord Chief Justice Phillips, speaking to the Criminal Bar Association in 2007, said the legal system should trust the common sense of British juries, and judges should simplify legal directions given to them, instead of trying to protect themselves from appeals on grounds of misdirection. Legislation and case law have already placed more trust in juries by allowing them to draw inferences, permitting hearsay evidence in some cases and admitting bad character references to correct false impressions. 'These steps have helped to move us away from a criminal justice system which seemed to favour the defence', he said.

Be that as it may, when comparing juries and magistrates, it should not be forgotten that all the worst miscarriages of justice in the last 50 years or so have been the result of jury decisions after receiving advice on the law from a senior judge. The Guildford Four, Birmingham Six and *R v Rowe* ((2008) 172 JP 585) were among the most notorious cases, but a BBC *Rough Justice* team (before it was disbanded in 2007) found that the verdicts in 37 out of 38 cases which they investigated were quashed on appeal. In some of the most notable examples, involving child deaths, the fault appeared to lie in the inability of the jury to distinguish between medical opinion and evidence. Would the same have happened if the cases had been heard and decided by a bench of trained and experienced magistrates? Unlikely. It may not be an entirely fair comparison, but it is perhaps worth mentioning again that substantially less than one per cent of magistrates' decisions go to appeal; and of those, only a small proportion end in the appellant's favour.

At one point in 1982, a Law Lord, during the miscarriages scandal, was heard to say that 'upholding the integrity of our system of justice is more important than the unlawful imprisonment of innocent people'. This was also at a time when there were cases of police corruption, much media hostility to the 'establishment' (including the magistracy), and a belligerent Thatcher government. When it comes to 'upholding the integrity of our system', there is no more reliable body in the country than the lay magistracy, which is one of the arguments for it to be allowed to take more cases from the Crown Court. However, if the pursuit of diversity on the bench has the effect of reducing the level of suitability and intelligence among its members, the success of such a change would be at risk.

Mr Justice Popplewell, a High Court judge between 1983 and 1999, said that 'in his experience' 40–50 per cent of jury acquittals, and a small proportion of convictions, are 'perverse' (i.e. given against the weight of evidence or judge's direction) which, if true, is quite alarming. In 1979, an enquiry by Baldwin and McConville confirmed that more than five per cent of those found guilty by juries are 'convicted in doubtful circumstances', but are left without the possibility of an appeal. Miscarriages of justice occur both when the innocent are wrongly convicted, and when the guilty are wrongly acquitted. Some years ago, the latter was well-illustrated by two Crown Court cases involving direct action by members of the public. In the first, a large group of Greenpeace demonstrators wiped-out a field trial of genetically-modified (GM) maize on a Norfolk farm. They were photographed in action, and admitted destroying the crop. The jury found them not guilty of criminal damage. The second case was brought against two disarmament protesters who were accused of damaging a Trident submarine in Barrow by spraying slogans on it and smashing equipment worth thousands of pounds with a lump hammer. They admitted attacking the submarine, but claimed their actions were justified. Again, the jury found them not guilty of criminal damage.

In both these cases, the jury used prejudice and emotion to ignore the law, their oath (such as it is), the evidence and the uncompensated losses and costs incurred by the farmer and the navy. The decisions were not made by those wicked old, unfair and 'unqualified' magistrates who are prone to 'getting matters out of proportion', but by 12 anonymous, unrepresentative 'pillars of the English justice system', exercising the 'collective wisdom' with which lawyers are so ready to credit them. Unlike JPs, jurors do not have to give reasons for their decisions, and do not swear 'to do right to all manner of people after the laws and usages of the realm, without fear or favour, affection or ill-will'; they only promise to 'give a true verdict according to the evidence'. In these two cases, as in many others, they appear to have shown favour and ignored hard evidence.

This is surely not the justice or democracy for which Britain has gained such a high reputation; it is the so-called justice of the critics who press for more diversity, representation and understanding on the magisterial bench, in the expectation that JPs will become more sympathetic to people like themselves, and more prejudiced like fallible jurors. If juries indicate that it is acceptable for protesters to take the law into their own hands with impunity, merely because they have strong feelings against GM crops or nuclear arms, how can we rely on them to respect the law, the evidence and judges' directions on other occasions?

CHAPTER 7

Trustworthy Justices[1]

'It is a principle of English equality that everyone should have the elevating and creative privilege of serving their country—an inducement to do their duty'

Benjamin Disraeli (paraphrased)

- Good and lawful citizens
- Merit and selection
- Recruitment, appointment and employment
- Training

Good and lawful citizens

A 1327 Act referred to 'good and lawful men appointed in every county to guard the peace', but the title justice of the peace (JP) was not used until 1361. Despite immense changes in the law, social conditions and the meaning of words during the subsequent 650 years, 'good', 'lawful' and 'upright' still carry the same significance when choosing today's JPs. To ensure continuance of respect and support for this unique public office, it is essential that we still require these attributes, above all others, in those to whom we entrust decisions of verdict and punishment. It demeans the office of justice to refer, as some do, to magistrates merely as 'sentencers'.

---

1. Magistrates are now appointed by the Lord Chancellor under the 2003 Courts Act which refers to them not as justices of the peace (JPs) but as 'lay justices'—in order, it is said, to distinguish them from salaried district judges (magistrates' courts). However, government nowadays maintains that 'lay' should no longer be used, because 'it fails to convey the professionalism of the magistracy'. While such a compliment is welcome, it remains necessary for a distinction to be recognised. Therefore, throughout this book, it is unpaid 'professional' lay justices or JPs to whom principal reference is being made whenever 'the magistracy' or 'magistrates' are mentioned.

JPs are members of the judiciary, and serve their country as unpaid lay judges and jurors. They are a committed, trustworthy and vital constituent of the democratic structure on which our nation is founded. They are independent, impartial, detached and objective. No other courts in the country represent a higher degree of justice and fairness than a mixed tribunal of trained lay magistrates. As the inheritors of a worthy public service tradition, they are proud to be part of a modest but important calling that ranks among the most honourable — and admired — in the civilised world. They comprise a popular branch of the judiciary which — in spite of criticisms, cuts and closures — remains at the forefront of summary jurisdiction in England and Wales, a resilient institution the enduring success of which owes much to the preservation of its voluntary status, to the broad-based composition of its courts and, in more recent times, to responsible leadership and training.

The reward, if any, for service as a justice is neither financial nor material, but a feeling of modest achievement and pride in searching for and finding justice on behalf of the law-abiding majority or the aggrieved, together with the inspiration of working with some of the most fair and sensible people to be found in our society. Those who become JPs are expected to work without reward or honour beyond the satisfaction of performing a valuable and interesting public service. However, after about 1950 it was accepted that magistrates could occasionally receive honours for outstanding service to the administration of justice in some other capacity.

JPs serve no-one but the sovereign, the embodiment of impartiality, the law, and their fellow citizens; they are independent of party politics, organizations and faiths; they have no privileges, other than the satisfaction of being entrusted with the administration of justice 'to all manner of people', the opportunity of regular involvement in an authoritative process of intelligent decision-making, and entitlement to appropriate use of the post-nominal 'JP'. Occasional calls for them to be set apart by some form of payment or the wearing of gowns have, rightly, been rejected; for either of these distinctions to be introduced would spoil the modest image and unique value of independent justice provided 'for the people by the people'.

For various reasons, not least the increased use of fixed penalties for minor motoring offences and the transfer of other duties to non-judicial bodies, fewer JPs are needed these days. In January 1975, there were 19,454 active justices in England and Wales (including the Duchy of Lancaster, where separate figures are kept) — 12,946 men and 6,508 women, sitting in 680 petty sessional divisions. By 1995, the number had reached over 30,000, about half of which were women; and in 2003 the Department of Constitutional Affairs was predicting that 3,000 more lay magistrates would be required in the following three years 'to improve the delivery of justice' — an astonishing miscalculation, as it turned out. In fact, between 2000 and 2012, there was a 25 per cent reduction, a significant decline which has continued. In addition to the diminished workload, the decrease was due to a rise in the 60 plus age group, and a 48 per cent increase of district judges (DJs) in magistrates' courts. When these figures are viewed alongside courthouse closures and bench amalgamations from earlier years, it can be seen what a profound change has overtaken the magistracy in the last half century. As a result, some extensive adjustments have had to be made; and more are likely to be necessary, not least in recruitment policy for both JPs and DJs, if lay participation in the justice system is to survive.

It is tempting to bemoan the marked reduction of magistrates and their workload in recent years. However, it should be remembered that the number of JPs has now returned nearer to that of 50 years ago, and that much of the work no longer carried out by them includes long lists of tedious licensing, rates and minor road traffic offences formerly dealt with in the defendants' absence.

Although the magistracy has continued through times of acute change to demonstrate its inherent value as a flexible public resource, there is a limit to the amount of disruption it can endure without crippling consequences, among which are loss of morale among JPs, especially those who have already been on the bench for some years, and the consequent disincentive to remain in unpaid service. These issues are reflected in the higher than usual number of resignations in recent years, the reasons for which were identified in a Department for Constitutional Affairs survey in 2007. This showed that the two principal causes of resignation were problems with employers (22.5 per cent) and disenchantment with the courts service (15.0 per cent); the training burden was third (4.8 per cent) Of the 'employment' leavers (average age 51), about half were due to promotion or change of job, and a quarter had problems with employers and managers who failed to support them. The disenchanted JPs (average age 61) gave as their main reasons for leaving early: administrative or bureaucratic issues (e.g. delays and ineffective trials), and concerns about judicial policy issues (e.g. ineffective sentencing powers, favourable attitudes to criminals, and lack of faith in the Probation Service). Significantly, many of those who cited employment problems said that they would consider applying again if their circumstances changed.

In an age when public marches, strikes and 'working to rule' are the all too frequent reactions of those whose livelihood or working conditions are threatened, JPs' apparent acceptance of unsettling change and loss of power may sometimes appear supine. But the magistracy must above all be trustworthy—its loyalty to the Crown, the law and the will of Parliament never in doubt. To take any action that might undermine these institutions, set a bad example or in any way interfere with the smooth running of the courts, would be unthinkable. The negative consequence of this unwritten guarantee is that, however unacceptable government policies may be and however damaging to the magisterial fabric, governments can usually take JP's ultimate compliance for granted, without offering them anything in return.

Unlike the political connections and property qualifications which applied to many JPs in former times, today's magistrates rightly attach supreme importance to their independence and to their freedom from overt affiliation. They can usually say with honesty that they do not know, and are not interested in, the political beliefs of their colleagues. The preservation of this tradition is crucial for the proper conduct and high reputation of British summary justice, and should mean that, with more experience and better training than ever, JPs can be entrusted with more—not less—discretion and powers. Instead, with the expansion of fixed penalties and the continuing, inexplicable failure of government to activate an agreed increase of justices' sentencing limits, the opposite has so far proved to be the case. Such unnecessary constraints not only reduce the exercise of fairness and flexibility in judicial decision-making; they also increase costs and transfer more power to executives and out-of-court regulators who are not bound by the judicial oath, and who are more open to corruption. The magistracy, meanwhile, is denied the opportunity to take on greater responsibilities.

Merit and selection

In a 1973 speech on *Selecting Magistrates*, Lord Chancellor Hailsham told Manchester justices, 'The greatest mistake is to regard JP after your name as an honour like the OBE, i.e. as a reward for past service or popular respect. It is not an honour, as such; it is a heavy responsibility involving arduous training, a heavy time commitment of 26 sittings a year, and constant keeping up to date with points of law and procedure. The first thing I ask advisory committees to look for is character — integrity, unimpeachable reputation, firmness, patience and, perhaps above all, wisdom'. Rightly or wrongly, modern committees are required to seek rather more specific attributes, but that does not make Lord Hailsham's standards any less relevant.

Personal qualities must remain paramount in selecting new magistrates. So much emphasis is devoted these days to the satisfaction of alternative, more fashionable criteria (e.g. diversity, representation, ethnicity) that the most important of all — suitability[2] — is easily overlooked. Any relaxation of this test poses a threat to the quality and future of the lay magistracy. The primary aim throughout should be to select JPs who are suitable in point of individual character, integrity and understanding, and who are generally recognised as such by those among whom they live and work.

In the absence of official guidance and the tyranny of correctness, my list of desirable qualities includes:

- Ability to express personal views and accept with good grace those of others.

---

2. The word 'suitability' is used advisedly here.

- Absence of prejudice, intolerance and pomposity.
- Dispassionate and discreet.
- Soberly dressed.
- Patient, good listener and measured in response.
- Personal integrity; good reputation in local community.
- Intelligent, 'savvy' and well-informed, with sound judgement.
- Reasoning ability, common sense; willingness to learn and take advice.
- Clear thinker; able to distinguish and concentrate on relevant issues.
- Socially aware and committed to serving the community.
- Respect for the rule of law; absence of criminal convictions.
- Freedom from overt party political or potentially controversial activity.
- Developed sense of justice and fairness, truth and honesty, balance and proportion, modesty and courtesy (none of these being the preserve of any particular type of person; they can be, and are, possessed by people of all colours, creeds, classes, ages and genders — but, to be candid, less often by younger people).
- Evidence of leadership potential (bearing in mind how important good chairmanship is for the reputation of the magistracy, and the fact that up to a third of all JPs may, with training, find themselves presiding over a public court after only a few years on the bench).

Although it is preferable to have a wide age-range on the bench and to recruit relatively young JPs whenever possible, it is irresponsible to compromise on the essential qualities by over-reacting to sterile scruples about age, class or ethnicity. Nobody should be surprised or concerned that the average age of any bench is unlikely to be much less than 50; however, it becomes a matter for concern if the average figure approaches 60. Apart from considerations of 'appearance', age has little relevance to the ability to do justice; moreover, the differences tend to even out within benches of three.

Senior members of the judiciary from time-to-time have added their views on desirable qualities for judges and magistrates. In general, they also paint a picture which has not changed much over the years. In 2010, Lord Chief Justice Judge said,

'We (judges) need to be intelligent, knowledgeable about the law but, more importantly perhaps, wise in the ways of the world, sensitive to others from different backgrounds to our own, fair, open-minded and balanced, independent in spirit, courageous to do what is right even when it will be unpopular; perhaps indeed most of all when it will be unpopular, whether with politicians, the executive or the media'.

A senior member of the Supreme Court has been quoted as saying that

'at the heart of being a magistrate are impartiality, objectivity and the ability to distinguish between what you feel and what you think (i.e. non-emotional self-awareness). To be a good judge, you need good judgement (i.e. the ability to concentrate on fact-finding, form sensible opinions and make sound decisions). We are ordinary people, living ordinary lives; others should appreciate that'.

Since 1998, selection committees have been required to assess candidates solely on merit under six key headings (no other factors may be taken into account):

- *Good character*
  E.g. personal integrity—respect and trust of others—keeping confidences—disrepute causes—willingness to be circumspect.

- *Understanding and communication*
  Effective contact—mental grasp of documents, relevant facts and evidence—reasoning and concentration.

- *Social awareness*
  Rule of law acceptance — understanding social issues, including causes and effects of crime — respect for ethnic, cultural and social differences — awareness of life outside own sphere.

- *Maturity and sound temperament*
  Relating and working with others — fairness, consideration and courtesy — open-mindedness — firmness and decisiveness — confidence — acceptance of alternative views and advice.

- *Sound judgement*
  Logical thinking, weighing argument, balanced decision-making — objectivity — avoidance of prejudice.

- *Commitment and reliability*
  Willingness to serve, meet minimum attendance and training requirements — undertaking regular duties.

These headings have been designed to identify current desirable characteristics, as well as to expose those that reveal unwelcome traits, such as political ambition or arrogant self-belief; however, concentration on key criteria alone may leave less room to achieve and maintain balance on the bench. The constraints of correctness make the task no easier for selection panels, and may increase the possibility of mistakes. Applicants are not obliged to answer (nor, presumably, to discuss) questions about gender, age, ethnicity or disability, even though they have to declare their title, date and country of birth, nationality, and any impairment. The reactions which magistrates may naturally feel at times during their work on the bench are difficult to gauge in advance, even under the best-designed interview system but, in addition to much patience, JPs need to have room in their temperament for overall awareness and the very occasional exercise of mercy, leniency, sympathy — and even humour. Vengeance should never feature among their feelings, while forgiveness belongs more appropriately with victims and the general public.

Because the necessary balance of age, gender, occupation, ethnicity etc. at any one time does not leave room on the bench for all those who possess the desired characteristics, the suitable but unlucky ones should not take it as a personal affront if they are not selected. For various reasons, not more than a quarter of applicants become magistrates but, of those who succeed, all would need to have met the standards to a high degree. If one asks what personal quality is considered most essential for a JP, nine out of ten people in the street will probably reply 'common sense'; yet, significantly, that characteristic is now absent from the key headings. This is because in 2004 the moral arbiters in Whitehall, in furtherance of a policy to remove subjectivity in the selection of candidates, and in shameful capitulation to prevailing mores, issued new guidelines to advisory committees in which 'balance' was to be discarded in favour of 'diversity', 'personal suitability' was downgraded by preference for 'representation', and common sense was condemned as 'likely to be heavily underpinned by background'. Big mistake. This type of 'appropriate' advice, particularly the demotion of personal suitability, constitutes one of the most serious threats to the future of the lay magistracy.

It may not be possible to define or measure common sense, but most people quickly recognise it in those who have it. Come to think of it, isn't the determination of 'good character' (see first 'key heading' above), and possibly some of the other five headings, just as dependent on 'background' as is common sense? It remains a debatable point; but it is apparently no longer enough—however overwhelming is the evidence—merely to conclude that any candidate 'would obviously make an ideal magistrate'.

'Common sense' also fell victim to the tyranny of political correctness in the *Equal Treatment Bench Book* issued to Crown Court judges in 2004; they were instructed not to use the term because it causes problems 'when there are parties from differing cultural backgrounds with differing world views'. The judges were also told—would you believe it?—not to use such words as 'postman' and 'chairman', for fear of causing offence; they should apparently be replaced by ridiculous non-sexist equivalents. In today's grievance-driven society, advice of this kind is now issued in such volume that it becomes more and more hazardous to open one's mouth in public in case someone is unintentionally offended. Who would have thought 50 years ago that judges (and magistrates for that matter) would need to be told that if they use wrong words they might upset criminals?

Hopefully, the typical magistrate remains likely to be intelligent, considerate, soberly-dressed and blessed with an abundance of common sense — the most favourable embodiment, one would imagine, of the 'Big Society'. If, in the eyes of some, this amounts to a dull character, it is likely to be because the magistracy has no room for emotional, attention-seeking or 'colourful' personalities, nor for those prone to public expression of strong views on controversial subjects; nor, indeed, for those who take pride in being 'non-judgemental', for this suggests unwillingness to exercise the very task for which they are appointed — i.e. judging. Unfortunately, there seem to be more candidates than in the past who have a view of themselves as paragons of judicial virtue which is not shared by the interview panel and does not sufficiently meet the above six-point description.

It has to be assumed that the investigation of candidates' good character and enhanced criminal checks will reveal any past infringements of the law, and that questions put to them under other core headings will produce an aggregate of ticked boxes which amounts to a modern 'objective assessment' akin to old-fashioned 'common sense'. If that is so, it is probable that the qualities sought in today's typical new JP are in the end little different from those of 50 years ago; it is just that descriptions and emphasis have changed. It is reassuring to hear from contemporary JPs in Kent that the quality of the few new recruits to the bench is still good.

In my 12 years on the Lord Chancellor's Advisory Committee in the 1970s and 1980s, when interviews were conducted at candidates' homes, and before dogma invaded the selection process, we often used our experience merely to ask ourselves, 'Would he or she make a good magistrate?' Usually, the answer was obvious, but today such arbitrary, simple but straightforward methods would be deemed unacceptable. Of course, we made a few mistakes, but probably fewer than result from the use of today's inflexible 'tick-box' methods.

Douglas Hurd, when Home Secretary in 1986 — and others since then — was guilty of pandering to those who accused the courts of racial bias, following a survey of the prison population that revealed a disproportionately large number of black prisoners. His ill-advised solution was to suggest the introduction of ethnic monitoring from the bench down to the court ushers, and to increase the numbers of black judges, magistrates and probation officers, a blatant example of positive discrimination that was strongly contested by Lord Hailsham who pointed out that this would interfere with the independence of the judiciary. Fortunately, the idea did not take root.

'Positive discrimination' is a deliberate policy, and 'affirmative action' a deliberate step, in favour of those who are deemed by their advocates to suffer from adverse discrimination. Such a policy and action should have no place in the choice of magistrates; the process of selection is emphatically not to appoint people just because they 'represent' black, Asian, teen-age, class or minority, but is to seek men and women from a wide range of backgrounds, jobs and life experience who are intelligent enough — without needing to be well-versed in the law — to weigh evidence fairly and interpret advice correctly; conscientious, well-balanced and respected citizens with a feel for justice, most likely to attract approval from any sector of society; sensible people who can be trusted to come to objective decisions whatever the case; discreet individuals by whom you would be content to be tried and sentenced if you had the misfortune to appear as a defendant in their court. There is no room for the bigot or the preacher on the bench, but broad scope for honest, well-informed, thoroughly fair-minded, otherwise ordinary, members of the public.

It is reassuring to note that the most common reasons expressed by people wishing to become a magistrate are 'to give something back to society' and 'to do something useful for the community'; another, more high-flown, motive is to contribute to what some regard as 'the highest form of civic duty'. One candidate went as far as to declare that her fervent ambition was to 'influence fairness and equality in the justice system' which, no doubt, she felt was just what the interviewing panel wished to hear, but which quite likely had the opposite effect.

Most newly-appointed magistrates are aware of what is meant by the 'judicial mind'; others acquire it through experience. The judicial mind is not law, but know-how. In essence, it is impartial and objective, thinks clearly and logically, recognises the relevant, has a sense of fairness and balance, weighs the evidence and comes to just conclusions. It is rational and unprejudiced, always aware of the necessary standard of proof; it judges not by intuition but on hard evidence, and is never swayed by emotion.

It is a mistake to equate lay magistrates with legally-qualified judges. Although three-quarters of the public are apparently unaware of the difference between JPs and DJs, part of the unique value of the former is that they are not lawyers, but creditable members of the public holding a voluntary part-time judicial office, in addition to their every-day lives and responsibilities, a position which does not require their freedom of expression to be constrained by professional codes or stringent directions from above. They must be trusted to behave in ways that befit their role as magistrates, and they rarely fail to measure up to that expectation. Experience of the last 50 years indicates that JPs have exercised this relative freedom and behaviour with at least as much responsibility as the professional judiciary, and certainly more than that which they have witnessed among MPs and others in positions of authority. Compared with politicians, churchmen and businessmen, the magistracy's record, both on and off the bench, suggests that it should be entrusted with more work and responsibility — not less.

Human fallibility ensures that mistakes sometimes occur, and unsuitable people may occasionally be appointed, but the risk is moderated by the practice of sitting in threes and by disciplinary procedures which can quickly be applied in extreme cases, a matter that is found less easy to resolve when dealing with unsatisfactory DJs. Although the number of grievances sent to the Office for Judicial Complaints against judges and magistrates has risen in recent years, they still apply to less than 0.5 per cent of all judicial office holders; about half are related to decisions rather than behaviour, and few actually result in disciplinary action. Most cases involving JPs are brought under the 'inappropriate behaviour' heading, and can usually be handled satisfactorily at bench chairman or local advisory committee level. In the more serious cases, voluntary resignation may follow, but outright dismissal by the Lord Chancellor is rare. However, it is disturbing to realise that a drink-driving judge may sometimes remain on the bench, while an equally-inebriated magistrate will certainly be dismissed. This is even more unacceptable than allowing judges to enjoy a higher retirement age than JPs.

Recruitment, employment and appointment

The Labour government in the early years of this century was persuaded by the Magistrates Association (MA) to take the recruitment of magistrates more seriously. There followed a number of initiatives which marked a peak in post-war government support. In 2003, the Lord Chancellor's Department published *Local Business, Local Justice*, along with posters and leaflets; in the same year, the National Recruitment Strategy was launched. Most regrettably, both these laudable moves were allowed to disappear in the mists of time, with few signs since then that politicians are genuinely interested in the magistracy's recruitment problems. Moreover, it remains unclear whether or not the relatively new Judicial Appointments Commission (JAC) — comprising 15 members of which seven are lawyers and only one is a JP — is well-disposed towards the lay magistracy.

Lord Chancellor Falconer wrote in his foreword to the Recruitment Strategy document,

'Magistrates are expected to demonstrate common sense, integrity, intelligence and the capacity to act fairly ... their role is pivotal to the administration, not only of local justice, but to our judicial system as a whole'.

The strategy, he said,

'aimed to highlight the importance of the work of magistrates, particularly to employers who must be persuaded that, by allowing staff who are magistrates time off to carry out their duties, they are contributing enormously to the maintenance of local justice and the value of good citizenship'.

A further potentially helpful lead came in 2005, when Lord Falconer issued *Supporting Magistrates to Provide Justice*, which included several ideas designed to improve recruitment and retention of JPs. These included:

- Supplying advisory committees with more financial and specialist support.
- A new website for applicants and employers.
- Establishment of a working party of senior employers' groups.
- Improving and shortening of the selection process.
- 'Lay' to be dropped when referring to the magistracy.
- Consultation on reduction of minimum sittings from 26 to 24 half-days.
- Introduction of 'good practice' guidelines for management of cancellations.

If the nation is serious in wishing to enrol younger justices and retain lasting lay participation in the judicial system, government and employers must be prepared to treat recruitment to, and service in, the magistracy more seriously, and with the same zeal and funding as are given to encouragement of service in the Territorial Army (TA) and certain other public offices. In 2000, £4.7 million was spent on advertising for the TA, compared to only £35,000 devoted to attracting members of the public to serve on the bench. If employers can be required to release staff for the armed services reserves, extended maternity leave, lifeboat duties, jury service, and other worthy purposes, without detriment to the employees under consideration, they should certainly be equally obliged to do so for the magistracy, unless exempted for special reasons, such as skills shortage or small company status. Voluntary public service is a great British tradition, and the envy of many other countries. Release for those who wish to do it must be seen and accepted by employers, not only as a duty, but also as a net benefit and honour for themselves and their company, and as a sign of corporate willingness to contribute to the common good. The solution to recruitment problems must be found, not by the irresponsible appointment of expensive lawyers to take over our summary justice system, but by creating more successful ways of attracting and keeping inexpensive JPs.

Even in areas where recruitment of magistrates is sufficient, solo-sitting DJs have been increasingly appointed to permanent posts. Such an unjustified policy has further weakened the lay magisterial base and caused much resentment, especially when JPs have been sent home while judges are retained for work which could — and should — have remained with the local bench. This makes one realise how disturbingly easy it is for government and others to enfeeble the magistracy, together with the whole system of summary justice.

Special and urgent attention must be given to recruitment, employing attractive procedures designed to increase the availability of ordinary citizens to serve on the bench, and especially to banish one of the most frequently-used excuses for appointing more DJs: chronic shortage of lay candidates. Advisory committees, bench chairmen and HM Courts and Tribunals Service must consistently plan in future for the long-term, and be adequately equipped to mount strong recruitment programmes before shortages arise. To meet the need for a sensible approach to the continuing demand for diversity, committees will require better access to demographic data and information on the make-up of local communities. While the need for 'diversity' must not be exaggerated, 'political affiliation' remains unsatisfactory as a measurement and ought, if anything, to be replaced by the use of socio-economic profiles.

Although the rise in out-of-court cases and DJs has brought about a huge reduction in the number of magistrates, the regular recruitment of new JPs and retention of experienced older members of the bench remain crucial for the future success of lay participation in the justice system. Much reliance will continue to be placed on finding a sufficient supply of citizens to come forward from a wide spectrum of society, willing to accept a degree of individual sacrifice, make personal adjustments and undergo training; but volunteers must be able to see in return at least some measure of stability, respect and satisfaction from their service. It may well be possible to recruit an even more socially representative magistracy, but it has to be born in mind that this may mean a more expensive service, because younger members cannot usually sit as often as older members and are more likely to claim loss of earnings and expenses.

Regrettably, a national survey in 2009 reported a fall in the standard of JP applicants. This was said to be due especially to signs among candidates of prejudice and 'chips on the shoulder', 'campaigners' and holders of immoderate views, disinclination to accept majority decisions, holders of previous convictions or general unsuitability. However, at a time when it has become quite common elsewhere for qualification levels to be reduced in order to accommodate a wider spectrum of entrants, it is essential for the future reputation of the magistracy that this is not translated into a lower standard of appointment merely to meet diversity criteria. If recruitment is a problem, ways must be found to overcome it without compromising quality or resorting to the appointment of more, but less diverse, DJs. It remains important that JPs as a whole should continue to be drawn from what Lord Hailsham described as 'the responsible elements in society'; important, too, that the magistracy is not composed only of good, loyal 'workhorses', but that it also attracts — and retains — leaders of sufficient calibre, independence and energy to hold their own at the highest level with senior politicians, lawyers and administrators, and be competent enough to challenge and mix with them when necessary.

Employers today, especially in small businesses, are less able to spare staff, especially when absence of one team member may disrupt production, cause targets to be missed and bonuses lost; nor are they so ready to regard it as an honour for their company when one of their employees is chosen as a JP. As temporary 'supply' teachers have become more expensive, schools have also become more reluctant to release staff for court duties. Such problems as these are particularly challenging for middle-managers — both those who are asked to release their staff and those who are magistrates themselves. Being a JP has become more onerous for those holding demanding work positions, so resignations have also risen. Unsympathetic employers, increased time-wasting in court, extra travelling, and more interesting cases taken by district judges have also combined to create a further obstacle in the search for recruits from more diverse backgrounds. This problem becomes especially serious when trying to attract busy younger men from industry, especially those in smaller companies; it is rather less difficult to find suitable middle-aged women who have raised a family and are looking for something worthwhile to engage their latent talents.

In 1988, Lord Chancellor Mackay urged employers to allow magistrates on their staff time off for court sittings. 'Whilst I fully recognise the difficulties faced by employers, I do most urgently request them to weigh in the balance their own particular interests and those of the community as a whole', he said. Thirteen years later, Lord Chancellor Irvine was also concerned about the difficulties some employed JPs were having. He told the MA that he might give public recognition to employers who encourage staff to become JPs, but nothing came of the idea.

On paper, employers are urged to 'play their part' and 'do their duty' by giving their employees agreed 'reasonable' time-off to engage in public service; for the TA, this is meant to allow for a couple of weeks' training each year and, for the magistracy, the minimum 26 half-day sittings. If such absence is unacceptable to the employer, the Safeguard of Employment Act 1985 may give protection from unfair dismissal, but that can never be an adequate answer; it has to be a last resort. Even when ultimate reliance is placed on goodwill, problems can arise with staff who become 'indispensable', and whose absence may cause resentment and snide remarks from managers and work colleagues.

Holiday entitlements for most employees these days are often generous enough to enable keen JPs to soften such problems by sacrificing a few days' leave. With so many people now entitled to as much as six weeks' holiday a year, it is surely not unreasonable to suggest that up to two weeks might be given to public service as a magistrate—and, incidentally, this alternative lessens the possibility of friction with employers; but it would be more acceptable if statutory provision could be made for introduction of a compulsory scheme of national service, whereby full participation in selected voluntary services (such as the magistracy and the TA) or other recognised purposes (such as parenting leave) would become part of every employment contract, without detriment to pay, promotion or pensions. Employers are already required by statute to make provision for parenting leave and the preservation of pension rights, in order that their female staff should not be disadvantaged; but a fully recognised 'national service fortnight' scheme would be a more effective way of reviving and strengthening the public service ethos and reducing friction between employers and employees.

Should consideration also be given, perhaps, to the payment of moderate compensation to small companies and organizations in return for the release of JPs for up to 26 half days a year, i.e. not a payment to JPs themselves, but an encouragement to employers to release staff for service on the bench? This would be a small price to pay for improvement in the number of applicants from business and industry in particular, and for strengthening the magistracy in general; again, it would also help to avoid the costly and undesirable employment of yet more DJs.

Declaring that one is a JP when applying for a job must not put applicants at a disadvantage. There is plenty of evidence to show that training for, and service on, the bench allows people to acquire marketable skills that are transferable to the workplace, including improvement in their confidence, decision-making, management ability and leadership. Making volunteering an established principle within the working environment should be recognised, not only as something which pays-off in employee satisfaction, but also as a route to improved performance, personal development and employer reputation. National policy in respect of service to the courts by the working public must leave employers in no doubt about the wholehearted commitment of all governments to support of the magistracy. This means that literature and advice must always be available to assist potential candidates when they inform their employers that they are thinking of applying to serve on the bench. Can we afford to risk losing such a valuable institution because, out of 30 million eligible people, we cannot find less than 0.1 per cent of suitable volunteers from that number to serve on the bench?

Fewer young and middle-aged people now feel tempted, or can afford, to be involved in voluntary public service. Indeed, it was found that voluntary work in general dropped by nearly a third between 1995 and 2000 in the UK, and has continued to fall. Even when such individuals are found, they are less likely than 50 years ago to meet today's refined selection criteria. All this has had a marked effect on the type of candidate coming forward. For good or ill, it has removed or kept out many younger and upstanding men and women from all walks of life whose background, style or occupation no longer fits the modern image of what an all-embracing magistracy should look like; casualties include so-called working-class or blue-collar workers for whom special recruitment efforts have been made, as well as people from the other end of the social and working spectrums. A typically broad 'waiting list' of candidates for the Ashford Bench in 1980 consisted of a surveyor, a farmer, an accountant, a postal officer, a bank manager, a personal assistant, a businessman, a postman, two engineers, a train driver, three school-teachers and three housewives. Yes, the magistracy was already practising 'diversity' 40 years ago, but never enough for its critics.

Although most candidates will view membership of the magistracy as a positive way of giving public service, it is less likely these days that a sense of duty will drive them to volunteer, and less still that they can afford to put the public interest before their own. Since the abolition of *ex officio* local authority justices in 1968, entrants are also, fortunately, less inclined to come with political labels. Party affiliation, although still permitted, does not sit comfortably with bench membership and should, in my view, be discouraged in the appointment of JPs; so it was most disappointing, to say the least, to hear in 1997 Lord Chancellor Irvine announce, under the pretext of trying to improve the political and social balance of the magistracy, that he intended to increase the number of Labour voters on the bench. That, surely, is not the way to rid the magistracy of party political influence.

Partial reassurance appeared in April 2004, when Lord Falconer revived the question of political balance in the magistracy by suggesting a combination of occupational and industrial classifications as a yardstick instead of political affiliation. But, although balance in such respects may be desirable, the future of the magistracy remains in danger if that objective becomes such an obsession that it over-rides personal suitability as the primary criterion for selection.

It used to be said that the particular knowledge brought to the court by locally-appointed JPs improved the quality of justice, and that this provided a strong argument against court closures and bench amalgamations. Looking back over the last 50 years, it is difficult to maintain that this was ever the key advantage that we believed it to be; now, with the almost complete disappearance of local justice as we knew it, this claim looks less persuasive than ever. I can recall only two motoring cases (out of, probably, thousands) in which I was able to draw usefully on my local knowledge; in both, I knew that the road layout descriptions given in the evidence were inaccurate and could significantly affect the decision; as a result, the accused drivers were acquitted of careless driving in both cases. But one wonders how many other occasions there might be when wrong sentences are given because the bench had no knowledge of the scene, and had to rely entirely on police and other witness evidence? Does this mean that benches should be more rigorous in questioning witnesses as to the accuracy of their impressions or measurements, because the decision may hinge on them, or must they stick only to the facts presented in court, even though at least one member of the bench knows them to be inaccurate? Consult the clerk.

Although the first women JPs were not appointed until January 1920, one matter today in which the lay magistracy cannot be criticized is the proportion of women in its ranks. There has been an approximate 50:50 gender balance for many years, and women contribute equally with men at all levels and in all positions. Fortunately, the results of a survey carried out by MORI in 1979 have continued to be ignored by selectors. In response to the question 'would you prefer a man or a woman as your local magistrate', 10 per cent of respondents answered 'a woman', and 40 per cent 'a man'—almost the same percentage as that resulting from a similar question asked in respect of doctors and MPs. There is little doubt that a poll, if carried out today, would show substantially less bias against women than 40 years ago.

It is entirely right in principle that disabled people should be eligible to serve on the bench, but they must be able to carry out the full range of magisterial duties, and the degree to which the system, layout and other provisions may have to be adjusted to meet their needs must be 'reasonable'. Those with impaired abilities often possess wonderful compensatory senses and are amazingly adaptable to particular situations (former Home Secretary, David Blunkett MP, being an outstanding example), but it is usually recognised that there has to be a limit, not only to the amount of re-arrangement needed to accommodate them, but also to the risk of discrimination charges (such as the partially-disabled magistrate who complained when expensive special provisions were not made for her at court, and when training times conflicted with her exercise routine).

Although hearing and eyesight play a big part in the work of justices in court, and are therefore particularly sensitive factors, it seems odd that interview panels are, apparently, not allowed to question candidates about the extent of their disability. While partially-sighted people (many perhaps possessing skills not so common in those with full sight, but which may be helpful on the bench) can apply to become JPs, much may depend on the degree of blindness, the technical equipment available to assist them, and the way in which the person, and those with whom they have to work, can cope with their disability. It is no more fair to either party to be asked to sit together on the bench than to insist that a professional symphony orchestra should include an aurally-impaired violinist. For obvious reasons, those with deficient hearing, should not join or remain on the bench unless they use reliable aids.

Problems sometimes arise, especially in 'honey-pot' counties such as Devon and Cornwall, when magistrates move home on retirement and apply for transfer to a new bench. As they are usually experienced, and money has already been spent on their training, it is understandable that many of them presume they will be immediately welcome in their new area. However, they need to appreciate that their hopes of re-appointment may conflict with established local plans and individual expectations. The balance of the bench may also be an issue, and aspiring local JPs may feel upset if faced with outside competition, particularly when they are finding it difficult to meet their minimum sitting obligations. On the other hand, there are inherent dangers in allowing recruitment to lag behind requirements. This can cause all kinds of consequent problems, such as shortage of mentors, excessive attendance by a few members, and calls for the appointment of yet more DJs.

Subject to the difficulties which can arise in connection with transfers, another solution could be to make provision for temporary retirement from the bench at the crucial period in younger JPs' working lives when absence may put at risk their prospects of promotion, a better job or the needs of their family. If they are later able to find more time to attend court, they could re-apply to serve another fifteen years or so, having taken a short re-training course to 'bring them back up to speed'. Naturally, such an idea would not find favour with those who maintain that the bench already has too many grey-haired members (the age factor is nearly always exaggerated), but it could have the effect of attracting more young applicants at the front end, who would otherwise be put off because of fears about employment difficulties in middle age. Furthermore, it has already been found that mature and widely-experienced late-comers (i.e. those appointed after 55) can be of particular benefit to the bench. It would be a tragedy if sensitivity to criticism of JPs' average age was to become an excuse for failure to take every possible step to increase the number and quality of applicants.

Although economic and employment conditions have made recruitment and retention increasingly difficult in some areas, it has been found on many occasions that a well-organized local advertising campaign, if sustained and adequately funded, can pay dividends in the search for suitable new applicants. For instance, in 1999 the Lord Chancellor launched a month-long national recruitment campaign, in order to raise the profile of the lay magistracy and to increase awareness, throughout the community and local organizations, of the fact that 'ordinary' people can apply to become JPs. The campaign was so successful that more than 15,000 enquiries were received; thus it is particularly deplorable when government seizes on poor recruitment as an excuse to allow district judge applications to proceed before every possible effort has been made to find suitable lay recruits.

Whenever recruitment problems occur, pressure increases among JPs for the mandatory retirement age of 70 to be raised, it being argued that these days many justices of that age are still perfectly capable, alert and willing to continue on the bench, and that in any case the magistracy can ill-afford to lose so much experience and talent unnecessarily. It is also felt that if a choice exists between allowing a few senior magistrates to continue for a little longer, rather than make up the shortfall by opening the door to even more DJs, the decision should be made in favour of JPs. Furthermore, it is pointed out, judges, although required to retire at 70, are still allowed to sit part-time until 75, the same limit as for jurors.

Why are JPs considered less fitted to sit in their seventies than presiding judges and jurors? A fairly recent proposition—that lay members of tribunals should be remunerated—could have fatal consequences for the magistracy. If that is accepted, how long will it be before it is suggested that justices should also be rewarded? No-one should be left in any doubt that payment to JPs would remove at a stroke one of the lay magistracy's greatest virtues. Nothing would bring about its demise more quickly. Fortunately, however, the idea has so far attracted little support.

Training

From its foundation in 1920, the Magistrates Association pioneered the training of magistrates. Without this, and subsequent dedication to the improvement of its skills, it is probably no exaggeration to say that the lay magistracy would not exist today. Even though there was some resistance among JPs at the time, the association persisted, and training became obligatory for newly-appointed justices in 1966. Fourteen years later, refresher training also became obligatory. At the end of the 1980s, the MA fostered the idea of training in structured decision-making, and the introduction of a competence framework followed in 1998, when it came to realise that, unless magistrates know and feel that they are doing their job as well or better than anyone else, they risk public criticism and unwelcome political interference. The magistracy cherishes its independence, but it has to earn it every day.

In spite of reduction in the number of justices' clerks, the various training and personal assessment programmes of the last 50 years have, if anything, enhanced the magistracy's professionalism and made it easier to accept suitably trained non-lawyers as legal advisers. The introduction of sentencing guidelines and structured decision-making (both Magistrates Association initiatives: the role of the association in training is discussed in *Chapter 12*) have also played a significant part in this progress. The more recent requirement that benches, unlike juries, should give reasons for their decisions has further concentrated JPs' minds on the paramount need for judicial competence. Paradoxically, the more professional, efficient and diverse the magistracy has become, the more it has been deprived of authority in its own house, the more its responsibilities have been pruned, and the less its potential has been recognised. Rather than gaining in strength and esteem, it has become more exposed to the depredations of bureaucratic rule, and to the notion that 'unpaid' is amateur and must therefore be inferior.

Training is one of the chief costs of keeping the lay magistracy up to professional standards of leadership and judicial decision-making; even so, it costs the country less than £40 per sitting JP—incredibly good value for the service rendered. Regrettably, however, training is often an early casualty of increased budget restrictions, posing a constant threat to the maintenance of magisterial skills and the efficiency of the summary justice system. Shortages of qualified trainers and reduced availability of legal advisers are further areas of risk. Moreover, since the withdrawal of the MA from a primary training role, the magistracy has become more vulnerable to the paralysing influence of central administration; as a result, funding cuts have weakened it while, as ever, strengthening the case for more DJs whose training budgets do not seem so vulnerable and do not come out of local funds.

CHAPTER 8

Public and Personal

'To serve and not to ask for any reward, save that of knowing that we do right to all without fear or favour'

Adaptation of a prayer by St Ignatius of Loyola.

- Standards and public service
- On and off duty
- Diversity and representation

Standards and public service

It can perhaps be said that being a justice of the peace (JP) represents a degree of privilege, not in the sense of right, advantage or power, but as granting an unusual opportunity to offer something of considerable benefit to society. Few JPs serve without making some kind of personal sacrifice — either of lost income or pension, time, pleasures or the pursuit of other, more rewarding, activities; they should not accept appointment to the bench unless they are prepared to make some adjustments or restrictions in their life. This approach is fundamental to the success of the voluntary service tradition in our country, and crucial to the conservation of an independent lay magistracy. It is also about maintaining a respected role in the process of democracy and justice. Public trust in the magistracy is important; it is better to be trusted than to be loved. By taking on such an office, JPs place themselves (and, to some extent, their lives and families) in the public domain. Potential and newly-appointed magistrates need to be reminded of this, and of its possible consequences. Before it is too late, someone has to ask them: Can you (and your family) put up with such exposure?

Politicians and bureaucrats — working, perhaps, under less onerous standards of public behaviour themselves — have shown few signs in recent times of appreciating the magistracy's special qualities, and how such a trustworthy resource could, and should, be employed more usefully for the benefit of the nation. Instead, many of them seem to regard magistrates, not as valued members of an essential service, but as misfits in a system measured only by crude numbers, cost and efficiency. Government should not take JPs' loyalty for granted. It should not, for instance, assume that those magistrates who still do not claim expenses (yes, there are still quite a few) will continue to be so generous when required to travel increasing distances to attend court; nor should it be insensitive to the demoralising practice of sending them home from court prematurely, so that their scheduled cases can be transferred to district judges (DJs) who must, it is maintained, be kept employed when their court lists collapse.

It is unfortunate in some ways that criminal justice is administered as a 'system', rather than a 'service', for it is to the latter concept that magistrates are more truly dedicated. There is a distinction between public service, such as that given by paid police officers and civil servants, and voluntary public service of the kind given by JPs. Full-time, salaried employees are usually expected to act within a recognisable 'public service ethos'. Lay justices are unpaid and part-time, their reward coming from the free and unrestricted nature of the service they provide. Additionally, magistrates hold a statutory office which sets them slightly apart from what are usually described as the 'voluntary services'. It is thus inaccurate to describe them as 'public servants'.

Regrettably, there persists in some official circles tacit disapproval of those who give their time and talents without receiving payment. Harold Nicolson, in his *Diaries 1945–62*, indicated that the National Trust shared this problem, when he wrote about the 'distrust of gratuitous public service shown by the (socialist) government's supporters, and the way in which those who give their services free are regarded with suspicion by the doctrinaires'.

There is no code of conduct specifically for JPs, although they are bound by the grand and familiar terms of the judicial oath to

'well and truly serve the Sovereign and do right to all manner of people after the laws and usages of the realm, without fear or favour, affection or ill-will'.

It can also be said that they are covered, at least in part, by the seven key principles or ethical norms, drawn up in 1995 by the Nolan Committee on standards in public life, which apply to anyone who works as a public office holder. This includes people who are elected or appointed to such an office and all those working in the Civil Service, local government, police, courts, Probation Service, non-departmental public bodies and other public service sectors. In summary, the Nolan principles are: Selflessness — Integrity — Objectivity — Accountability — Openness — Honesty and Leadership. However, the advice given to JPs by a former Attorney-General of Western Australia would perhaps be even more appropriate. His guidance said, 'We, the JPs, will:

- Maintain and promote, in both our public and professional lives, standards of conduct that uphold the integrity and independence of our office.
- Respect and comply with the law, and conduct ourselves in a way that promotes public confidence in the integrity and independence of our office.
- Act impartially, not allowing conduct in our role to be influenced by political, business, family or social interests.
- Separate the functions of our office from any personal or political interests.
- Not convey, or permit others to convey, the impression that we are in a special position of influence.
- Perform judicial duties without bias or prejudice.
- Respect confidentiality ... and not disclose information of a private, confidential or commercially sensitive nature received in the course of our duties.

- Disqualify ourselves from proceedings in which our impartiality might reasonably be questioned.
- Not accept any payment or gift in the course of our duties.
- Not use our office to advance our personal or business interests.
- Participate, whenever possible, in training offered to increase our knowledge and professionalism in relation to our role'.

The presence and influence of local politicians on the bench has declined since the abolition of ex-officio JPs, and this has been a good thing for the image of an independent, non-party magistracy. Although some local authority members are still appointed through the normal selection process — and most of them are assiduous in keeping their political views to themselves — it would be even better if those holding public positions involved with party politics were expressly precluded from applying to become, or remaining as, JPs. In my humble view, party politics and the magistracy are incompatible. They should be kept apart. Justices should behave more like judges or members of public boards, and be governed by the advice given under 'political activity' by Nolan. For instance, they should:

- Be, and be seen to be, politically impartial.
- Not occupy a paid political post or hold a high-profile role in a political party.
- Abstain from all controversial political activity.
- Refrain from making political statements or engage in other political activity.
- Exercise proper discretion and remain conscious of their public responsibilities.

In other respects, JPs should remain free to associate with organizations that do not conflict with the holding of judicial office, while being careful not to express themselves in any forum on matters that may be perceived as politically sensitive, nor to act in ways that might raise doubts about their impartiality on the bench. They must be aware of the need to maintain the high reputation of the magistracy at all times.

With the best of motives, some magistrates join bodies with an interest in the courts, such as the National Association for the Care and Resettlement of Offenders, the Prison Reform Trust, the Howard League for Prison Reform, and even Liberty, the human rights campaigning organization. However, these groups may sometimes be less than complimentary about the magistracy, and JPs therefore need to be aware that membership of them may lead to conflicts of interest, and may prove awkward when trying to balance the needs of effective sentencing and punishment with genuine concern for offenders or the reform of custodial regimes. Magistrates do not have to declare their membership of organizations although, for eleven years from 1998, they were required to reveal if they were freemasons. This was an unjustified piece of selective discrimination, introduced after a parliamentary Home Affairs Committee raised 'a perception that there could be a problem', although no evidence whatever had been found of impropriety or malpractice by magistrates or judges in this respect. A large number of JPs, including those among the massive majority who were not freemasons, refused on principle to answer the subsequent question about membership; the government in the end was left to calculate that less than seven per cent of them belonged to the organization anyway, and the requirement was then dropped.

Because JPs are often quite well-known, recognisable and sit in judgement of other's behaviour, they are naturally expected in their personal affairs to keep within the law, be of good character and exemplary conduct, to have a clean record, and to avoid using (or appearing to use) their status to promote personal interests. We all know how easy it is to break speed limits with impunity, but magistrates have to keep in mind that every time they do so, the driver behind them or in the car they pass may be someone known to them who will be saying to themselves: 'How can he have the temerity to punish me for speeding when he doesn't keep to the law himself?' It is a salutary thought which should always be in a JP's mind.

Unless candidates are prepared to accept the necessary constraints on their behaviour without reservation, they should not seek appointment or remain on the bench. Discipline applied to personal conduct has become an unpopular code for many people, and some aspiring JPs may find the strictures attached to public office too much to accept. In general, magistrates should refrain from behaving in any way that could bring their own reputation or that of the magistracy into disrepute—a rule which has sometimes placed both the institution and individual JPs at a disadvantage when invited to join public expressions of opposition. Regrettably, more (though still few) magistrates are having to be reprimanded than was the case 50 years ago. There are probably a number of reasons for this, not least the demand for greater diversity among members, a general dilution of the public service ethic, and a weaker sense of duty and personal commitment, occasionally amounting to quite shameless irresponsibility.

Nearly half of the disciplinary matters relating to magistrates now arise as a result of failure to maintain competence or to meet minimum sitting requirements, something that was unheard of 50 years ago. The next highest category (c.20 per cent) is misconduct or behaviour which falls below the required standard; but, although the number of complaints as a proportion of total JPs appears to have risen in recent years, the overall picture relative to modern behavioural standards remains satisfactory. Whatever the degree to which individual JPs measure up to the ideal, the reputation and future of the whole magistracy may also be affected by their behaviour, and it may be necessary for this fact to be more strongly emphasised before they accept appointment. For instance, if they make a habit of phoning-in irresponsibly at the last minute to cancel a scheduled court attendance because of other commitments, they may not only be jeopardising their own competence level and the efficient operation of the courts system, but also be adding to the case for appointment of yet more DJs.

To some—especially those permanently conditioned by a hostile attitude towards 'authority' and 'the establishment'—JPs are always likely to be regarded unfavourably, however modestly they behave, and however competently they perform their work. Even though they are unpaid, and sometimes unfairly referred to as 'amateurs', it is essential that they conduct themselves and their courts in every way as true 'professionals'. At all times they have to prove that they are not only well trained, but able to do the job as efficiently or better than others. They must also show that their voluntary, unpaid status is a strength, not a weakness, and never use it as an excuse for less than professional behaviour and performance. Skilled and unfailingly courteous chairmen are the key to the provision of an effective answer to criticism of the magistracy; they must never be overbearing when exercising firmness; never pompous when preserving the authority and dignity of the court; never verbose when simplicity and clarity are needed. JPs should always be conscious of the obligation to protect the integrity of the law and respect for their authority as judges. To do this, a degree of detachment is necessary, and temptations to 'popularise' justice or abandon formality should be resisted. Magistrates who mistakenly believe that it is an advantage to exercise special understanding of criminal motives, or to have sympathy with offenders, are always at risk of breaching their judicial oath.

Critics and reforming politicians sometimes like to create the impression that the magistracy is so inept that there is a call for change, but a study by Morgan and Russell in 2000 found that only eight per cent of regular court users had 'very little' or 'no' confidence in the lay magistracy. The main reason for lack of faith was 'inconsistency in sentencing decisions', which is perhaps not surprising. Interestingly, the most common criticism of DJs arose from their 'different personalities and styles'. The survey concluded that 'JPs need to improve in showing command and in addressing questions to lawyers and the CPS' (Crown Prosecution Service); it also highlighted how ignorant the general public and media are about the magistracy and justice system (e.g. a third of a MORI poll thought that lay justices are legally qualified), and how frequently researchers rely on the uninformed views of unrepresentative members of the public to make recommendations for changes designed to satisfy the critics.

JPs can — and, I believe, should — derive some inner satisfaction, even modest pride, from being regarded as unpaid professionals, skilled in structured and impartial decision-making and, frequently, chairmanship; participants in an intelligent process for which they are well trained to ensure that everyone is treated fairly, without prejudice or discrimination. Yes, of course, being chosen as a JP is an honour, but it is above all a substantial responsibility. It is not, and must never be, about power, influence, money or charity. It is a duty, not a job or opportunity for self-aggrandisement; nor is it an undertaking for which everyone is suited.

On and off duty

There is no better indication of what is meant by 'the judicial mind' than the words of the judicial oath. If its simple precepts are fully respected and faithfully observed—as they are—most concerns about the lack of diversity and the fear of injustice become irrelevant. Experienced or well-trained magistrates have no difficulty in putting aside their prejudices when sitting on the bench. However, deciding the appropriate meaning of 'reasonable', when looking for proof 'beyond reasonable doubt', can be quite a challenge. If a constant diet of crime stories, unpleasant events and the corrupt conduct of mankind threatens to become too depressing after a day in court, it is helpful to remind oneself that the criminal members of our society are a tiny proportion when compared to the millions of law-abiding, honest people, who never offend, but look to the police and the courts for protection and relief from the threats, violence and obnoxious behaviour of the sinful minority. The great majority go about their lives peacefully, keeping within the law and treating their neighbours and colleagues with civility; it is these, if anyone, whom JPs represent—not just those of their own class and background. Magistrates fail in their duty and let these good people down if they do not deal firmly with the few who—often deliberately, needlessly and selfishly—wreck the universal wish of the majority to live in a virtuous society.

Among the personal tools needed by JPs are fairness, patience and courtesy. For chairmen, the greatest of these is courtesy; it almost always evokes a civil response, even from the most belligerent occupants of the dock. Readiness to show mercy (helpfully described in the dictionary as 'compassion shown by one to another who is in his power, but has no claim to kindness'), when appropriate, is another useful resource, but there should be no room in the kit for emotion nor for tolerance of criminal or anti-social behaviour.

In regard to patience, the Earl of Birkenhead, as Lord Chancellor addressing the inaugural meeting of the Magistrates Association in 1921 at Central Hall, Westminster, gave the following advice (paraphrased): 'Be patient with the presentation of the case by the advocate if he is at all competent for, believe me, no greater disservice can be done to the administration of justice than that he who comes before the court should go away feeling that the magistrates begrudged the necessary time to reach a conclusion based on a full consideration of all the facts. Never be in too much of a hurry to make up your mind that you know the facts of the case. It is very easy, when you have heard the opening address, and when you have heard perhaps the first witness, to think that you know all about the case. You can never be sure until you reach almost the very end of it'.

However, patience should be rationed when the court is confronted with long-winded lawyers. Chairmen should always be ready to tell them — politely — when they are being unnecessarily tedious and the bench's tolerance is running out, e.g. in Crown Court parlance, 'Mr Brown, I think we have absorbed your point to the limit of our ability'. Perseverance used to be needed in addition to patience when faced with a boring session of nothing but unpaid road tax, council tax or TV licences, all civil matters, none of which ought really to have been brought before criminal court justices in the first place — and today, thankfully, are not.

There are inadequate or less good JPs, too; but their contribution to decision-making in the retiring room is usually minimised by the input of other magistrates. One hopes that JPs who are unsuited to the job are never allowed to become court chairmen, in which position their faults may be magnified by symptoms of partiality, failure to understand presumption of innocence and burden of proof, tendency to believe or disbelieve the prosecution, inattention to what is being said, inability to distinguish what is irrelevant, and excessive leniency or harshness. Their greatest problem is that usually they do not recognise their own failings.

Although magistrates have shown themselves remarkably patient and adaptable to changing demands, and the majority have indicated they are 'quite satisfied' with their work, a higher number than ever express dissatisfaction (leading in some cases to resignation), due to a combination of delays, late starts, wasted time, inefficiency, late cancellations, poor administration and lack of consultation; quite a few complain of being undervalued, under-appreciated, and even badly treated. Younger JPs may have little option but to accept the new roles which may be allocated to them in the future, but the older ones are likely to find it more difficult to come to terms with algorithms and reforms which may include strange new roles, such as 'dispute resolution', 'problem solving' and more reliance on 'restorative justice'.

It is one of the enduring strengths of the lay magistracy that it is adaptable enough to allow older, experienced JPs to sit more often when there is a temporary shortage of recruits, and when younger ones may be struggling to meet their minimum requirements because of work commitments or cancelled sittings. This flexibility, and the dedication that goes with it, extends to the occasional need to sit on a Saturday morning, and at other times out of normal working hours. Several ideas for holding courts at unusual times have foundered, not on account of JPs' unwillingness to sit, but on the difficulties raised by one or other of the salaried participants in the court process.

Dress is also important in the courtroom. There are no uniforms, but magistrates and officers are expected to dress soberly and in a way that reflects the dignity of the court, which usually means for the men a suit, shirt and tie of neutral appearance unlikely to attract attention, and for the women suits or dresses of equal sobriety. The women's hats and gloves of former years have long since disappeared. If JPs do not keep to the unwritten rules of dress, it might renew the occasional — so far, resisted — calls for them to wear gowns; but although these would help to cover up the more extreme differences of personal taste, they would detract from the image of relative informality, and of a court consisting of respectable ordinary citizens.

By and large, the conventions are sensibly observed but, if JPs arrive unsuitably dressed, it becomes a matter for a quiet word from the chairman. His advice may need to include the banning of club ties, badges or other symbols that might raise questions of bias or prejudice. It is inappropriate to wear signs of sympathy or allegiance to any cause or organization when on the bench; it would be particularly wrong, for instance, to wear a CND badge when adjudicating in a case involving nuclear weapons protesters, or a National Farmers' Union tie when trying a local farmer for subsidy fraud. The chairman must also be prepared to intervene if he and his colleagues feel that a defendant or witness is dressed in a way that offends the dignity of the court, especially when it is obvious that the wearer is deliberately being disrespectful. Fifty years ago, failure to remove a hat came into this category, but such an order would not be enforced today. A contempt of court charge should always be considered if defendants ignore a chairman's reasonable request.

Even though some may agree with American Justice Stevens that 'anonymity is a shield from the tyranny of the majority', no-one should seek appointment to the bench unless they are willing for it to be known that they are a JP. A few magistrates in the past have sought anonymity, but have had to be told firmly that this is not acceptable. The matter became the subject of correspondence in 1985 between the MA, the Law Society and the Guild of Newspaper Editors, following threats of violence at that time from militant organizations, including the self-styled Animal Liberation Front, and a spate of refusals by justices' clerks to reveal names of their magistrates. The MA Council responded by saying that 'the names of adjudicating magistrates should normally be available on request by persons having a *bona fide* interest during or after proceedings in court, but there will be a small number of occasions when it will be in the interests of justice for the names to be withheld'.

Disallowing anonymity on the bench is also part of the openness of our courts. 'There is in my view no such person known to the law as the anonymous JP', said Lord Justice Watkins. Magistrates themselves abuse their power if they or their clerks try to keep their names secret; they should be as keen to espouse open justice as to expose injustice. Neither magistrates, as judicial office holders, nor the advisory committees who recommend them for appointment, can expect to be anonymous. Although, for security reasons, the names of serving JPs are not given more publicity than necessary, transparency is also important. Names may therefore be disclosed at any time to genuine enquirers but quite rightly, not addresses or telephone numbers.

The confidentiality of Advisory Committee membership ended in 1988, when the Lord Chancellor (Lord Mackay) announced that the aura of secrecy surrounding the selection process would be removed, thus allowing the public to see that the Committees are fairly composed of members drawn from different sections of the community. 'No member is, or should regard themselves as, a representative of any organization, group or political party', he said.

It cannot be denied that, as holders of a public office, there is a small risk of personal abuse or assault. It is likely to be much less these days than for nurses and ticket collectors, but perhaps greater than it used to be when I was appointed in 1962. In some circumstances, JPs may feel assailable, or will have witnessed a violent or threatening incident in the courtroom, but relatively few have been intimidated or attacked in or outside court; that probably still leaves over 80 per cent who have never felt themselves to be more vulnerable than usual as a result of being a magistrate.

It can be said that magistrates (whose names are public, and whose chairmen speak in court) are more exposed to personal scrutiny and potential danger than either bewigged judges or anonymous juries. I was occasionally called uncomplimentary names in court by troublesome offenders, but in nearly 40 years on the bench, I never felt unsafe, and never received abuse from any member of the public elsewhere. However, verbal attacks on JPs drawn from 'working-class' areas have been known to occur when friends and neighbours feel they have 'joined the enemy' and are no longer 'one of us'.

The MA was highly critical of the government in 1987 when police protection was withdrawn from courts, but it is difficult to measure what effect this, or any of the subsequent changes in security arrangements, may have had on the behaviour of defendants, witnesses and members of the public within courtrooms. Because family and youth courts are designed to be more intimate and informal than the adult criminal court, there is perhaps more likelihood that magistrates in those courts will feel less safe and potentially more intimidated on some occasions. Good chairmanship can have a substantial beneficial influence in this respect.

To maintain public confidence and avoid compromising the impartiality and independence of both the bench and themselves, it is equally important that justices refrain, not only from taking part in a case involving friends, relatives, employer or anyone with whom they have dealings, but also from one in which they might find they have close personal knowledge or a conflict of interest; whenever there is any doubt, it is always preferable not to sit—or at least to consult the chairman or clerk before doing so. When agendas are no longer issued in advance and justices have no knowledge of the business before arrival at the court, this problem is more likely to arise at the last minute.

In general, it is unwise for JPs as such to give interviews or express opinions to the media; even if invited to do so in other connections, thought needs to be given in advance to ensure that reference is not made to the magistracy nor to anything that could bring it into disrepute. Bench chairmen may occasionally feel obliged to say things in public, but never to comment on individual cases; they rarely have training in press relations or details of the law so, unless they have considerable experience, it may be necessary for them to consult the clerk. Guidance is also available from the MA, especially for those wishing to give general talks about the magistracy. In recent years, the Judicial Office (JO) of the MoJ has also produced guidance which amounts to further tightening of restrictions on the relationship between the judiciary and the media. The advice now is based apparently on the presumption that any request for an interview should be declined, and certainly that none should take place without the prior knowledge of the bench chairman, the JO press office and the senior presiding judge. Even if JPs are invited to speak on behalf of the MA, the JO have to be notified; this threatens to become a level of constraint on the chairman and senior officers of the MA to which they have not previously been subject. Experienced, responsible JPs should not be put through censorship of this kind.

It is to be hoped that magistrates will never be found lacking in a sense of humour—or be thought not to have one. Although they have a deep responsibility and serious purpose—and must never give the impression that these are not uppermost in their mind—this should not prevent them from seeing the humorous side of things when appropriate, and fellowship between magistrates should always be a pleasure.

Diversity and representation

In 2003, the average composition of benches in England and Wales was 20 per cent aged under 50, 49 per cent women and 94 per cent white. For many years the magistracy has enjoyed gender equality and the benefit of female JPs, which is, for what it's worth, more than can be said of many other national institutions. In the early days of women on the bench, there was criticism that they tended to be too severe; others feared that they would be too soft and sentimental but, 100 years later, it cannot be claimed that there is any clear correlation between gender and attitudes to crime and sentencing. Furthermore, during the UK's corporal punishment debate at the end of the last century, women were prominent on both sides.

In regard to gender and race, magistrates are significantly more representative of the general public than any other group within the criminal justice system, and critics need to be reminded that the composition of the magistracy is more diverse today than at any time in its long history. Yet the slaves of political correctness, and those who smell injustice in every corner of public life, claim that the process has still not gone far enough. Some of them can even be heard to suggest that diversity should take precedence over suitability for the job—a recipe for the ultimate failure of any institution, such as the magistracy, that relies on a high level of competence for its continued existence. The reality is that the critics will remain dissatisfied, because no-one will ever be able to agree or determine when 'far enough' has been reached.

One of the silliest remarks made about JPs by the media and other fault-finders is that they are 'disproportionately middle-class' (the middle-classness of journalists is, of course, never questioned). This meaningless description appears to ignore the fact that almost all JPs are drawn these days from among the ranks of 'ordinary working people' (that favourite phrase of politicians) who form the great majority of our society—a broad centre band of the population, known as 'the middle-classes' within which the widest diversity and the least prejudice are likely to be found. Why therefore should such a conventional label for magistrates be regarded as anything but good and desirable? 'Disproportionality' is sometimes a sensitive issue for black and ethnic minorities (BAEMs), but a 2011 report by the MA's Youth Courts Committee found that this group are themselves already 'over-represented' in all areas of the criminal justice system—certainly in the youth justice system. At the same time, BAEM JPs are said to have a higher than average resignation rate; when given the opportunity, too many of them seem to find it a harder task than they imagined, or fail to measure up to the standards required, which is perhaps a matter for even greater concern and attention.

Professor Zander of the London School of Economics, in his response to the 2001 review of the criminal courts by Lord Justice Auld, brought some welcome sanity to the subject of balancing the composition of benches when he wrote: 'In so far as the main thrust of government policy is to achieve a magistracy that is more balanced in terms of age and class … I doubt whether there is much likelihood of any significant improvement. The struggle to broaden the social class mix of the magistracy has been going on for decades and has made little headway. It seems inevitable that magistrates (like judges) will in the main continue to be middle-class and middle aged. If that is right, it seems pointless to agonise over it or to regard it as a serious problem. Moreover, the idea that the magistracy would have a better image if more magistrates were working-class or younger is politically correct wishful thinking. The public is hopelessly ignorant on the subject. Whatever the actual composition of the bench, it will have the image of being broadly middle-class (even the working-class magistrate will tend to wear a suit)'. There is nothing of which to be ashamed in being a middle-class or middle-aged JP. We have to continue asking ourselves—and especially the critics of the magistracy—what is so wrong with being in the middle? Isn't that the most suitable place for a magistrate to be? The criticism of course arises from the ridiculous idea that 'justice' can only be met if criminals are tried by those of similar age and background, i.e. those most likely to be partial and prejudiced in favour of the defendant or the victim. This is one of the routes to the creation of one law for the young and disadvantaged, and another for the rest.

The ethnic minority component of the magistracy roughly matches that of the population as a whole, and new justices are drawn from an increasingly wide spectrum. From time-to-time MPs, in the misguided belief that the bench should be composed entirely of representatives, demand to know why more effort is not made to select JPs from among 'working people' and minorities, but selection has to give priority to the achievement of balance between diversity and personal suitability. As a result, today's lay bench is more varied and well-qualified than at any time in its extensive history. The long-term 'quality' of the magistracy is not enhanced by slavish concentration on its composition. In fact, such attention is more likely to condemn it to perpetual inferiority, in which competence, experience and authority are secondary, at a time when such qualities are needed more than ever to maintain high standards of leadership, judgement and efficient administration.

One of the myths proclaimed by black, Asian and ethnic minority (BAEM) groups is that the relatively high number of their members in prison arises because of an 'unrepresentative' and 'institutionally racist' judiciary. They assume that this situation would automatically be overcome if more black people were to be appointed as magistrates and judges. In parallel with this fantasy, they fail to consider or accept that there may be other far more credible reasons why courts convict or imprison more BAEMs than their proportion of the population would indicate. They imply that benches with stronger minority representation would be more inclined to apply positive discrimination, bias and greater leniency towards favoured individuals — a travesty of the judicial oath, and a threat to the essential impartiality of the courts.

Of course, it is important that the composition of the bench is sufficiently mixed to attract public confidence and that the range of people available is kept as wide as possible, but there are signs that the diversity 'tail' is too readily used to 'wag the magisterial dog'. Much irrelevant nonsense is spoken about diversity. It is, for instance, unrealistic to expect JPs to be a mirror image of society, but some penal and social reformers are never satisfied; they persist in demanding more diversity, while ignoring the narrow background of DJs and senior staff in other departments of the justice system. They seem to imagine that fair treatment from the courts can only be gained by a perfect blend of magistrates, representing every one of the numerous parts from which society is composed, available to sit every day, so as to demonstrate affiliation with every offender, an approach which, if pursued to logical conclusion, would lead to teenagers, drug addicts and habitual criminals becoming majority members of the bench. True, the magistracy may now contain a majority of people from the middle-classes, but no longer, as at times in the past, is it dominated by landowners, politicians, churchmen, housewives, schoolteachers or traders.

It is interesting to note in this connection that in the county of Kent in 2004 the principal occupations of JPs were:

Not in paid employment	38 per cent	57 per cent
Self-employed	19 per cent	
National and local company employees	15 per cent	25 per cent
Civil servants & local government	10 per cent	
Health care & other professionals	9 per cent	9 per cent
Lecturers and teachers	6 per cent	6 per cent
Others	3 per cent	3 per cent

The spread under these headings may not be all that different today, but the diversity within them is likely to be greater. How many other national institutions contain such a wide variety among their recruits?

The Auld review of the criminal courts said, without mentioning why, that benches should reflect more broadly the communities they serve—a statement that has, it seems, become obligatory whenever the future of the magistracy is at issue. For years, great play was made of the continuing need for more diversity when selecting JPs, and this was considered a matter of such importance that government even forgot on occasion to remind advisory committees that—above all else—they should continue to seek and recommend the individual candidates they consider most suitable for the work. Meanwhile, the appointment of district judges is apparently immune to the dogma of diversity. DJs are not chosen to reflect the communities where they sit, nor are they selected with this in mind, nor can they ever demonstrate diversity in practice like a bench of justices. It is ridiculous therefore to apply the stricture only to JPs.

Nevertheless, it is right to keep diversity in the forefront because, at its most sensible, it resembles the traditional advice that membership of benches should 'broadly reflect the community they serve', a view endorsed by Lord Chancellor Irvine in 1999 when announcing his campaign to attract a wider range of candidates for the lay bench. Unfortunately, 'diversity' has become a fashionable component of the sanitised speech used by social reformers on both sides of the Atlantic, along with other loaded words like 'empowerment', 'accountability' and 'entitlement'. Beware those who talk about diversity, when what they really mean is wider representation. 'Diversity' has also been hijacked in recent times by those who wish to exert political influence over appointments, and by those who find it a useful antidote to charges of elitism, racism and being 'too middle-class'. On the way, its scope has also been broadened to include a variety of unrealistic aspirations, ranging from the disabled and young to 'sexual orientation', 'under-representation' and faith—enough in total to make it less likely than ever to satisfy the critics.

By all means, let us celebrate the principle of diversity, but if the magistracy ever allows it to be advanced at the expense of suitability, it will be sowing the seeds of its own destruction. Similarly, in trying to achieve the perfect reflection of our community on every bench, we must be careful not to perpetuate division and separation, nor confirm minorities as permanently distinct and isolated from the rest of society. It may in practice be more difficult to achieve greater diversity from day-to-day in court if there are fewer magistrates, while larger benches sometimes make it easier. Be that as it may, one cannot help but ask again why it is so much more important for JPs to be diverse than other influential decision-makers in public life? In most cases, people are elected or appointed primarily because they are perceived to have the necessary character and qualifications for the specific job in hand. The niceties of diversity are, at best, secondary.

The cult of diversity apparently also afflicts the diplomatic service. The following extract from Sir Andrew Green's valedictory message on leaving Saudi Arabia in June 2000 could almost have been composed with the magistracy in mind. He wrote:

'I have viewed with dismay the spread of "political correctness" in recent years. Intellectual honesty is the foundation of our Service; political correctness its antithesis. "Diversity" is the latest of several rather fashionable fashions. The truth is that diversity is irrelevant to diplomacy. No foreigner I have ever met knows or cares whether the service has 50 per cent women, 10 per cent homosexuals and 5 per cent ethnics. Their only interest is whether a diplomat has something useful to contribute. Furthermore, "targets" are but a thinly disguised form of positive discrimination, which undermines the fundamental principle of public service that promotion should be based on ability alone. The risk is that "minorities" will be promoted because they are (just) credible, not because they are the best. If so, they will become symbols, not of inclusion but of incompetence'.

Political correctness, diversity, targets and positive discrimination are also irrelevant to justice.

A study of the procedure for selection and training of lay justices by the law faculty of Dundee University in the 1980s concluded that 'while the experiment produced justices with different characteristics, those selected could not (any more than their predecessors) be said to constitute a random sample of the population at large'. While it is accepted that diversity is a desirable aim when considering the overall composition of the bench, in reality it is impossible to guarantee on a regular day-to-day basis. Those who think that some attainable ideal exists are likely to remain as permanently disappointed as those who yearn for equality in mankind. Belief that justice cannot be achieved in the absence of this ideal is misconceived; but a partial concession can be found by paying some attention to appearance, e.g. by avoiding three justices of the same sex sitting together. In striving to keep a balance that is acceptable from all points of view, the 'look' of the bench has to be among the objectives of advisory committees' — but not if it can only be achieved at the expense of individual suitability. Meanwhile, there is still room for better media and public appreciation of the wide base from which JPs are actually recruited, and of the fact that they are not paid, nor need to be lawyers or have degrees.

Biased researchers, with nothing better to do, and relying on unfounded opinions, declare periodically that they have discovered a low level of public confidence in the magistrates' courts, from which they naïvely conclude that JPs need to be more representative. However, wider representation does not actually improve the quality of justice; it merely threatens to undermine the courts' reputation for impartiality, and increases the possibility that lawyers will claim (as they already do re juries) some JPs to be unacceptable to their client, because they are known to have been appointed to the bench to represent certain groups or views. Homosexuals, for instance, may insist that they be tried only by magistrates believed to favour their particular 'orientation'. Surely, such a situation must not be encouraged to occur in the magistrates' courts.

Lord Justice Auld agreed that it is unrealistic to expect the social composition of the bench to be close to that of the general population, and he was scathing about results of research on public confidence: 'It is one thing to rely on uninformed views as a guide, but another to rely on such views as an argument for fashioning the system to meet them. Public confidence is not an end in itself; it is or should be an outcome of a fair and efficient system', he said. It is of course still desirable that JPs should, so far as is practicable, reflect or broadly mirror the population of the area in which they live, work and adjudicate, but this is quite different from the representation of specific types or groups of people. There is a grave danger that those who persist in demanding the latter, without distinguishing between collective and personal, will do more harm than good to the future of the magistracy, and that an obsession with diversity and representation will lead to the appointment of unsuitable magistrates and a lower standard of justice. Ministers should constantly make it clear to advisory committees and the public that 'representation' as such is not a valid criterion for selection of JPs.

Among the magistracy's habitual detractors is the Howard League which, while repeating *ad nauseam* out-dated references to composition of the bench, sometimes misinterprets 'judgement by peers' to question the adequacy of its diversity, as if believing that there is some ideal mixture out there which, when reached, will satisfy the critics. In reality of course they, too, will never be satisfied. Ignoring the fact that, in the original Magna Carta, 'peers' meant noblemen, not laymen, and that the 'legitimacy of professionals (among whom, presumably, are district judges) may be undermined by their lack of representativeness', they single out lay magistrates, because (to quote Crawford's *Criminology and Public Policy*, 2004) 'representation has a slightly different order of importance for lay people … as against professionals whose primary justification lies in their accountability and expertise'. Again, pure nonsense. Why should lay people have 'a slightly different order of importance'? The league might better justify its funding from the Legal Services Commission if it concentrated on matters of far greater concern to the justice system, such as the increasing replacement of lay justice courts by single, unrepresentative lawyers.

There is a serious risk that the influence of 'new' criteria, designed to meet the call for more diversity and representation in place of intelligence, personal integrity and suitability will create more problems for advisory committees than solutions, not least a temptation to lower standards — or, worse still, pressure for JPs to be paid — so as to attract the kind of people deemed necessary to make the composition of the magistracy more acceptable to a few vociferous critics. By all reasonable means, recruitment policy must continue to preserve as broad a base as possible without compromising core standards. It is infinitely preferable to accept minor imperfections in the selection system than to destroy the whole institution in the pursuit of 'politically correct' fantasies. If the magistracy itself gives support to the concept of 'representation' among its members, it will be making a major contribution to its own destruction.

Bearing in mind that the 2011 UK Census forms listed nearly 20 ethnic groups, the suggestion that the magistracy needs to be more representative of all ages, colours, races, sexes, religions, classes and minorities looks even less realistic and potentially more ridiculous than the obsession with diversity. Perfect representation is a myth nourished by partiality. It poisons the essence of impartial justice, and threatens to undermine judicial independence and the integrity of the oath taken by all JPs on appointment. It has more to do with politics and power than with equity and fairness, and everyone needs to be aware of this. Those who know or believe that they have been chosen as a representative find it harder to act impartially; no-one should seek to be appointed to the bench if they do so with social prejudice or political influence in mind. Magistrates are chosen to speak and act for no-one other than the crown and the law, and to represent no-one other than the diverse general public from which they are drawn; if they ever feel or behave otherwise, they are in danger of betraying their oath. If JPs are deemed to represent anyone else, it can only be the victims of crime and the long-suffering public majority who have never been inside a courthouse, and who long to conduct their daily lives in an atmosphere of honesty, peace, goodwill and freedom from intimidation, untroubled by crime and anti-social behaviour, and protected against violence and abuse.

Every system of election or selection has its cynics and critics. Among the latter are those who think that people who are unelected or without legal education should not be entrusted with decisions affecting the lives of others, and those who claim that JPs should not be engaged in recruitment, because 'all they do is create new magistrates in their own image'; but what is so wicked about that, so long as the image remains sound? Many of those who persist in demanding even more changes in selection criteria—and who will never be appeased until they themselves make the choices—believe that if JPs were to become more representative, they would have more understanding of criminals; if they were more understanding, they would be more sympathetic; if more sympathetic, more lenient; if more lenient, more just.

Such a chain of reasoning may be attractive to some, but is inappropriate as a major indicator of suitability for the bench. Insight to the criminal mind may sometimes help in deciding the most suitable sentence, especially in regard to the difficult question of intent, but JPs who try to comprehend the minds of defendants and reasons for their behaviour may be much troubled in coming to just decisions on verdict. Someone once said 'If you understand all, you will pardon all', which is hardly applicable to a court of law.

CHAPTER 9

Bouquets and Brickbats

'I have never found that criticism is ever inhibited by ignorance'

Harold Macmillan

- A jewel beyond price, or a bunch of amateurs?
- The cornerstone of our society
- Undeserved criticism
- Amateur, unrepresentative and 'out of touch'
- White, too old, too middle-class . . .
- 'Muddled' magistrates and 'repellent' lawyers

As a national institution, the lay magistracy inevitably attracts occasional attention in the form of both praise and adverse criticism; much of the former, while always welcome, is disappointingly unmatched by official support, and much of the latter is based on ignorance or prejudice. For obvious reasons, most of the compliments come from government ministers and senior members of the judiciary when addressing magistrates, but it is noticeable that some of the most vitriolic comments come from minor lawyers. Some of the criticism seems to arise from the common divide between amateur and professional—the latter believing that those who are unpaid cannot possibly be competent—and some from those who insist that justice is unsafe in the hands of anyone but themselves. In the event, JPs alone are the only people consistently able and willing to 'beat the drum' for the magistracy; regrettably, neither government nor the senior judiciary, nor anyone else associated with its distinguished contribution to the life of our nation, can be relied upon to express unqualified support.

However, the magistracy has shown commendable resilience and flexibility during years of struggle to maintain its position and self-esteem against repeated government and bureaucratic disruptions, endless new legislation and needless incursions. As Lady Justice Hallett wrote in *The Magistracy at the Crossroads* (2012), 'The magistracy has proved its worth, and deserves to survive'.

A jewel beyond price, or a bunch of amateurs?

Lord Chief Justice Bingham said that the magistracy is 'a democratic jewel beyond price'. An Open University report described JPs as 'a bunch of amateurs'. These quotes illustrate the breadth of view that can be held of an institution that is, after more than 650 years, a source of pride for some and an anachronism for others. However, magistrates are by no means alone in attracting such variable descriptions; they just seem sometimes to be an easier butt for the critics.

A 1982 article in the *Justice of the Peace* also reflected this disparity. It described attitudes towards the magistracy as divided between the 'officially sycophantic' and the 'aggressively critical'; both, it said, missed the point, but it was not clear what point was being missed. Be that as it may, aggressive criticism is unlikely to destroy the magistracy any time soon, nor will sycophancy guarantee its future. The point that matters most is that it should remain fit and unchallenged as a vital and respected part of our judicial system, our democracy and our national culture. Ministers and law lords who tell magistrates that they need have no fears about their future, because the country could never afford or find enough lawyers to replace them, are probably trying to be reassuring, but they risk leaving the impression that if a cheaper alternative using lawyers could be found, it would be preferable. However, if the profligate appointment of expensive district judges in recent years is anything to go by, some people already think the country can afford lawyers to replace magistrates anyway, even when they are demonstrably more expensive than a bench of unpaid JPs, and there is no evidence that they perform superior justice.

From time-to-time senior members of Parliament and of the judiciary make lukewarm references to their support and admiration for the magistracy. Jack Straw MP, for example, addressing the Magistrates Association's 2007 AGM as Lord Chancellor, could only say, 'I am aware of, and appreciate, the work that magistrates do'. Perhaps such meagre recognition is all that could be expected from someone who had previously made no secret of his aversion to the magistracy; but, sad to say, there is quite often a whiff of insincerity around such compliments from politicians. A year later, Lord Justice Leveson, then a regional presiding judge, said 'I cannot envisage a future without magistrates. I am a great believer in the magistracy'. Hardly enough to make JPs feel highly valued, especially when in almost the next breath he sanctioned the appointment of yet another unnecessary district judge in the south-east, having approved without comment an obviously deficient business plan. Ministers, too, have been guilty of duplicity on many occasions in the last 50 years; one minute they are heard to say how 'committed' they are to the lay magistracy and how 'wedded to the concept of local justice', but in the next they are shown to be impotent in resisting further cuts to the CJS and the closure of dozens more courts. If local justice is so important to government, we have to ask: Where is the logic or efficiency gain in shutting so many local courthouses and sending local JPs to sit, and defendants to be tried, 50 miles away from home?

The magistracy cannot expect any sympathy from civil servants either. Far from it. Those with inside experience of Whitehall have reported that at best they are indifferent, at worst openly hostile. If it suits them, ministers and politicians may genuinely try to be encouraging, but they are fair weather friends, too dependent on the fickle winds of election and economic climate changes. Appreciation of JP's services to the nation are obviously welcome from any quarter, but they are rarely enough to sustain confidence in the intentions of government. The steady demotion of the magistracy during the last 30 years or so has shown how big the gap can be between words and actions. It is unfortunate that MPs and civil servants are not often in a position to take a long-term view; five years at the most is the limit of their vision.

While ministers, and senior judges with responsibility for executing government policy, occasionally make reassuring and supportive statements, they seldom express any misgivings about the introduction of changes that are certain to damage the magistracy, or venture to promote measures that would strengthen it or increase its powers; they are less inhibited in praising the costly and inefficient jury system, a bias which is not lost on unpaid JPs from whom so much more is expected and demanded. This view appeared to be shared by a Kent JP, and former Whitehall civil servant, who perceived that 'lay magistrates have always been seen as a necessary evil—inefficient and uncontrollable, but cheap. Rather than a clear agenda to replace magistrates with district judges, there is a lack of interest in preserving the lay magistracy; decisions are made about particular initiatives on the basis of whether or not they are 'a good thing' in cost and efficiency terms on their own merits'. 'The impact on magistrates is more or less disregarded', he continued, 'as the view is that people will always come forward for this role; if it withers on the vine, all well and good, but the MoJ cannot afford to replace it lock, stock and barrel'. When it comes to civic matters, Parliament and local authorities usually stop short of openly criticising justices, but politicians, local and national, are never keen to come out in support of those who may sometimes be in a more powerful position than they themselves.

As for the media, many provincial journalists are now keener to write banal 'human interest' stories than routine court reports. If they mention magistrates at all, it is more likely to be in criticism than in praise, because that is the easier way to create eye-catching headlines and sell newspapers. The striking thing about most articles unfavourable to JPs and their work is the boring predictability of their descriptions and the incredible ignorance of the authors. In general, it is difficult to understand why journalists, who are in a position to witness the worth of the magistracy more readily than most, do not support it more strongly, especially bearing in mind the helpful contribution they and a free press can make to the process of local summary justice.

In spite of government claims to the contrary, the public also remain relatively ignorant and unconcerned about the magistracy. References to 'public demand' for this, that or the other reform in regard to justices and their courts are usually bogus. Only a small proportion of the population ever see the inside of a courthouse or are interested in what goes on there. Actually, this is a pity, because the magistrates' courts (except for family hearings, where only accredited press are permitted) are open to the public and are, in a sense, the people's courts. Magistrates provide a public dimension to the justice system. The 1997–2010 Labour MoJ spent millions in trying to bring the judicial process closer to the public. Unfortunately, the idea was expensively advertised as if by a commercial organization promoting a new product, using slogans and vision statements to reaffirm the government's solid support for justice and the people against crime and the criminal. The torrent of glossy publications issued by the ministry, written in 'delivering justice' jargon, probably made the politicians and civil servants feel good, but it appeared to have little effect on public opinion.

Magistrates should not expect to be loved. The most they can hope for is respect and appreciation from Parliament and people for doing a difficult job competently and dispassionately in what can be testing circumstances. To achieve this with honour, they need constant support from government, and confidence that they are acting on behalf of an overwhelmingly law-abiding and supportive public. Although they are accused occasionally of being unsuitable for the task, they know that 'they cannot please all the people all the time' — nor should they be expected to do so. This acknowledgement of reality should not be taken as an excuse for complacency, but it is hard these days for magistrates to perform more efficiently or effectively than the law, the judicial system and the Treasury will allow.

The cornerstone of our society

When opening new courts at Blackpool in 1971, Lord Chancellor Hailsham said,

> 'My advice to the English people after 40 years of experience of the law is: Do not try to get rid of your old-style justices of the peace. If you do, you will get rid of one of the most valuable and stabilising of your social institutions. Insist that they go through the new training courses, if you please. Exact stiff standards, certainly. Ask them to retire to the Supplemental List

when they become deaf, infirm or reach the age limit, by all means. But abolish them, I hope never'.

In 1983, he told the AGM of the Magistrates Association (MA) that 'for every complaint I get about lay magistrates, I get ten which concern the professional judiciary'. A year later he said, 'I verily believe there is no people's court … anywhere in the world which is as representative of the responsible elements in society as the lay bench of England and Wales'.

Lord Denning, Master of the Rolls for 20 years (1962–82), and often referred to as 'the people's judge', was of the same view when praising Sir Thomas Skyrme's *History of the Justices of the Peace* saying:

'The JPs and their clerks are an essentially English institution. There is nothing like them all the world over—not even in the British Commonwealth. They have proved their worth over the last 600 years. It is sometimes suggested that they should be replaced by stipendiary magistrates. I would scorn the suggestion. A good layman is better in trying fact than a middling lawyer. We must keep them; we are proud of them and of their long history'.

The Bishop of Lincoln in a 1990 sermon referred to the magistracy as 'providing us all with a living symbol of what justice means within the community', and Lord Chancellor Falconer touched on the same theme in the foreword to his 2005 initiative *Supporting Magistrates' Courts to Provide Justice*. 'It is difficult', he wrote,

'to over-estimate the contribution they make to their local communities. They are a permanent part of our justice system … Magistrates themselves demonstrate a particular commitment to public service and to making their communities better and safer places to live. They show fairness, decisiveness and the ability to apply reason and common sense … The magistrates' courts are an important and valued part of the justice system. I recognise and value the work of magistrates … and the diligence with which they carry out their duties'.

JPs at that time could well have asked what more could they wish to hear than that, but the smooth talk and unusually generous praise were deceptive. It turned out to be the beginning of a long down-hill slope for the magistracy.

It may or may not be significant that Lord Falconer's emphasis (at least in the title of the publication) was on support for the magistrates' courts, rather than for the magistracy itself, but his initiatives included a number of improvements for the recruitment and retention of JPs. It looked at first as if he was going to be one of the most helpful Lord Chancellors with whom the MA had worked for many years; however, while such encouraging noises were coming out of the Department of Constitutional Affairs (motto: 'Justice, Rights and Democracy'), yet more courthouses were being closed, more justices' clerks made redundant, more administration centralised, and more district judges appointed. As has so often been the case, ambivalent ministers sought to praise the magistracy while continuing to pursue policies which undermined it.

Such reservations would have been absent in July 1999, when Lord Bingham of Cornhill, then Lord Chief Justice of England and Wales and one of the most respected lawyers of our time, spoke at a London Mansion House dinner for HM judges. In that speech, he asked, 'What are the most distinctive features of the English legal system developed over the last 1,000 years?' 'Many different answers might be given', he said,

'but mine would be: the lay magistracy and the trial jury. They share of course one common quality, of inestimable value to the democratic strength of the nation, that they bring the ordinary citizen, unsullied by professional legal education or training, into the very heart of what would elsewhere be judicial decision-making. The lay magistracy is such a familiar institution that we tend to take it for granted. But JPs administer the only justice which the mass of the population ever experience; without reward, they dispatch well over 90 per cent of all criminal business, to say nothing of their family work, and they have no counterpart anywhere in the world outside the United Kingdom. Those who criticise the professional judiciary as unrepresentative and elitist have here their answer. Successive Lord Chancellors have striven, with considerable success, to appoint local benches which include women as well as men, people from a very wide range of social and professional backgrounds, members of ethnic minorities as well as of the white majority, members of all political parties or none, the youngish as well as the more mature, and now and again the disabled'.

'Above all', Lord Bingham continued,

'the justices are chosen for their qualities of fairness, judgment and common sense, alert to the needs and concerns of the communities they serve, and enabling issues to be determined locally by local people. In the eyes of the public, they have one great advantage: that they are free of the habits of thought, speech and bearing which characterise professional lawyers, and which most people find to a greater or lesser extent repellent. The existence of 30,000 citizens—more if one counts the retired—distributed around the country, all with a sound practical understanding of what the law is and how it works is, I think, *a democratic jewel beyond price*'.

These all-encompassing words, from such a highly regarded source, must surely rank as one of the finest tributes paid to the magistracy in modern times—hence the title of this book.

Lord Bingham's successor, Lord Woolf, was also a fan of the lay magistracy. He is quoted by Trevor Grove, author of *The Magistrate's Tale*, as saying, 'It is a unique and marvellous system ... I value it immensely ... any reforms would have to be ones which preserved the strengths of the system ... I see the magistracy as a huge champion of independence in the administration of justice ... (the cost) is worth it, because of the involvement of the public and the independence'.

In 2005 Lord Phillips, as Lord Chief Justice and President of the MA, said that

'the fundamental principle the magistracy reflects is that lay people should be involved at the heart of our justice system, ... that local justice has always been of central importance to the magistracy, ... that those sitting in court should be members of the local community sharing local concerns, ... that our courts are and must remain locally based, and that the magistracy, drawn from local communities, is the lynch pin of delivering justice locally'.

Regrettably, government was deaf to his lordship's entreaties, for 'local' has continued to become an increasingly inappropriate word for use in connection with the magistracy.

At about the same time, Lord Chancellor Irvine said, 'The magistracy is the cornerstone of our society... in which we can all take pride; we remain fully committed to the future of the lay magistracy and to local justice'. While this appeared at the time to be a most welcome fillip for the magistracy, it was later felt to be little more than political rhetoric, as little or no evidence of positive 'commitment' appeared.

It is noticeable that all the above bouquets were given by Lord Chancellors, Lord Chief Justices and other senior office-holders in the judiciary or government—all members of the so-called 'establishment' to which, critics maintain, the magistracy also belongs. Left-wing lecturers are among those who feed the minds of young law students with a different brand of rhetoric; for example, 'lay participation is mere tokenism by the establishment' or 'magistrates are often portrayed as part of the establishment, there to deny defendants a basic human right' (i.e. jury trial).

However, a Lord Chancellor's Department (LCD) minister in 1992, displayed genuine enthusiasm when he said, 'There's hardly any country in the world that has the lay magistracy that we have; and I actually think that it is a very wonderful thing. It is to be nurtured, encouraged. The magistrates themselves are to be made to feel—by society as a whole and the LCD in particular—how much they are valued, how important it is what they do. I have a real feeling for magistrates' courts'. The British lay magistracy is indeed highly regarded—and envied—throughout the world, especially by countries such as those in eastern Europe that spent decades under totalitarian rule. The Minister's reference to the importance and value of the lay magistracy should be reprinted in large letters, framed and hung as a reminder in every MoJ office today.

Following an exchange visit in 1995 to some English courts by a group of American federal and supreme court judges, a Kent JP related their experiences: 'The Old Bailey apparently left them very unimpressed', she said. 'The proceedings, they considered, were far too long-winded. They couldn't believe barristers were on their feet for days pleading the same case (the limit for advocacy in the US supreme court is 90 minutes). Then they went off to see some lay magistrates at work. This time, they were beside themselves with wonder — the speed, the common sense, the brevity, the simplicity — and all this before they heard the most astonishing news of all: No-one received so much as a penny for their time'.

An internet 'blogger' — *The Anonymous Prosecutor* — wrote refreshingly in February 2010 to disagree with a lawyer colleague about his experience of lay benches: 'It is a waste of time stereotyping a lay bench, the diversity is astonishing', he said.

> 'The quality of decisions is very high; I rarely encounter decisions that I think are wrong, and I rarely encounter wild departures from the sentencing guidelines — district judges are more prone to that, if anything. For a long list or a juicy trial, you can't beat a good lay bench. They are well trained, sensible, unvaryingly polite, usually quite jovial, and I have almost always enjoyed appearing before lay benches. They have a healthy dose of cynicism where required, and usually grasp the human aspect of the case very quickly. For me, a sensible way forward would be to extend their sentencing powers, keep more work out of the Crown Court, and have more lay benches doing trials'.

It is always easier to publish articles and stories designed to criticise rather than praise the magistracy, but Morgan and Russell, in their report for the Home Office and Lord Chancellor's Department in 2000, in acknowledging the office of JP as an important tradition of voluntary public service, said that at no stage in their fieldwork was it suggested that magistrates' courts do not work well or fail to command general confidence; whatever the lay magistracy's imperfections, it manifests the concept of 'active citizens in active communities' favoured by successive governments. What many journalists and commentators do not seem fully to understand is that the judiciary must retain significant detachment in order to preserve the neutral authority of the law, and to be seen clearly as separate from both the executive and legislative branches of government.

All these examples of praise and endorsement from varied sources at home and abroad, might suggest that the magistracy is as safe from destruction as the jury, the Health Service or the National Trust; that everything possible would be, and is being, done to preserve the concept of tribunal lay justice for the benefit of the nation; and that the highly unwelcome consequences of failing to do this would be recognised and deliberately avoided. But no. JPs continue to be left with the feeling that they are not sufficiently valued — at least, not by government — to be sure of their future.

Those who genuinely hold the magistracy in high esteem, and wish to see it supported and strengthened, too often appear unable to organize themselves effectively enough to match the influence of well-established lobby organizations and pressure groups (all of whom are themselves, of course, beyond reproach?) who habitually find little to say in its favour.

Undeserved criticism

Bearing in mind its visibility, and because over 90 per cent of criminal cases are handled through its courts, it would be surprising if the magistracy received more bouquets than brickbats. Like it or not, periodic criticism of major national institutions is a feature of the disparaging age in which we live. The judiciary and magistracy cannot expect to be exempt from this, but it is never pleasant to be criticised, especially when the remarks are gratuitous, insulting or rooted in ignorance. Unless it is malicious, those in the firing line have little option but to accept it as part of modern public life, and to hope that little attention is paid to it.

Crude generalisations about magistrates actually have little effect; nevertheless they erupt from time-to-time and are kept alive by prejudiced individuals and those with left-wing or anarchist tendencies; even respectable sources of information like Wikipedia are guilty of repeating untrue facts. A variety of familiar descriptions, intended to be uncomplimentary, are regularly served up by the media, e.g. white, middle-aged, middle-class, unrepresentative, out-of-touch, amateur, unqualified, too lenient, too harsh, undemocratic, secretly appointed, self-perpetuating, inconsistent, racist, prosecution-minded, unaccountable, muddled. At least, these days, one never hears magistrates described as corrupt, which is the curse of judicial systems in so many other countries, nor can they be accused of male dominance; there has been a roughly 50:50 balance between men and women on the bench for many years now. Otherwise, the most frequent accusations — still occasionally trotted out monotonously by ill-informed critics — are little different from those raised 30 or more years ago, and are as wide of the mark as ever.

A 1988 editorial in the *New Statesman* highlighted the ignorance, prejudice and exaggerated language frequently used by liberal activists wishing to denigrate the British judicial system in general and the magistracy in particular. It contained the following excerpts: 'Routine justice doled out by unqualified, unpaid burghers, selected by a mysterious process ... daily dispensation of punishment by middle-class men to the working-classes ... a fundamentally undemocratic Tory model of active citizenship that stinks'. Only an ill-informed hack, let alone the editor of such a well-known publication, would get satisfaction from writing such rubbish. As usual, not a shred of an attempt was made to suggest a constructive alternative, and the editor declined my invitation (as Chairman of the MA at the time) to spend a day in my court, to see for himself how totally inaccurate his views were.

Unquestioning magisterial support of the police and political bias on the bench no longer appear among criticisms of JPs. Charges of secrecy also arose in the past from the way in which appointments to the bench were made by anonymous Advisory Committees. However, since 1993, that censure has also virtually disappeared; the names of those serving on the committees are now published, and one third of them are required to be non-magistrates. Furthermore, misuse of JP membership lists has not proved to be the problem that some people forecast 30 years ago.

Criticism is not unusual from disillusioned social reformers, ethnic minorities and occasionally the police; concerns in these sectors usually focus on topics related to over-use of custody, excessive leniency, unrepresentativeness and distorted perceptions of the magistracy. Others who tend to express hostile opinions towards the courts and legal process from time-to-time include contributors to *The Guardian* and *The Observer*, and liberal-leaning groups, such as the National Association for the Care and Resettlement of Offenders, the Howard League for Penal Reform, the Prison Reform Trust and Liberty. Some of their work is praiseworthy, and their membership includes a few JPs, but these organizations are not above criticising the magistracy; and, because there are few comparable lobbies representing victims or the law-abiding majority, their one-sided views frequently appear to receive undue attention from the media.

Many newspaper columnists, even today, seem unable to write about crime, the courts and the penal system without invoking a grossly out-dated stereotype of JPs; but, when doing so, they invariably expose their own ignorance of the modern magistracy, and repeat *ad nauseam* the notion that, if magistrates were younger, darker-skinned and a different class, they would somehow demonstrate more understanding, act more justly, and send fewer criminals to prison. It is sensible that JPs should be drawn as widely as possible from the communities in which they live or serve, but the bench is not intended to be representative or prescrip-tive; some journalists — themselves unrepresentative — seem incapable of grasping, or unwilling to accept, this fact. Meanwhile, they bask in the luxury of freedom to criticise without responsibility or engagement.

With the loss of so many former duties, the status of the magistracy has undoubtedly been weakened. This in turn has sometimes encouraged ancillary agencies — bundled into government-controlled talk-shops like Criminal Justice Boards — to indulge in unfair criticism of the local mag-istracy, as a means of diverting attention from the shortcomings of their own organizations, and without apparently realising that they themselves are usually the cause of the systemic failings for which they blame JPs. For example, a frustrated Superintendent from Middlesborough, addressing a Harrogate conference of his association in 1986, said: 'Almost every day files come across my desk, marked "Perverse decision by Magistrates". Lay magistrates, in my experience, are a total wash-out ... [we] should support the principle of stipendiary magistrates'. That was a particularly rich comment coming from a police force, senior officers of which were themselves later charged, but acquitted, of serious malpractice.

Censure often comes in spates, triggered by a tendentious newspaper article or letter, with one outburst fuelling another. I recall some bad patches in the 1970s and 1980s. Unfavourable books published at the time included Pat Carlen's *Magistrates' Justice* (1976), Elizabeth Burney's *JP: Magistrate, Court and Community* (1979), and *Unmasking the Magistrates*, published by the Open University (OU) in 1989 and described by the *Daily Mail* as 'a punishing new report', which branded JPs as 'a bunch of amateurs' and some courts as 'stinkers'. There was nothing new in the authors' criticisms; they merely repeated, even more boringly than usual, the standard pattern of stale invective and predictable references to old, white, middle-class magistrates, clichés faithfully repeated subsequently by the *Daily Mirror*.

Dr Carlen was a writer on sociology. The flavour of her book, much of which needed translation into plain English, can be gauged from the following extract:

> 'A magistrates' court is an institution rhetorically functioning to perpetuate the notion of possible justice in a society whose total organization is directed at the maintenance of the capitalist exploitation of labour, production and control, and where the only alternative allowed is that of power and privilege'.

The introduction claimed that the contents 'critically exposed the "justice" constructed, propounded and imposed in these courts'. It is unlikely that the book was intended to be complimentary to the magistracy, but the contorted language ensured that little damage could be done. JPs have never before seen themselves described as 'rhetorical functionaries'; nor did they realise that 'transformation of the ritual display of justice into the socio-legal technology of coercion is the first step in the manufacture and celebration of all magistrates' justice'. Now we know.

Typical of Miss Burney's superficial concerns was her assertion that benches are secretly appointed, self-perpetuating groups of politically biased people, 'isolated from the public at large'. Her ignorance of the facts was profound. However, she was generous enough to admit in conclusion that stipendiary magistrates are, if anything, even less in touch with ordinary life than JPs, and that lay justice is a valuable and unique inheritance.

By the end of 1989, the magistracy had had enough of gratuitous unmasking, and the MA issued a press statement to coincide with the publication of the OU book. As chairman of the association at that time, I described it as 'sensationalist, based on out-dated research and prejudiced opinion—a negative and unhelpful contribution to the important current debate on the principles of sentencing and the role of the magistracy'. So far as I was aware, my portrayal proved true, and little notice was taken of the book thereafter.

Understandably, justices are sometimes criticised for inconsistency in sentencing but, thanks to the Sentencing Council's guidelines, much less so than in the past. These assist magistrates and judges in the process of structured decision-making, but sentencing is not a precise art; there are sometimes enormous differences between individual cases, and courts thankfully still have some discretionary powers. Mandatory sentences and fixed penalties apart, JPs also have to consider seriousness of offence, mitigation, circumstances of the offender, ability to pay, whether to exercise mercy, and so on, factors rarely mentioned in media reports. Inconsistency is raised by critics as if only the magistracy is guilty of it. But the police (especially when dealing with offenders on-the-spot), the Probation Service, local authorities, and many other public bodies are equally culpable—or even more so. It is a difficult problem to avoid totally, without risking the even greater perils of uniformity and rigid regulation.

In 1999, some articles appeared in *The Times* and *Financial Times*, causing an uproar by throwing doubts on the future of the magistracy. Jane Kennedy MP, a minister in the former Lord Chancellor's Department (LCD), was invited to attend the MA Council to deny the rumours, to admit that the LCD was appalled by the articles, and to state that recent government projects and research were not designed in any way to suggest possible abolition of the magistracy, but to ascertain if the criminal courts are fit for their role in the twenty-first century. 'We want to remove some of the criticism … and to rebut the ignorance', she said. 'We cannot manage without lay magistrates … we appreciate (that) you are an easy target'. Council then passed a motion deploring the attacks. Both Ms Kennedy and the Lord Chancellor also made supportive speeches in Parliament at that time.

Immediately afterwards, Ms Kennedy also wrote an article in praise of the magistracy, but the LCD was apparently unable to get a single broadsheet to accept it; nor did *The Times* see fit to print supporting letters from both the chairman of the MA and the Justices' Clerks' Society. This was a good opportunity for the press to champion the magistracy, but it failed to take it. Imagine, by contrast, the reaction if it had been the future of the jury that was at issue.

It is a disturbing fact that, in spite of regard for its unpaid status — formerly assumed to be an advantage — and all that it has done in recent times to improve its image, the magistracy still lacks natural allies, making it more of a soft touch for government and critics alike. It enjoys neither the guaranteed support on which the higher judiciary can rely from the large number of lawyers in Parliament, nor that on which the jury system can rely from the bar. Isolated between the unassailable and the sacrosanct, it can find it difficult to mount sufficiently effective defence against the combined forces of politics, bureaucracy, lawyers and penal reformers without having its motives misrepresented. Meanwhile, the government — aided at times by a compliant senior judiciary — can continue to ignore magisterial requests to make changes in its favour, e.g. to stop appointing unnecessary district judges, abolish either-way cases that needlessly clutter the Crown Court, and increase maximum prison sentencing powers of magistrates from six to 12 months.[1]

The magistracy may sometimes be disparaged, but today's JPs have nothing of which they need be ashamed. On the contrary, they have a great deal of which to be proud. They are trained and proficient, they exemplify popular justice at its best, they are paragons of unpaid public service and 'The Big Society', and they are selected from an increasingly wide range of local and national life. Yet, surprisingly, support is often qualified. If one asks, who are the friends on whom the lay magistracy can rely, the answer is equivocal. It may be thought that fellow members

---

1.   This was technically enacted in the Criminal Justice Act 2003 but never implemented.

of the judiciary and the legal profession would be obvious supporters, but senior judges are usually little more than mildly reassuring, while some lawyers are openly hostile. Politicians are opportunistic, the Civil Service indifferent, the police volatile, the media unreliable, and the public unconcerned. Many of the justices' clerks, on whom JPs could invariably rely in the past, have joined the rival camp as district judges. It is therefore a stark irony—and a significant worry—that, when the chips are down, one of the nation's greatest institutions, central to the democratic justice system and much admired by the civilised world, could find itself without sufficient friends at home to ensure its future.

There are few signs that the public would 'go to the stake' in support of the magistracy, or that there would be riots if it was proposed to abolish it. In spite of occasional government claims of 'widespread public demand' for changes, most people are quite agnostic about the justice system; again, probably because most of them have so little to do with it. Results of recent questionnaires suggest that, when asked to choose between trial by jury or by magistrates, about two thirds of the public would choose the former. However, it is probably true to say that, although there are still sporadic outbreaks of media-led criticism, the magistracy now receives less of a 'bad press' than at any time in the last 50 years. In these circumstances, it is difficult to fathom why government does not do more to strengthen recruitment of JPs, give it more powers and extend its jurisdiction.

Amateur, unrepresentative and 'out of touch'

Before magistrates were removed from administration of the courts service, the *Guardian* in January 1977 carried an article quoting the chairman of the Howard League for Penal Reform. He, having admitted that compulsory training had had 'a profound effect in bringing magistrates from being pure amateurs to a quite considerable degree of professionalism', nevertheless went on to describe them as 'nice, ordinary people on the whole who have no kind of idea what it is to administer criminal justice'. So far, the highly-paid expert alternatives, when given the opportunity, have shown no signs of doing the job any more efficiently or fairly than lay justices.

For obvious reasons, 'amateurism' is the favourite weapon of lawyers seeking to attack the magistracy, but this charge has looked increasingly irrelevant since JPs have been trained, mentored, re-trained and assessed. The accusation sometimes reappears, especially when the replacement of magistrates by 'professionals' is being promoted by those who assume that, because lay justices are not paid, they cannot be proficient. It seems not to occur to these critics that a bench of magistrates is actually a professional jury, and that size of salary is no guide to competence — sometimes quite the opposite. It is one of the strengths — not a weakness — of the lay magistracy that JPs are judges, but not usually lawyers. Derogatory reference to 'amateur' is also sometimes made alongside fallacious claims that justice cannot be obtained in a magistrates' court by anyone unless they are represented by a member of the legal profession.

In August 1980, a *Guardian* article, titled 'Too serious to be left to the amateurs', declared wildly that justices should be abolished and replaced by stipendiary magistrates, on grounds of excessive cost (a bench of three JPs costs much less) and miscarriages of justice (very rare in the magistrates' courts). Neither of these reasons were supported by facts. It therefore attracted a robust reply from the chairman of the MA, who took the opportunity to remind readers that professional judges' decisions vary just as much as laymen's, and that the Lord Chancellor receives many more complaints about professional judges than he does about lay justices. When money becomes the sole measure of value, and we show less respect for things that come free, there is more pressure to justify the relative need for every activity. Although free labour may sometimes bear the stigma of social inferiority, and 'amateur' may be a convenient way to describe JPs, this label becomes an insult if used to imply that the modern trained magistracy is in reality anything but professional.

A *Yorkshire Post* contributor opined in 1989, 'We are running the system with amateurs ... Every solicitor knows that some of their decisions are crazy ... They play a significant part in sending more of the population to jail than in any other EC country ... It is high time that we brought in far more professional lawyers to do the job properly'. Again, truth was a casualty. Such an exaggerated remark if made today would of course look even more ridiculous than 30 years ago. However, to his credit, the paper's editor allowed me to reply at some length. When condemning the lay magistracy and deploring 'the fact that JPs run the system', ignorant critics usually seem unable to avoid the words 'amateur' and 'untrained', while preferring to overlook the truth that the whole country is run by untrained, amateur councillors and politicians — 'perhaps the only profession for which no preparation is deemed necessary' (Robert Louis Stevenson: *Familiar Studies of Men and Books*).

The Times in 1999 gave space for a naïve article by a former executive of BOC Gases, a member of the Glidewell Committee on the Crown Prosecution Service, who seemingly knew little about the magistracy. He used it to trot out the standard drivel about 'an unaccountable, out-of-touch, middle-class elite, ill-equipped to deal with the problems of an increasingly complex multi-ethnic society', in which JPs 'need to reflect the age, ethnic, religious and educational background of the local population in such a way as to justify the claim that those charged with an offence are judged by their peers'. The 'peers' whom he seemed to prefer were the expensive, solo-sitting stipendiaries, whose class, ethnicity, religion and education were even less likely to reflect the background of local offenders than a mixed bench of JPs. In what way, one wonders, can a single paid lawyer possibly be more democratic, representative and accountable than a bench of three intelligent, trained men and women from widely different backgrounds? The *Times* article provoked one enraged JP to reply: 'In the ethnically mixed area where I sit, my entry year group comprised one male Jew over 50, one male Muslim under 35, a West Indian male over 40, a Hindu male under 35, a female Roman Catholic under 40, and a similarly aged Presbyterian. Two of that number were born in Scotland, and three were born outside the UK. All resided within seven miles of the courtroom'.

Less than two weeks before the *Times* article appeared, the Lord Chancellor told JPs, 'You are selected for your representativeness, as well as for your personal abilities. You are part of the local democratic constitution'. He was right about the last two points, but surely wrong about the first — or maybe he just picked the wrong word. He should perhaps have used the word 'diversity' instead, because magistrates are not chosen to represent anyone or anything (except justice and the Queen). They, and those who appoint them, strive hard to ensure that they are, and are seen to be, independent and deliberately unrepresentative of any particular grouping. The traditional guidance for advisory committees on the selection of magistrates goes no further than to say that they should 'broadly reflect' the communities from which they are drawn. It cannot, and must not, be otherwise.

It is unfortunate that this subject continues to be regarded as synonymous with justice and is demanded as a token of true democracy and fairness. The mistaken equation with political election is compounded by the misconceived notion that magistrates allow their own background and political beliefs to affect their decision-making, whereas in fact their judicial oath, selection, training and experience ensures that they are likely to do exactly the opposite. The built-in ability to be detached, impartial and objective is one of the advantages and real strengths of a court consisting of three magistrates. It is a myth to suppose that crime is miraculously reduced if the courts are made 'more accountable' to the public.

The charge that JPs and judges are 'out of touch with ordinary people' is linked to the 'representation' myth. It echoes the perennial bleats of the disgruntled minority who can never find anything more imaginative to say. The inference is that one can only be an acceptable judge of others' behaviour — let alone be fit to determine guilt or innocence — if one shares the same age, colour, background and experience as the accused. Clearly nonsense. No-one ever prescribes what magistrates and judges need to do in order to prove they are 'in touch' or 'representative'. Show blatant prejudice and wear t-shirts on the bench, perhaps?

JPs are probably among the least out-of-touch people in the country. Not only are they drawn from a wide spectrum of society and expertise but, after a few years on the bench, there is not much they have not seen or heard about people and human behaviour. Collectively, they are certainly more broadly experienced than most of those who come before them in the courts, and they have every right to ask why it is always the magistrates who must adjust their role to suit those whom they are appointed to judge without favour. It should be seen from the opposite direction, for it is the offenders who are out of touch with, and unrepresentative of, the rest of society, the overwhelming majority of whom deplore criminal behaviour and wish to see it punished.

White, too old, too middle-class ...

Among criticisms of the magistracy, the most overused clichés of all are: the idea that white and indigenous people cannot judge black and ethnic minority people fairly—and vice-versa; the false equation of young age with suitability to do justice; and the nonsense that middle-class people cannot understand, and therefore cannot do justice to, so-called working-class people. It is said that 'young working-class black and minority ethnic (BME) men feel they will not get justice from a middle-aged, middle-class white bench'. Whenever this sentiment is boringly repeated by the critics, the confusion between 'understanding' and 'fairness under the law' is exposed, alongside the absurd implication that BMEs can only be treated justly if they are tried each time by a bench of teen-age, working-class, coloured magistrates.

Contrary to the impression given by detractors, the composition of the magistracy currently reflects that of the nation as a whole. Over 90 per cent of the English and Welsh population are white, less than 15 per cent are ethnic, well over 50 per cent are middle-aged, and a huge majority are described as 'middle-class'. Yet, at a time when ageism is 'an offence', the average age is rising, and class is immaterial, it is, according to the critics, a sin to be 'white, middle-aged or middle-class', especially if you are, or want to be, a magistrate. If you do not satisfy these criteria, and are not legally qualified, you are not considered fit by some to deal with what are referred to as 'the complex problems arising from today's multi-ethnic society'. Such is the idiotic theme of the magistracy's most unintelligent critics.

Much of the criticism on grounds of age, colour and class arises from a misconception of the essential function of a court of law, and ignores the pledge and training which govern the attitude and behaviour of every magistrate. The complainers—including those who persist in calling for more and more 'representation'—construct a false equation between justice and the composition of the bench. They seem to suggest that the judicial oath—requiring magistrates to be fair to all—should be variable, so as to match the personal characteristics of the bench to each offender. Thus, they infer, justice can only be done if youths are dealt with by JPs from a similar age group, if members of ethnic minorities are sentenced only by magistrates from a like culture, or if those from the 'working-class' are tried only by fellow workers. Such a fanciful idea could never be made to work fairly in the way they imagine.

Unfortunately, some non-white defendants claim 'discrimination' whenever they are found guilty and sentenced by an all-white court. Provided JPs always act judicially, there is little that can, or should, be done about this, and they have to live with such criticism. Race can only become an issue if the court has ignored the judicial oath by showing prejudice when dealing with offenders of a different skin colour. In spite of many efforts by detractors, there is no evidence whatever to show that black or brown skinned are treated by magistrates any less justly than white people. Sheffield University conducted widespread research on discrimination in the criminal justice system in the 1980s and early-1990s, concluding that 'racial discriminatory behaviour was not an obvious or noticeable feature of courtroom interactions'.

Since more than 85 per cent (2011 Census) of the UK population are white, it is reasonable to expect that benches will continue to be predominantly white, and that this will have no effect on their sworn duty to adjudicate 'without fear or favour'; for what it's worth, the current proportion of JPs drawn from ethnic minorities is believed now to be more than 12 per cent, and continuing to rise.

'Magistrates are too old', the critics say. First, one has to ask: Too old for what? Taking into account the fact that around half of the UK population are aged over 50, and that for various reasons most JPs are appointed after 30, and have to retire at 70, it would be surprising if their average age was less than 50. What is so wrong about that? Those who make judicial decisions require maturity and experience, not youthfulness. As with most leaders in other walks of life—including politicians, industry, academia and public services—magistrates in their 50s have acquired useful knowledge and are probably at the peak of their mental ability; and, on a normal adult bench of three, there is usually a spread of ages and other characteristics anyway. Furthermore, apart maybe from appearance, there is nothing fundamentally wrong or unjust in having a bench of 60-year-old JPs—all of whom have themselves been young once, and probably have children of their own—to deal with teenagers for the same crimes as are committed by adults. Nevertheless, magistrates who sit in the youth courts are drawn from the youngest on the bench, and they are all obliged to receive special training for youth court work.

The retirement age for magistrates was reduced from 75 to 70 years in 1968, and for appointment from 27 to 18 in 2004 (a 19-year-old law student was appointed to the Pontefract bench in 2006). These changes were generally welcomed at the time, but the effect on the average age of JPs was unlikely to be significant or to satisfy everyone. Of course, it is always desirable that there should be more younger people on the bench, but it is patently unrealistic to think that this can ever be easier to achieve in the magistracy than in any other comparable national institution. It has to be admitted, however, that appearance may at times count for something, and partial recognition of this is reflected in the general practice of appointing the younger magistrates to Youth Court panels. If this point were to be further conceded, it would become unworkable—and, in respect of district judges, totally impossible.

If the age theory is carried to the extreme, it means that only very young magistrates, gifted with superhuman maturity and wisdom, can fairly try and sentence young criminals, because older magistrates are said to become deficient in 'understanding'. This is of course a ridiculous notion, which could lead to a situation in which youths would be treated—not more justly—but more leniently, because the juvenile bench has been directed to take a more perceptive and sympathetic attitude towards them. While understanding of human behaviour can be useful in sentencing, it should not be allowed to influence verdicts. If it were ever to be thought that justice could only be done in the youth courts by finding and appointing younger and younger magistrates, capricious and harsh decisions based on prejudice would be commonplace, and youths would be handed an even greater incentive to continue offending.

What is meant by 'middle-class'? What is so unacceptable about the majority of JPs being drawn from the majority group in society — as are MPs, judges, teachers, civil servants, and leaders from all walks of life? The population is said to be overwhelmingly middle-class these days; therefore magisterial appointments and the diversity of bench membership reflect that fact. But this does not mean that those who feel they belong to a different class are likely to receive anything other than the impartial treatment given to all defendants in the magistrates' courts. Again, the Auld Report — falling, surprisingly, into the institutional stereotype trap — seemed anxious to criticise the magistracy for being 'disproportionately middle-class', the unavoidable implication being that this disqualifies JPs from doing justice to those considered to be members of other social groupings.

We continue proudly to assert the principle of 'trial by our peers' as one of the chief reasons for supporting the lay justice system, based on courts of three justices. But actually this is only true in the sense that we are tried by fellow citizens. If we were strictly to be tried by 'peers', we would have to make provision for countless tailored benches, over the composition of which there would undoubtedly be endless argument, as there is already sometimes over juries. Clearly, this would be both unachievable — and undesirable — in the magistrates' courts. Equally, it is nonsense to portray JPs as members of the so-called 'establishment', implying that this somehow means defendants will be denied a basic human right when tried in a magistrates' court.

'Muddled' magistrates and 'repellent' lawyers

Contrary to impressions which may sometimes be given, courts do not exist for lawyers — nor for magistrates — but JPs are among the few members of the community who are in a position when necessary to mediate between the general public and pretentious advocates. This may be one of the reasons why lawyers sometimes appear among the leading critics of the magistracy, which many in the profession have been brought up to regard as amateur, no matter how well JPs are trained or how competently they perform. Some of the nastiest attacks come from junior barristers, with little experience of the magistrates' courts, and some from immature law students who have already acquired that arrogance with which lawyers in general are sometimes labelled. However, as Lord Chief Justice Bingham said, 'Justices of the peace are free of the habits of thought, speech and bearing which characterise professional lawyers, and which most people find, to a greater or lesser extent, repellent'.

Surprisingly, the editor of the Law Society's *Gazette* in 1990 gave space to the opinions of an ignorant student, in which he claimed to have been allowed to observe magistrates and their clerk at work in the retiring room (which is forbidden) and in training. Having heard that magistrates (properly) take ability to pay into account before fining, and that defaulters' courts (correctly) do not ask for details of the original offence, he concluded that all magistrates are 'muddled' and 'unable to view the system as a whole'.

Members of this fine profession — the legal profession — undeniably represent the more intelligent strata of society, which enables them to become essential to the conduct of many human activities. For a start, they draft our laws in their own language, which also gives them a monopoly of interpretation, and grants them special power and influence over our lives, from government to private relationships. It is hardly surprising therefore that some lawyers — exhibiting Lord Bingham's 'characteristics' — come to feel that they possess a superior 'habit of thought' which gives them a divine right to judge.

On the other hand, there are few things more impressive than the professionalism of a judge's summing-up after a long trial, a skilled defence lawyer's cross-examination of prosecution witnesses, or a beautifully constructed legal 'opinion'. In the magistrates' courts, there is nothing more pleasing than to see and hear the courtesy and clarity with which most advocates conduct themselves, especially those who (whatever they may think of JPs) show due respect for the bench and assist in upholding the dignity of the court.

Unfortunately, even in the legal profession, there are members who let the side down. They cannot resist the temptation to score points off the magistracy and write insulting letters about JPs to *The Times*. One such solicitor and erstwhile deputy judge wrote in 2010: 'It is not far short of bizarre that in the twenty-first century justice is still being dispensed by the modern equivalent of tinkers and tailors'. At a guess, he had recently lost a case which he had been sure of winning in a local court; but, needless to say, JPs were outraged. Is it jealousy, selfishness or professional arrogance that makes some lawyers so ready to subvert the lay magistracy while continuing to give unequivocal support to the fallible jury system?

A criticism of magistrates, particularly from defence lawyers, which used to be heard more than today, is that of 'prosecution-mindedness' or 'police-mindedness'. Before World War II, and in the days of police courts, there may have been some grounds for this; there were credible stories of magistrates saying that they 'always believed what a police officer said'. But recent changes, the introduction of JPs' training and, sadly, some serious cases of police unreliability, have combined to remove any magisterial bias of this kind.

CHAPTER 10

A Great National Institution

'One of the great and abiding institutions of our nation'

Lord Judge, Lord Chief Justice (2011)

- Independent authority
- Respect and appreciation
- The people's court
- Good value for the nation

The lay magistracy, during a history spanning more than 650 years, has evolved to become one of the world's most effective forms of popular justice, and one of Britain's most valuable institutions, respected for its integrity, admired for the unpaid service given by its members, but inadequately recognised for its importance in the fabric of a mature democracy. Regrettably, its powers and status have been considerably reduced in the last 50 years, during which many advantages have been discarded in favour of economy and administrative convenience. The principle of popular involvement in our judicial system, and the tradition of voluntary public service on which it relies for recruits, are probably still strong enough in most areas of England and Wales for the lay magistracy to survive, provided that apathy and political indifference can be overcome and transformed to ensure a presumption in favour of a summary court system based on JPs, selected as broadly representative of the areas they serve and sitting as a 'bench' of three.

The magistracy may appear at times to play a relatively small part and cost little in the totality of national life—so much so that its wellbeing can too easily be neglected—but this belies its immense contribution and importance to the maintenance of our internationally-admired judicial system. As the House of Lords is to Parliament, so the magistracy is to the judiciary: a leavening influence on the democratic process which ensures that decision-making is shared by a larger number of more widely chosen people than would otherwise be the case. It is difficult to measure the value of such civilising institutions, but it is certain that without them the nation would be much the poorer. Lay participation in the justice system is a strength, not a weakness, and lay magistrates are selected to do an important job for our society. They do it well, and at little cost to the nation. It therefore ill-behoves politicians and reformers to support actions which may be designed to improve the justice system as a whole, but which devalue the magistracy in the process. Likewise, the sustainability of the magistracy can only be assured if the popular demands of the present (e.g. the excessive attention given to the desirability of diversity) are met without compromising the future of the whole institution.

Independent authority

Alongside that of the jury, the magistracy's history can be said to begin with the 1215 Magna Carta, by which for the first time the rights and freedoms of the individual citizen, as opposed to the unfettered power of kings, became established under Parliament. About a hundred and 50 years later (1361), Justices of the peace became a national institution in their own right, a permanent office for lay people at the heart of the justice system which continues to the present day. However, many changes affecting the status and powers of JPs have taken place during the intervening 650 years; other regimes have come and gone, and volumes of legislation have been added to the statute.

Some of the power formerly wielded by monarchs, churches and barons has, unfortunately for the ordinary citizen, been replaced in modern times by other tyrannies, such as trade unions, political parties, big business, lawyers, the media, 'political correctness', self-righteous mobs and odious class distinction. The British judiciary as a whole, including of course the magistracy, has remained remarkably independent and incorruptible, but politicians are constantly tempted — in pursuit of power, control, economy, impatience, or administrative convenience—to transfer authority from court to executive or to restrict freedom of discretion. In the last 50 years, many powers, formerly confined to magistrates, have been passed to police, justices' clerks and other officials, none of whom are subject to the same degree of judicial constraint and public scrutiny as JPs. Handing over powers and responsibilities to people or bodies making arbitrary decisions behind closed doors, and accountable only to their supervisors, opens the way to the dishonesty and secrecy for which the magistracy was itself criticised in years gone by, but from which it is these days totally free.

I joined the bench at a time when the magistracy was regarded as part of 'authority', based on reputation, respect and legitimacy, whose voice generally carried sufficient weight to be accepted without undue question. Not so today. The voice of authority is now subject either to instant challenge, or it becomes just another expression among many that are ignored or unheard. We live in an era of distrust—especially regarding anything which smacks of power—and even representative democracy is now questioned at every turn by those who feel that MPs have become too distant from those who elect them.

The British form of democracy still relies substantially on the numerous institutions, including the magistracy, that go back too far for any modern political party to claim as its own. However, the potential always exists for conflict between government and judiciary. In the end, it is about power and the mechanisms for keeping power in check. Although Parliament makes the laws, judges and magistrates usually have the final word over the interpretation and enforcement of them. From time-to-time, over-zealous politicians are tempted to rebel when they discover that, in spite of parliamentary privilege, even they are not above the law, and that there remain some non-elected people in the country who can occasionally tell them what to do. Friction is most likely to occur when government is being held to account, or judges are called upon to make sense of badly drafted legislation. It is then that frustrated MPs may be heard accusing the judiciary of 're-writing the law', being 'unelected', 'unaccountable' or 'out of touch'.

Even in a democracy, liberty and human rights are always at risk. Each person and society as a whole have to be protected against frequent infringements, and this can only be done effectively through strict separation of powers. As the French judge and political philosopher Montesquieu wrote in *The Spirit of Laws* (1748), 'There is no liberty if the judicial power is not separated from the legislature and executive'. Surprisingly, it was relatively recently (in the 2005 Constitutional Reform Act) that a more or less full separation of powers was achieved in England and Wales, after hundreds of years during which it had been taken for granted. In a genuine democracy, final power must rest with the people. For administration of the law, it is difficult to imagine a better way of achieving this than by the use of juries (for indictable offences) and lay justices (for summary offences), the latter being particularly selected for their freely-given dedication to the qualities of fairness, impartiality, dispassion, and common sense; amateur in status, holding the respect of fellow-citizens; trained and professional in practice, not only as assessors of innocence and guilt, fact and fiction, truth and falsehood, but also as judges of appropriate punishment and treatment of offenders.

The independence of the judiciary from Parliament and the executive, and from all forms of outside coercion or interference in judicial decision-making, is fundamental to the maintenance of justice and respect for the rule of law; the integrity of the magistracy and its ability to do justice without fear or favour depends supremely on its ability to remain independent. But this essential characteristic has been under threat during the last 50 years, as governments have continued to erode magistrates' responsibilities, and ancillary agencies have sought, and been granted, a larger share of the judicial process. Even the higher courts are not immune from ambitious politicians seeking to meddle with the separation of powers. A former Home Secretary and Tory leader, Lord Howard of Lympne QC no less, was heard to say on a radio programme in 2011, 'The power of the judges, as opposed to the power of elected politicians, has increased, is increasing and ought to be diminished. More and more decisions are being made by unelected, unaccountable judges, instead of accountable, elected MPs who have to answer to the electorate for what has happened'. The rule of law, an independent judiciary and a free, responsible press are essential for the maintenance of a true democracy and the survival of liberty. The ordinary individual citizen is the real loser when judicial independence does not exist; he must be able to rely on the total impartiality of those appointed to sit in judgement between him and the state.

Independent lay magisterial jurisdiction, with legal advice, is one of the most democratic and effective systems through which the law can be summarily administered without excessive reliance on expensive bureaucracy or dominance by lawyers. So, every time government increases centralisation, restricts discretion, appoints another district judge or hands power to executive officers, democracy and independence are jointly compromised. Moreover, if it is accepted that the success of our brand of democracy owes much to a system of justice which encourages the maximum participation of ordinary citizens, it follows that, every time its role is diminished, so is the quality of our national life. The unpaid, voluntary magistracy needs always to be sensitive to the danger on the one hand of becoming a subservient branch of government, and on the other of being looked upon as incapable of making independent rational decisions, on account of its members not being trained as lawyers.

High among the most persuasive reasons for sustaining the lay magistracy is simply that it has developed into one of the fairest, most flexible and most incorruptible, systems of independent justice ever devised. This is a more powerful argument than reliance on its long history, the merits of public service or its relatively low cost. If long-established institutions like the magistracy seem too old to be relevant, it is probably because they still work rather well. During the last century—unlike politicians, bankers, businessmen, police, priests and doctors—the magistracy has been one of the few among the country's great institutions that have managed to retain a reputation for integrity. This cannot be measured, but we must agree that in times of falling standards it has greater value than ever. Why undermine or destroy something that has proved, and continues to be, so worthy?

My brief membership of the Commonwealth Magistrates Association Council, and the opportunity which this gave to meet magistrates and judges from many younger countries, brought home to me how fortunate

we are to have an independent judiciary with substantial public participation, a free press and a democratic government unaffected by endemic
corruption. We are liable to take for granted such advantages, but many
judges and magistrates from emerging democracies envy our good fortune, and long for the same degree of freedom, fairness and—above
all—independence from political interference.

When immigrants who have been accepted as new British citizens are
asked why they chose the UK as their future home, a commonly recur-
ring reason is the independence and fair play they associate with our lay
magisterial and jury systems. This reminds us how easy it is to become
casual about our most familiar institutions, and how deep is the yearn-
ing in many countries to possess similar tokens of a free and civilised
society. We may criticise our own system, and seek to find fault with our
magistracy, but we must never allow this to devalue the very qualities
that are so admired beyond our borders.

The magistracy cannot exist in a vacuum. It has to operate from a position of confidence and strength, rather than power, safe in the knowledge
of uncompromising government support to carry out the work with
which it is entrusted. It does not expect favour or protection for its own
sake, but it does deserve the special attention that any civilised country
would devote to the preservation of a unique national asset. Alarmingly, in modern times it often seems that the magistracy is treated like
a cherished but eroding coastline on which government has decided to
abandon the sea defences 'for environmental reasons'.

Great national institutions in democracies must neither be neglected
nor allowed to rest on their laurels. They have to be ready to adapt
constantly if they are to survive. In the last 50 years, it can be said that
the magistracy has done as much as could be expected to remain fit for
purpose and resilient, in spite of unwelcome change and interference.
Because of its innate reserve and befitting reluctance to campaign in its
own cause, it has not always resisted as well as it might the less sensible
changes, particularly those that threaten its own long-term future. But
if the nation values it as highly as it appears to treasure other great institutions—such as the jury system (with all its faults)—the magistracy
should not have to face constant challenges to its very existence.

When they were a more important part of the courts' organization, most justices' clerks would have been willing to give genuine backing to the magistracy, but those days have long since passed. Thus, one of the nation's greatest institutions now has to rely all too often on its own members for justification and support. It should not have to do this. JPs should not be placed in the invidious position of having to defend themselves and their role in the judicial hierarchy; they should not be disadvantaged because they give their services for nothing; they should not be expected to accept lower expenses than others in the public sector. Even more unacceptable is that the lay magistracy is not represented on some boards of national bodies with which it is closely involved, such as HM Courts and Tribunals Service.

In defending its position in the justice system, the magistracy itself has to be careful to avoid giving the impression that it is motivated merely by the instinct for self-preservation. It must constantly strive to conduct itself in a dignified and 'professional' way, so that its outstanding value to the nation is self-evident; so that a trio bench of trained JPs is acknowledged to be inherently preferable to a single lawyer; so that the principle of unpaid judicial public service is seen to be a vital part of a healthy democracy; and so that local trials of local people, by local people, remains the most desirable option for the achievement of true summary justice.

It is a sad fact that, when major re-organizations involving the magistracy are announced, many hard-working JPs do not have the time or inclination to consider seriously the long-term consequences for its future. They react with mixed feelings of frustration, anger and acceptance of the inevitable. Most would be truly upset if the magistracy failed to survive, but are, unfortunately, not in a position to provide effective resistance. Why should they be bothered? An increasing number take the easier option and resign. In departing, they do not forfeit an income; they do, however, leave the magistracy much the poorer for their absence, and lose the regular satisfaction of working professionally with valued colleagues in the demanding work of the courts. Every time a JP leaves the bench prematurely, the injury is not only to the magistracy and the state, but also to the public service tradition, local justice and democracy itself.

The core strength of the volunteer magistracy lies in its unpaid but trained status, and its independence from politics, pressure groups—and, dare I say, lawyers. Although a full member of the judiciary, the magistracy has the advantage of being outside the legal establishment, and thus 'free of the habits of thought, speech and bearing which characterise professional lawyers' (see page 198). It is, therefore, a mark of strength, not of weakness, if the senior judiciary can have enough respect for its magisterial colleagues to leave them with maximum independence, devolved powers and free speech within the judicial system. Such trust, in turn, requires the quality of magisterial leadership and practice to be maintained at a constantly high level.

Respect and appreciation

There are few 'rights' attached to being a magistrate and few at all receive honours, or recognition beyond that of their court colleagues, but it can surely be agreed that JPs at least deserve respect, adequate training for their work, personal security within their courthouses, and adequate allowances for travelling and subsistence. They should also be entitled to expect that, when required to attend court on rota, they will not be sent home and deprived of court work in favour of district judges, nor receive any less favourable rights and privileges than those granted to salaried senior members of the judiciary and other public servants. As JPs themselves are voluntary and unpaid, the nation should at least do everything to uphold the status and dignity of their office; and, in the accepted absence of individual honours, it should never fail to show genuine recognition of their collective service.

Magistrates have been allowed to retain one modest distinction, in that they are permitted to use the post nominal 'JP', but even that was nearly taken from them in the 1990s. Some are rewarded after a while by invitation to a Royal Garden Party, and a few may receive minor honours for outstanding service in other areas connected with the justice system. Before direct links were severed, these included the prison, probation and magistrates' courts services, for which honours such as OBE and MBE were awarded for 'services to the administration of justice' or 'services to the community'. Otherwise, it appears that in the last 25 years the level of official recognition given to JPs, for whatever reason, has declined.

This apparent reduction in regard for the magistracy's contribution to the justice system seemed to coincide with a rise in official belief that people who are not professionally qualified, or do not charge for their services, remain 'amateur' and somehow less competent — which of course is not only untrue but insulting. The reason may also lie in a re-allocation of automatic awards to state and legal post-holders, leaving less room for recognition of those in the lower ranks of the judiciary. Whatever the case, magistrates have sometimes watched with dismay while others — often incompetent — have continued to collect automatic honours in addition to the generous financial rewards they already receive. Although highly paid for the positions they hold, lawyers, social service directors, penal reformers, police chiefs and offender charity directors are elevated to, and thus represented in, the House of Lords; Probation Service and victim support leaders receive knighthoods or damehoods, and courts service personnel (including district judges) collect CBs and CBEs for fulfilling their job descriptions.

Many JPs make considerable personal sacrifices in valuable ways outside the courts, and for these there is no logical reason why they should not rank for full recognition alongside other forms of voluntary public service. Meanwhile, national leaders of commerce and industry, while ignoring their shareholders in continuing to award themselves inflated salaries and bonuses, receive national honours in addition; peerages and knighthoods are still given in return for donations to political parties; MPs feather their nests with inappropriate expenses; and ridiculously overpaid sportsmen and broadcasters make the headlines for all the wrong reasons. People can now even be rewarded merely for popularity, celebrity status, or whatever they are held to represent, rather than for what they actually do. Senior civil servants continue to receive the usual accolades, even when palpable failure in their department costs the country billions of pounds (e.g. mismanagement of the foot and mouth disease crisis at the beginning of this century). On the very day in 2008 that Network Rail was fined a record £14 million for 'shocking incompetence', its chairman was receiving a knighthood at Buckingham

Palace. At the same time, it was announced that the company's directors had awarded themselves bonuses of £700,000.

Notwithstanding the apparent imbalance, it is true to say that there is no jealousy or resentment on the part of unpaid justices, because they usually know the score by the time they qualify to sit on the bench. But the unsung service, integrity and loyalty associated with the magistracy exists in marked contrast to the highly-paid selfish world around them, frequently tarnished by suspect personal relationships, dishonesty, hypocrisy, inflated salaries, money laundering, strikes, phone tapping, paedophilia, drug dealing and alcohol abuse.

The MA is well respected by government as an essential and representative charity on whom it can always rely for helpful consultation, sound opinion and responsible leadership; its national chairmen occupy a high-profile position as the recognised leader of the lay judiciary in England and Wales. As such, they carry a substantial responsibility, exercise numerous public skills, travel widely around the country, and devote most of their free time. They usually merit a place in the honours list after at least six years 'on the ladder' or in office but, since the beginning of this century, at no higher level than that given to Crown Prosecution Service area business managers, committee chairmen or senior staff.

In the past, most MA chairmen were deemed to merit a CBE (Commander of the Order of the British Empire) but, although high awards are regularly made to senior judges and civil servants responsible for the magistracy, no appointment higher than that has ever been made to a JP solely for service to the judiciary, however exceptional. The first chairman (1920) was a peer, Lord Merthyr, who was thus able to speak frequently on behalf of the magistracy in the House of Lords; Sir William Addison, who was chairman from 1970 to 1976, but also a prominent historian and author, was knighted 'for services to public life'. However, a chief stipendiary magistrate received a knighthood in 1998, as did the already well-rewarded leaders of the probation, social, prosecution and Prison Services during this period. Prominent members of almost every other major organization in the country—professional and charitable—have also become knights, dames and peers from time-to-time, many of them having received titles that automatically go with the appointment, regardless of the quality or scale of the service rendered.

Most of the country's principal institutions and organizations have representatives of one sort or another in the houses of Parliament but, since Lord Merthyr's time (more than 90 years ago), there has been no-one there who could speak at first hand for the magistracy. This has made it much harder for the voice of lay justices to be heard in public debate, and the MA has needed to go to some length on many occasions to brief uninformed MPs and peers. It is ironical that, while critics complain interminably about the magistracy being 'unrepresentative', JPs themselves, who carry more than 90 per cent of the criminal caseload, are not directly represented in our legislature; and it is not unreasonable to suggest that the current recession in the magistracy might well have been less severe if it had been. Furthermore, there is not a single lay justice on the board of HM Courts and Tribunals Service (the executive agency responsible for running all the magistrates' courts in England and Wales) and some other important organizations connected with the management and training of JPs. What a difference 50 years ago, when magistrates had the oversight of their training and courts administration!

By comparison, lawyers have been over-represented in Parliament for centuries. For instance, the 'barrister-infested' 1650 House of Commons, in which half the MPs were lawyers; and even today, around 15 per cent of the lower House are members of that one profession; but maybe, for the nation as a whole, that is not such a bad thing, because lawyers are at least usually cogent and articulate. But imagine what a stir there would be if it was found that 15 per cent of MPs were psychiatrists — or, indeed, if 15 per cent of JPs were found to be members of the clergy.

Compared with the past, it has become more difficult to serve as a JP, more difficult to retain the essence of summary justice, and more difficult to satisfy the combined demands of reforming MPs, ambitious civil servants and a querulous public. Even the unpaid status of JPs has not been enough to overcome this trend. Indeed, it sometimes seems that — because of the independence which they enjoy — they are more likely to be dismissed as 'reactionary' or 'obstructive', if they have the temerity to challenge grandiose official schemes for further centralisation or re-organization of the courts; it is also much easier to ignore those who are unpaid and uncontracted, because their livelihood is not at stake. Each time the magistracy's concerns about threats to its status are not taken seriously by government, the respect on which JPs have to rely for their role in the justice system is diminished.

For a long time, there has been a system by which most JPs on retirement qualify for inclusion on the Supplemental List and may, if they wish, continue to use the post-nominal 'JP'. They also receive a standard letter of thanks for their services from the Lord Chancellor; but, welcome though that is, it suffers from being rather impersonal and does not usually take into account the wide variation in length and degree of service given by each recipient. In the days of smaller benches and relatively few retirements, most chairmen wrote to thank long-serving colleagues; and Lord Lieutenants, who normally chair the local Advisory committees on JP appointments, often still try to compensate for insufficient official recognition by sending their own, more individual, letters to express at least their county's gratitude.

The people's court

'The power of kings and magistrates is nothing else but what is only derivative; transformed and committed to them in trust from the people to the common good of them all, in whom the power yet remains fundamentally, and cannot be taken from them without a violation of their natural right'

John Milton, The Tenure of Kings and Magistrates.

In a democracy, power stems from the people. They choose the representatives to whom they are willing to delegate authority for law-making. However, for a well developed democracy, it is essential that the people are also enabled to participate fully in the administration of the laws. In our case, this has been achieved for hundreds of years by retention — under the Crown — of a judicial role for ordinary citizens through the magistrates' courts and the jury. When the former is described as 'the people's court', it is easier to understand why replacement of a lay magistrates' bench by a single lawyer, and the transfer of judicial powers to members of the executive, are both perceived to be incompatible with the notion of democracy and of 'justice for the people by the people'. It is usually a backward step to transfer inherited power away from those who are using it responsibly for the benefit of the community.

Whatever may be the public perception, the magistracy may not be quite 'us', but it is certainly not fully 'them' either. It is not designed for the employment and convenience of JPs, police, lawyers or social workers, but for the efficient administration of justice by and on behalf of the community. Normally, magistrates' courts should be public and easily available to all, as are libraries, medical centres and other civic services. The principle and advantage of local summary justice are lost if those attending courts, for whatever purpose, are required to travel unreasonable distances at unreasonable hours to reach them.

Amalgamations and centralisation, often carried out for little more than administrative convenience, are clearly a major setback for the image of lay and local justice. Nevertheless, our magistracy, and the model of summary jurisdiction it represents, remain among the most notable achievements of the civilised world. It is one of the key pillars of British democracy and culture, and is still ranked among the most enduring of our institutions, alongside the monarchy, church, Parliament and the other great organizations of state—an invaluable asset that has helped to shape the character of our nation and its high reputation for justice.

One of the major reasons for its success and survival is our long tradition of public service by individuals from all walks of life, and the unpaid, unattached status of JPs. Unlike most west European countries, we still have a modest reserve of loyal and selfless people in Britain who are prepared, in most areas, to continue serving the community on this basis, often at considerable disadvantage to themselves. This goodwill should not be squandered or taken for granted. Removal of judicial powers from selected ordinary citizens, combined with indifference towards the magistracy, merely increases fears for its future.

The voluntary element is crucial to the continued existence and success of our lay justice system; if JPs were paid, it would quickly bring about its demise. Furthermore, it must be recognised that 'doing it for nothing' has become part of the honour of being a JP. This is public service at its best, and a crucial weapon in the struggle to maintain the independence and integrity of the institution. Voluntary service remains an admirable way of retaining public participation and confidence, and it can (just) still be claimed that the relative localness of lay magistrates is an advantage.

The value of the magistracy to the nation is incalculable; certainly greater than the sum of its parts. Is it too much to hope that we will, sooner rather than later, realise that what matters is not the outward features of the magistracy, but its unique overall contribution to our national culture and tradition of public service? If it is allowed to wither, not only will access to a wealth of wisdom and common sense disappear, but a free, irreplaceable human resource will be lost for ever. As part of the foundations of our democracy, this asset is too important to neglect; it must somehow be conserved and strengthened against the destructive efforts of those who think that the courts should belong only to the lawyers and the management executives.

The future health of British justice and democracy lies not in lawyers' courts, but in people's courts; not in more highly-paid barristers and solicitors, but in more volunteer citizens; not in more centralised bureaucracy, but in more efficient local organization. Our lay justice system does not need to rely for survival on a proud history of more than six and a half centuries; it has proved in the last 70 years or so that it can still provide a modern, flexible and relatively inexpensive service, provided that it is allowed the benefit of enlightened leadership and the unequivocal support of politicians, civil servants and senior judiciary.

Governments may come and go, laws may change, courthouses may be closed, but the magistracy — perhaps needing again to be more involved in its own administration — must be confirmed as the principal avenue for summary justice, using the most modern technology. The lay system has done as much or more than any other institution to uphold the liberty of the people, and to prevent the creation of dictatorships, monopolies and tyrannies of all kinds. It should be given every encouragement to continue doing so.

Good value for the nation

There are a number of impressive reasons why we should continue to have a lay magistracy, and why the nation derives huge benefit from it. In the criminal courts, it already comprises over 90 per cent of the judiciary, handles 95 per cent of the cases, and spends less than 1 per cent of the courts service budget. Far less than one per cent of justices' decisions go to appeal, and of those, more than half are disallowed. Among other notable features are the magistracy's flexibility and the opportunity it provides for widespread public participation in the justice system. Reformers and critics—hell-bent on discrediting the lay magistracy—have attempted for many years to manipulate the figures so as to construct unfavourable comparisons between a bench of three JPs and a district judge (DJ) sitting alone, but the report *Strengths and Skills of the Judiciary in the Magistrates' Courts* (compiled by MORI in 2011) found that DJs are significantly more expensive to employ than JPs, and that their much-vaunted speed does not compensate for the extra cost. So, even if generous allowance is made for the obvious fact that DJs (not having to consult or retire) may work faster on guilty cases, the cost argument remains clearly in favour of JPs. Cost and speed are not everything; and at least one presiding judge was of the view that speed is actually irrelevant.

I have referred to the enviable and well-established tradition of public involvement through voluntary service in Britain, and there is no finer example of this than the magistracy. There was perhaps a time when it seemed as if the work was becoming tedious for busy JPs, too technical for non-lawyers, and 'unsuitable for middle-class amateurs'. But since compulsory training was introduced in 1966, and membership has become more diverse, such fears appear exaggerated and are now rarely heard. It is probably true to say that today's lay justices are more competent and better equipped for their judicial role, and less blameworthy, bigoted, prejudiced, prosecution-minded and ambitious, than at any time in their 650-year history. Training and good leadership can probably take much of the credit for this.

A further attribute—not as vital as 50 years ago, but still valuable—is the relative localness of JPs. The meaning of 'local' in this context has become somewhat devalued, and benches are now drawn from wider areas, but local knowledge can still count for something in deciding verdicts and in choosing the most appropriate sentences for a particular area or circumstance. It should also not be forgotten that advisory committees still try to recommend JPs that are 'broadly representative' and resident in the area where they sit.

Membership of the magistracy when I joined in the 1960s was something of which one could be quietly proud; it was acknowledged as a great national and local institution, attracting some of the finest people one could wish to meet from all walks of life, giving opportunities to participate in a wide range of associated public service. We were still at that time largely in control of our own affairs, and had many other responsibilities, but we were well-aware all the time of the need to improve our image and performance. We strongly supported training for JPs and the constant search for administrative improvements. We strove hard to reduce inconsistency in sentencing through the production and use of guidelines; and, through increased professionalism, we successfully countered those who criticised us for being 'amateurs'.

In addition to its unquestioned integrity and independence, the most persuasive reason for having a lay magistracy is that, in this country, it manifestly does a good job at a very low cost. Magistrates themselves know this, and so do all those with sufficient knowledge of its record.

CHAPTER 11

Whither Lay Justice?

'If we could first know where we are, and whither we are tending, we could better judge what to do, and how to do it'

Abraham Lincoln

- Missing the point
- Safeguarding the lay magistracy
- Stop dismantling; start rebuilding
- Questions for the future

The following is adapted from an article I published in *The Times* as long ago as 8th April 2010.

More than 55 per cent of criminal offences are now dealt with outside our courts, on-the-spot fines exceed 200,000 a year, and more than a fifth of offenders who breach conditional cautions are not pursued by the CPS. A Commons Select Committee described this as representing 'a fundamental change to our concept of a criminal justice system'.

Such a change is potentially terminal for the concept of justice itself, and especially for the summary jurisdiction of our magistrates' courts. It is, therefore, essential to review and arrest the damage being done to both.

Few things define a nation more clearly than how it reacts to internal lawlessness. Faced with persistently high levels of crime, reoffending and anti-social behaviour, embarrassed by burgeoning prison numbers and under police pressure, the Government has resorted to out-of-court and other desperate measures, but its reaction has created vastly more law while reducing opportunities for justice. Long-established procedures are being discarded under resource-driven policies that place the system above the needs of fair practice. At the same time crime figures are made to look rosier and performance targets easier to meet.

Repeated cautions are now given for quite serious offences, including violence; worse still, some people are not charged at all. Widespread use of new powers enables the police, supplemented by a third tier of assorted officials, to mete out instant 'justice' on a take-it-or-leave-it basis. No argument, no mitigation, no means testing, no compensation, no transparency, no consistency—and, of course, no need to go to court.

Arbitrary decisions and diversion offer little room for the exercise of true justice. Pressure on offenders to accept easy options is inevitable, thus opening the door to the corruption and injustice we so despise in many other countries, while more than half those charged fail to pay their fine.

There is a role for out-of-court disposals, but their inappropriate use is leading to the abandonment of deliberative summary justice, as is the undesirable practice of trials conducted by district judges sitting alone. Intentionally or otherwise, the normal court of three JPs is being made to look increasingly inconvenient. Simultaneously, we are devaluing justice, threatening the future of the (lay) magistracy, and increasing the hegemony of lawyers at the expense of democracy in our courts. The nation should be alarmed by this trend.

Our unpaid magistracy has shown remarkable adaptability to extra burdens, disruptive changes and constant financial restrictions. Furthermore, JPs are subject to appointment and working constraints—designed to ensure the practice and visibility of high quality justice—that do not apply to most of those now permitted to act arbitrarily on their own behind closed doors.

Diversion and the effects of budget cuts emphasise the vulnerability of a compliant magistracy to the depredations of reforming politicians and bonus-driven civil servants who have little interest in whether valuable institutions survive or not. The magistracy needs strengthening, not further decimation; yet, successive governments have steadily eroded its powers and status, apparently without concern for the long-term consequences.

Although not perfect, the magistracy serves the nation well. It remains one of the world's fairest and most efficient forms of summary justice, and many countries would give their soul to possess the tradition of voluntary public service and personal dedication that have sustained it for hundreds of years.

Nevertheless, all too frequently, we seem ready to discard this unique national asset in favour of speed, economy and short-term administrative convenience. In contrast, whenever the relatively costly and inefficient sacred cow of the justice system — the jury — is under threat, the legal profession and much of the media are outraged. It is not unreasonable to suggest that the magistracy merits equal concern.

This should start with more determined action to boost recruitment of JPs, priority being given to provision of easier release from work commitments. Another imperative is compulsory impact assessment of the damaging effects on the magistracy arising from proposals for big changes in the justice system. If such plans indicate that the institution as a whole could be further weakened, they should be favourably amended. This is not to say that the magistracy should be preserved from change, but that greater regard than at present should be paid to its well-being and potential.

Substantially more than a narrow review of cautioning is needed to restore confidence in our criminal justice system. The approaching 650th anniversary of the first appointment of JPs is an appropriate time to reaffirm our belief in the supremacy of popular justice over reformist bureaucracy, and in the plural magistracy as the preferred custodian of our summary jurisdiction.

More than 70 years ago, and well before training of JPs was introduced, barrister and politician Lord Merthyr (1901–77) submitted a minority report to the Royal Commission on Justices of the Peace, in which he forecast that 'it is merely a matter of time before lay justices disappear; it is a question, not of whether but of when they should be replaced'. Ironically, having experienced, it is said, a 'Damascus conversion', he became one of the lay magistracy's strongest advocates and longest-serving chairmen of the Magistrates Association (MA).

Actually, the strength of the magistracy increased during the 50 years following the commission's report. Latterly it has declined, and its future again appears threatened, although probably for different reasons to those which Lord Merthyr had in mind. It beggars belief that our country might at any time be so stupid as to abandon or further neglect such a key constituent of our justice system and essential component of our democracy. At a time when the ideals of popular government are under strain, the lay magistracy is more relevant, and has potentially more to offer the nation, than at any time in the last 500 years. Indifference must therefore give way to action at the highest level if its distinguished position among our great national institutions is to be restored.

It is unfortunate that some present-day commentators on its future seem prepared to accept its current weakened status as good enough, and thus to condemn it permanently to a minor role. Much of this book (*Our Magistracy*), on the other hand, while exploring the reasons for the present unsatisfactory situation, is intended to support the belief that the magistracy's strength and unique role can, and should, be enhanced, not for its own sake, but for the benefit of the whole nation.

Missing the point

Reacting to the uncertain climate surrounding the magistracy, a number of well-informed thinkers in 2012 suggested some answers to the question of the future, but they appeared to attract little attention in Whitehall. The opinions were contained in a book of essays on *The Magistracy at the Crossroads,* published by the Waterside Press, and in a survey titled *Active, Accessible, Engaged: The Magistracy in the 21st Century,* which was produced by the MA. Disappointingly, neither of these publications appeared to recognise that the magistracy's survival depends first and foremost on its acceptance as an irreplaceable part of our national infrastructure. Unless this assumption is adopted as the starting point for discussions on its future, the danger is as described by David Faulkner in his perceptive introduction to the aforesaid Waterside publication, that 'the magistracy's role, influence and significance could be gradually attenuated until the very idea of volunteer judges comes to be seen as a quaint historical relic, existing on the fringe of an ever more professional, managerialist and mechanical ... system of justice'.

The wide range of contributors to *The Magistracy at the Crossroads* correctly analysed the reasons for the current situation and put forward a number of ideas but, far from making a compelling demand for reinvigoration of the whole institution, many of them seemed to suggest that the only way its continuance could be justified might lie in finding minor, uninspiring alternative occupations for under-used JPs, such as:

- Strengthening links between them and probation officers.
- Membership of problem-solving, neighbourhood justice and crime panels.
- Monitoring of compliance with parole conditions and court orders.
- Reconnecting the magistracy with local communities.
- Involvement with rehabilitation and restorative justice.
- Oversight of out-of-court penalties.
- Return to prison monitoring.

The need for restoration of a close relationship with the Probation Service has substance, and some of the other suggestions may appear to be useful, but none would be viable if those undertaking them had to be paid for their services, and it is hard to imagine worthy citizens flocking to volunteer for such unrewarding tasks. In the notable absence of demands that some of the magistracy's original powers and responsibilities should be restored or increased, readers of the book are left with the impression that some of the authors were hard pressed to think of suitable new jobs for JPs, thus appearing to accept from the outset that their future lies on the periphery of the criminal justice system (CJS), leaving the lawyers to command the more interesting work at the centre, as predicted by stipendiary magistrate Peter Badge (see *Chapter 5: Lawyers: Allies or Rivals?*). While the huge increase of district judges (DJs) is briefly mentioned in the book, few contributors seemed prepared to admit the seriousness of its threat to lay justice. Several of them seemed merely to regard an increase in the magistracy's popularity as the answer to its future, by suggesting that JPs need to become more dynamic, more involved with the public and community justice, less remote, better understood etc. Surely, they are missing the point.

It is said that the magistracy already enjoys the confidence of a majority of the adult population, and is perceived to be fair in its conduct, but it is unrealistic to believe that it will ever be able to satisfy all peoples' expectations of justice all the time especially when, as we have already seen, 'justice' can come to mean anything or nothing these days, depending on where you stand. In recent decades, huge efforts have been made, and success achieved, in making the magistracy more independent, more diverse and more professional; but the critics are never satisfied. Among the worst damage that government might cause to the justice system in general, and to the magistracy in particular, would be to base future reforms on the demands of those who naïvely believe that justice is dependent solely on confidence in the courts, and that this would be substantially increased if JPs are encouraged to become even more socially representative than they are already. Yet again, we have to remind ourselves that the primary duty of the magistrates' bench is to act as a judge and jury of summary jurisdiction, not as a specialist tier of the social services.

Typically, some of those searching for reform and new roles for unwanted magistrates flirted with the American concept of 'problem-solving', which envisages specialist courts for domestic violence, drugs, and mental health, alongside intensive alternatives to custody and 'integrated' offender management projects. Under this heading, it is also suggested that JPs might visit and monitor community pay-back projects and drug rehabilitation programmes 'to see how they work, learn more about what happens outside the courtroom, ensure that accountability conditions are met, and show that they care about them'. There is much to condemn in this vague, wishy-washy kind of approach, and there are fortunately few signs at the moment of enthusiasm for it. It also has to be said that American innovations in this field have rarely turned out to be suitable in Britain, and it is quite difficult to visualise magistrates welcoming a situation in which their role is reduced to mundane monitoring, reviewing and visiting. Fobbing-off the magistracy in this way, far from offering improvement or progress, would merely hasten its total redundancy.

Many of the 'fresh' ideas and titles are little more than 'old wine in new bottles'. 'Problem-solving' looks like just another way of describing what magistrates already do in court most of the time; and, in the days of truly local justice, JPs were widely involved with the life of their communities, were often engaged with rehabilitation through their close relationship with the Probation Service, regularly visited local prisons, and their activities on behalf of their fellow citizens were reported weekly in the local press. Few people claimed in those days that they needed to be less remote, better understood or more in touch; and, of course, such ethereal words as 'transparency' and 'accountability' had not yet entered the vocabulary. In any case, it remains questionable whether these fanciful concepts are the key to a successful search for truth or the reduction of crime.

The survey conducted by the MA in connection with its publication on *The Magistracy in the 21st century* was also disappointing in its limited coverage of macro-policy for the future. In parts, it seemed more sensitive to image and communication issues than to the crippling realities of ever-more centralised administration, external control and competition from DJs. However, the survey did offer some encouragement, among which was that:

- Both victims and offenders had few criticisms of the magistrates' courts; there is less cynicism than was thought.
- Plenty of confidence remains in the tradition of lay justice, but public awareness is insufficient.
- JPs are seen as central to public trust in the law; but they need to be given more information about effectiveness of sentences, and to keep victims better informed.
- Local justice should remain local.

- Support for restorative justice is limited.
- Experienced JPs should be allowed to act singly on guilty-plea no-mitigation offences; cases to be 'digitally-managed with access to a legal adviser'.

From all the most recent researches, it becomes clear that the magistracy has nothing of which to be ashamed. It does not need to be apologetic or submissive. A false impression is gained — as so often happens — if undue attention is given to the critics, because surveys have consistently found that those who work in the magistrates' courts have 'confidence' or 'a lot of confidence' in lay justices — the degree varying from 80 per cent (Probation Service) to 65 per cent (police) — while DJs are censured for 'variation in personality', whatever that means. In regard to the lower figure for police confidence, and their readiness to criticise magisterial inconsistency in sentencing, they perhaps need to be reminded of their own inconsistency in the use of 'diversions' from prosecution, which in 2011 ranged nationally from 26 per cent to 49 per cent. Public confidence in the CJS as a whole is said to have fallen, but this view has everything to do with the prejudiced opinions of the media, and little, if anything, to do with the magistracy.

Far more to the point — but boring and un-newsworthy for the media — is the need to focus on ways in which the lay magistracy, its courts and its procedures can be strengthened and enabled to take maximum advantage of digital technology, not as an excuse for radical reform, but as a tool for gradual improvement of the system.

It is misguided to believe that allowing cameras into the courtroom would be a useful way of improving confidence. Televising the decisions made on completion of prominent cases may have a limited place in the future, and cameras may be useful in contests involving children, but American experience (e.g. O J Simpson in 1995) suggests that filming a trial, in whole or in part, is likely to distort impressions, especially if the presence of cameras leads witnesses, defendants or advocates to 'play to the gallery', if the media use edited highlights to colour the evidence, or if viewers try to second-guess the jury. When any such devices are employed, there is a risk that the serious process of justice is replaced by the temptations of sensation and entertainment. Social media, already being manipulated for political and commercial purposes, threaten to have an even more damaging effect on judicial process if used, for instance, to target and influence juries, or to mount campaigns against the judiciary based on 'false news'.

Safeguarding the lay magistracy

Over the years, Lord Chancellors and government ministers have sought to allay fears of grand designs, hidden agendas and 'master plans' for the dismantlement of the magistracy by making splendid references to 'a cornerstone of our society', and 'a great future to which we remain committed', but such words have little value unless backed by deeds. A notable feature of recent years is that, in spite of evident goodwill from almost every quarter, this has not been translated by government into effective support for the magistracy. Quite the opposite. Maintenance of its status as a cherished national asset has been neglected. There may not have been a grand design, and there may be understandable reasons for the reduced workload, but it cannot be denied that there has been a general deterioration of the way in which the magistracy is officially regarded; several major policies which could have helped to restore its position have been shelved or inexplicably delayed, and others allowed to go ahead without heed to serious opposition from those most affected.

Politicians, civil servants and the legal profession should be stopped from continuing to edge the lay magistracy out of existence. More should be done to halt the decline, strengthen the defences and keep JPs firmly at the centre of the national response to crime, anti-social behaviour and family disputes. The nation's wholehearted belief in the institution should be re-affirmed, starting from acceptance that the magistracy is not just admirable, but irreplaceable. Like other national treasures, it should be 'kept in good repair' at almost any cost. There must never be doubts about full government commitment to provision of the relatively modest resources necessary to enable JPs to operate with confidence, free from the enfeeblement of perpetual austerity and a questionable future. Positive action should follow closely on the rhetoric, and emphasis should be given to the continuance of the magistracy as an active source of individual and national pride in public service and collective justice; not as a cherished anachronism, but as a vital part of our modern democracy; an adaptable, evolutionary body of citizens that can continue to be relied upon—inexpensively—'to do justice to all manner of people without fear or favour'.

One method of protecting it from further erosion lies in proofing and impact assessment. Nationally, we already give priority to the conservation of certain critical traditions because they are deemed to be an irreplaceable part of our inheritance, culture or natural environment. Where this status is recognised by government, a presumption is maintained in their favour, which means that 'proofing', including an impact assessment, is a compulsory part of policy-making. As the lay magistracy is of special value to the nation it, too, should be subject to rigorous proofing and in-depth assessment whenever proposals impinging upon its wellbeing or long-term future are being considered, so that the likely impact can be fully taken into account from the outset. This has not always been the rule, with the result that the magistracy has remained alarmingly vulnerable to the depredations of cavalier policy-makers, hell-bent on cutting costs, centralising administration and transferring power. As has been shown, government can—and, on occasions, has—allowed the courts to become paralysed, or so obstructed as to ensure that they cannot function effectively.

Many UK procedures in other spheres specify that regulatory impact assessment (RIA) must be carried out and key questions asked before changes are made to vital elements of national life, public services, natural resources etc. RIA is now a well-established UK government tool for evaluating the costs, benefits and risks of proposed changes in certain business, charity and voluntary sectors. Timing is critical; so it must be applied early in the planning process to identify consequences and encourage full public debate. Proofing is increasingly used where for instance vulnerable wildlife, cherished countryside or ancient buildings are deemed to be in need of protection. Policies and projects are screened for possible damage to ecology and the natural environment; and plans are sometimes conditioned by presumptions in favour of certain courses of action, e.g. preservation of amenity or historical buildings. 'Proofing' may also be required in order to anticipate the effect of future developments, so that action can be taken to avoid any negative or unintended consequences. Occasionally, certain items are simply declared to be non-negotiable or 'ring-fenced', and there is no reason why this principle could not be applied to some features of the magistracy.

There are also numerous examples in international legislation where 'proofing' is enshrined for the protection of certain core elements. For instance, under the European Union Habitats Directive, changes to natural sites are forbidden before proper assessment has been made of the impact on the conservation status of certain species of plants and animals. If proposed changes cannot be modified, there is a procedure for the identification of such objectives as 'purpose' and 'alternatives', and for the measurement of effects. In practice, therefore, proposed changes are much less likely to go ahead if 'spurious purposes', 'satisfactory alternatives', or 'detrimental effects' have been identified in advance.

There is no good reason why impact assessment and proofing should not be applied to the magistracy as standard practice. Therefore, published results should always be available early in the discussion when changes are in mind. If such examinations reveal potential damage to the institution, guidance must be given as to how proposals might be modified so that the core objective—maintaining a strong lay magistracy—remains secure. Shallow 'consultation', followed by disregard of the magistracy's expressed views, should no longer be considered acceptable.

Proofing in the magistracy's case should be particularly aimed to ensure that cost and convenience are always subordinate to the need for, and encouragement of, the strongest possible lay participation. To avoid further damage from careless government action—and to reinforce a common 'duty of care'—specific proofing and RIA should be compulsory in all policy consultations and proposals which could affect the magistracy's future. No excuses should be accepted for attempts to avoid this provision. Politicians and others concerned must be made to think through fully (and publish) their assessment of the long-term consequences of their plans.

In regard to any change in policy, practice or funding, the same searching questions must be asked and answered. For example: Why is it proposed to appoint another unnecessary DJ, costing seven times that of a lay bench, in an area where JP recruitment is strong and the local advisory committee have not requested it? Or, what short-term and long-term impact will this, that or the other have on the operational quality, recruitment, essential strength etc. of the magistracy, locally and nationally? If the answer is deemed likely to be detrimental in any respect: Can the proposal be modified to avoid damage, or should it be abandoned? An example of an adverse proposal would be the suggestion that funding should be linked to the time taken per court case, which could have the effect of forcing magistrates to retire less, give poor consideration to decisions, reduce the quality of justice and make way for even more DJs.

Stop dismantling; start rebuilding

Streamlined procedures and the benefits of micro-technology have already brought laptops on to the bench, halved the average time between charge and trial, reduced the number of hearings, introduced earlier disclosure and identification of real issues, enabled more one-day probation reports and first-hearing sentences, and retained more either-way cases in the lower courts. Remote witness connections, and use by the Crown Prosecution Service of iPad tablets with 'bundling tools' (allowing for easier navigation of case material), are also being used increasingly. Undoubtedly, there is more to come in the use of computers for streamlining the judicial process, and the Internet will continue to change the way courts operate, by giving JPs easier access to information, such as case law, average sentences, guidelines and availability of community punishment and treatment facilities.

The adoption and development of better case management practice has brought huge benefits; however, many cases are still taking longer than 50 years ago. It must not be forgotten that the CJS is primarily about people, their behaviour and the cost of maintaining law and order in a free country, and this can slow things down. Concurrently, we need to question whether we are placing excessive emphasis on buildings, equipment and digital technology at the expense of open justice and vital personal services. We are quite good at reducing the costs of construction, tools and paperwork, but the cost of people — be they lawyer, police officer, prison warder, probation officer, social worker or criminal — continues to rise inexorably. As a result we are sometimes deluded into thinking that we are making progress by closing more courthouses and using cheaper technology, while failing to spend enough on the human requirements for success in early education, crime prevention, effective punishment in the community and treatment of offenders (especially, for example, on release from prison).

The overall cost of lay justice in particular remains a tiny fraction of the total departmental budget. This ought to mean that greater use of JPs is automatically included in any plan to reduce the cost of the CJS. Paradoxically, the last 20 years have shown this not to be so. Instead, arbitrary interpretations of 'efficiency' and 'effectiveness' have been permitted to make magistrates' courts look expensive, inconvenient and dispensable, while cases continue to be sent unnecessarily to the costly Crown Courts. Although not identified as the primary target for reform, lay justice has become a victim by association. When trying to improve the efficiency of the system, the magistracy should not automatically be seen as a problem, but as an important part of a preferred solution inspired by a change in political and official attitudes. JPs have frequently accepted or initiated change, and have shown remarkable adaptability; they do not deserve to be targeted as scapegoats for failure in other parts of the judicial and penal systems. Change by means of constant evolution, not radical reform, should govern progress and development.

Future government policy in regard to the summary justice system must perceive the magistracy, not as the reason for change, but as the primary vehicle for change. Measures needed to strengthen the current position include:

- Establishment of an overall presumption in favour of a lay magistracy.
- 'Proofing', to safeguard the lay element at the heart of our democracy.

- Abolition of either-way offences, and the transfer of all but the most serious cases from the Crown Court to summary courts.
- Implement existing provisions to increase prison maximum sentencing powers from six to twelve months.
- More research, and distribution of more information, on effects of sentences.
- Decentralisation of administration; more involvement of local magistrates.
- Closer, more responsive consultation on CJS changes affecting the magistracy.
- Strengthening of recruitment and retention, especially of younger employed JPs.
- Improvement in conditions attached to absence from work to attend court.
- Phased reduction wherever possible in the number of district judges (magistrates' courts).
- Ending closures, amalgamations and increasingly long-distance travel to courts.

Meanwhile, the magistracy itself must:

- Continue to train conscientiously and act professionally.
- Embrace computer technology.
- Provide consistently competent leadership and chairmanship.
- Support the Magistrates Association as the primary representative body for JPs.
- Uphold high standards of appointment, and reject all forms of political interference.
- Never allow 'diversity' and 'representativeness' to surpass 'suitability'.
- Insist on close adherence to the judicial oath.
- Be sensitive to, but not obsessed by, image.
- Avoid behaviour which brings disrepute.
- Respect and maintain good relations with the senior judiciary.

- Maintain independence in keeping with full membership of the judiciary.
- Foster good relationships with DJs, but work towards reduction in their number.
- Seek closer liaison with the Probation Service.

Questions for the future

In the past, the nation gained much from the leadership of those in the magistracy who understood the significance of dependable public involvement in the judicial system as a major contributor to the character of our democracy. That recognition was the inspiration for their devotion, not only to public service in general, but to training and the increase of magisterial competence in particular. It is tragic now to observe that the beneficial results of their work, experience and advice have been seriously eroded by a flood of thoughtless reform and false economy, leaving a weakened lay magistracy to contemplate an uncertain future in a less efficient system, dominated by lawyers and centralised bureaucracy.

We must still hope that—before too long—there may yet be someone out there with enough foresight, ambition, courage and influence to ensure that one of the nation's greatest institutions is successfully diverted from the path to obscurity. The magistracy has been in a similar position before. In the nineteenth century, following the 1832 Reform Bill, it had to face a similar period of radical change and lost many of its former duties for no better reason than that it was felt to be outdated; but it survived to see an enormous expansion of summary jurisdiction, culminating in the creation of petty sessions in 1849. Meanwhile, for those contemplating the future and a reinvigoration of the lay magistracy in the twenty-first century, it may be helpful to consider some of the following questions:

- Do we really wish to forsake the lay justice principle, which has taken us centuries to develop, and has become the envy of the civilised world? Will we have the wisdom to recognise it as the fairest and most efficient system yet devised?

- Do we wish to see the courts and justice system subject to even more dominance by the legal profession at the expense of public participation?
- How can government attitudes towards the magistracy be changed from frequently negative or indifferent to sustained positive? How can official support for it be made as consistent as that given to the jury by the legal profession?
- Why should JPs themselves, rather than the government, have to bear the burden of promoting the virtues of the lay magistracy?
- How will it benefit the future of the magistracy and quality of justice if JPs 'communicate better with the public', become more 'diverse', 'representative', 'active, accessible and engaged'? Who is to measure such aspirations, and how relevant are they?
- Do we wish to abandon the great British tradition of voluntary, unpaid public service, manifest at its best in the office of JP?
- Are we prepared to continue seeing expensive DJs kept in employment, while inexpensive JPs are sent home when court lists collapse?
- The cost of a trial by a district judge is seven times that of a trial by a bench of three JPs. Why therefore do we persist in appointing unnecessary and costly DJs; and why is their number not reduced in the same proportion as JPs in response to decreasing workload?
- In order to avoid unjustified fears that a bench of experienced JPs might become 'elite' or 'too professional' if allowed to sit more often, would we rather see them replaced by yet more expensive, single lawyers?
- Are we content meekly to accept shortages of JPs in some areas without first spending more on exploring every possible way of increasing recruitment to the lay bench?
- Will we ensure that 'diversity' and 'representativeness' are never allowed to surpass 'suitability' as criteria for recruitment of new JPs?

- The average cost (excluding legal expenses) of a Crown Court trial is nine times that of a magistrates' court. Up to 70,000 cases a year could be transferred from the Crown Court to the magistrates' courts — a relatively simple way to save money. Why therefore do we persist in denying the magistracy increased sentencing powers and permanent transfer of either-way offences from the higher court?
- How can high standards be maintained while keeping costs down?
- Will we have the good sense to search more seriously for solutions which reinforce the lay magistracy and the quality of justice with which it is associated?
- In future, will we actively resist the temptation to take easy, short-term, expedient decisions that weaken the magistracy, threaten its independence, and hasten its collapse?
- Will we continue to take major policy decisions in the justice sector without properly considering the long-term effects on the wellbeing of the magistracy?
- Crime and lawlessness are eating away the fabric of our democracy and costing our economy billions of pounds unnecessarily. What prevents us from recognising the net benefit that would accrue from spending more attention and money on this sector in general, and on prevention in particular?
- As a nation, we are proud of our reputation for fair and transparent justice. How is it therefore that we can so easily accept that more than half a million cases a year are diverted from the courts to the police, acting as prosecutor and judge, issuing cautions and penalties 'behind closed doors', without any mechanism for accountability?
- Is it really necessary to spend time and resources on trying to educate the public about the magistracy, merely because surveys suggest 'lack of confidence' in the justice system, or to mollify critics who are never likely to be satisfied?

- Are we going to remain silent while centralisation and regionalization continue to destroy the character of the magistracy and what remains of local justice?
- Do we really wish to see the lay magistracy further demoralised, diminished and eventually destroyed as a result of persistent replacement by DJs, more solo decision-making, and an end to voluntary unpaid magisterial service?
- The lay justice system is outstanding for its low cost, transparency, independence and lack of corruption. Why allow such a trustworthy institution to be enfeebled? Why destroy it? Why not do more to strengthen it and encourage its use?

My overall answer to these questions is unequivocal. The nation should be encouraged above all to rebuild faith and pride in the triple magistrates' model; this should be the default system, not only as the fairest and most acceptable form of summary jurisdiction, but also as a safeguard against the corrupt and inefficient forms of mono justice practised in so many other countries, and now increasingly in our own. Substitution by professional lawyers and empowered officials may seem smart, practical and economical but, in the context of British judicial and democratic history, it can only be viewed as a massive backward step. We must not allow ourselves to be deceived into devaluing, diminishing or discarding such a priceless asset.

CHAPTER 12

Voice of the Magistracy

'I always pay great attention to the Magistrates Association'.
Sir Patrick Mayhew, Home Office Minister

- Pioneer of training and guidelines
- Influence and reputation

Pioneer of training and guidelines

The Magistrates Association—the only independent voice of the lay magistracy—was founded 100 years ago to represent and support justices of the peace (JPs), while promoting high standards and sound administration of the law; it should not be confused with government sponsored and financed organizations claiming to speak for the magistracy, nor with the Council of District Judges (Magistrates' Courts). The majority of JPs belong to the MA, which has had charitable status since 1968 as a provider of training and guidance for lay justices, and of information about the magistracy for the public and media; it is also closely concerned with matters such as recruitment and retention of magistrates, working conditions and relationships with the senior judiciary, courts service management, and membership communications.

Nineteen-twenty was a notable year in the history of the magistracy. On 1st January, the first six women JPs were appointed, and in the following October the realisation that magistrates needed to be trained and better informed was the incentive for a conference of over 200 justices in the London Guildhall which led to the foundation of the MA. An inaugural meeting was held in the following year. Their foresight probably ensured the future of the lay magistracy for at least the next century. With the invaluable help of the justices' clerks, the association quickly became the leading organizer of training meetings, courses and conferences, a role which it maintained up to and beyond the introduction of compulsory training in 1966.

At one time, Magistrates' Courts Committees (MCCs) and the MA, together with the justices' clerks, were the chief providers of training for all JPs (whether they were members of the MA or not), and the association received substantial grants from government—amounting to between 15 per cent and 50 per cent of the cost—for this purpose. Regular, well-attended training conferences and courses were organized by branches throughout England and Wales but, at the end of the 1990s, this responsibility was assumed by the national Judicial Studies Board (later the Judicial College). By 2003, the JSB had become the principal organizer and source of material for magistrates' training, and the MA's contribution inevitably declined; however, while government has steadily reduced its support, the association has maintained a significant (unsubsidised) role, especially through *The Magistrate*, in helping and encouraging JPs to keep up-to-date and become more proficient, and in assisting the development of law and practice affecting the magistrates' courts. More than 96 per cent of members say that they consider the provision of up-to-date information now to be the main purpose of the association.

Membership of the MA, which was only 2,000 in 1933, grew steeply thereafter. It was 16,354 by 1970, 24,578 on 30th June 1982, and reached a peak of around 30,000 in the 1990s, when it represented more than 90 per cent of lay justices. The number has since been halved as workload has been reduced and fewer JPs appointed. This, in turn, has challenged the MA's role, restricted its income and activity, necessitated a few uncomfortable management decisions, reduced branch meetings attendance, and increased the need to examine internal costs and services. Such changes are necessary every now and again but, after a few decades, some of them have a way of returning full circle. Thus some people in both government and magistracy are beginning to suggest that the MA might resume a significant role in training. *Plus ça change, plus c'est la même chose.*

Implementation of the Charities Act 2011 had a profound effect on the governance of the MA. It confirmed that, as a charity, all its council members assumed the duties and responsibilities of charity trustees, an undesirable position analogous to company directors under common law. This was contrary to the provisions of the association's former charter and bye-laws, making it necessary to amend both in due course. Until then, the national council of 100 or so elected members from its branches was the governing body, but the Act made it necessary for this function to be passed to a small board of trustees, thus depriving the council and its executive committee of responsibility for control and management, and leaving it in reality with no more than a consultative and advisory role at a time when the branches were seeking closer involvement. Instead, the ordinary membership was likely to become more distant, and this had to be compensated in the end by change to a one-member-one-vote system of electing national officers and trustees—an unfortunate development, in my view.

To its credit, the MA has generally managed to avoid becoming a reactive, self-interest or lobby organization. Like the justices it represents, it has simply got on with the job of serving the institution and enabling JPs to do their work as competently as possible. Without the grants in return for its contribution to national training and consultation, it has had increasingly to rely on income from members and investments for its livelihood, while ensuring that it remains truly sovereign and free from political or commercial influence. Fortunately it has been prudently led and managed over the years, so that it has been able to preserve its independence and influence through difficult and changing times.

In spite of limitations, the MA can continue to take pride in the significant contribution it makes, not only to the training, support and increased 'professionalism' of the lay magistracy, but also to the development of sentencing practice, court procedure, and numerous initiatives designed to improve summary criminal justice, youth and family courts regimes. Specific efforts on behalf of its members have included beneficial adjustments to travelling and subsistence allowances for JPs, and success in persuading the Lord Chancellor (LC) that immunity from civil actions enjoyed by salaried judges should apply equally, if not more so, to unpaid

JPs—a matter which came to a head when £3,200 costs were awarded against Wareham magistrates following a 1989 High Court decision.

It has been said more than once that if the association did not exist, it would quickly have to be invented; without it, the magistracy would undoubtedly have found it more difficult to survive the onslaughts of politics and bureaucracy during the last 50 years. This reflects, not only its obvious role in representing JPs, but also its dedication for 100 years to public service and the principle of independent, local lay justice. It has also come to be respected by successive governments as a reliable consultative body, a position recognised by the grant of a Royal Charter in 1962, when the membership had reached 14,600.

Among its most far-sighted decisions (after a successful £75,000 appeal in 1968) was the freehold purchase for £50,000 of 28 Fitzroy Square, an elegant listed (Grade 2) Georgian property in London W1. This served as the MA's headquarters for the next 50 years, before being sold for about £5m in 2017. Other notable houses in the same terrace include No. 29, the home of George Bernard Shaw from 1887 to 1898, Virginia Woolf from 1907 to 1911; and Prime Minister Robert Cecil (later to become Lord Salisbury) lived at No. 21 for some years.

The association pioneered the issue to members of sentencing guidelines in a commendable move to increase consistency of approach and confidence in the CJS. In the 1980s, with the approval of the Lord Chancellor (LC) and Lord Chief Justice (LCJ), and in addition to occasional guidance from the Court of Appeal, it published its first *Suggestions for Traffic Offence Penalties,* applicable to first offenders of average means, and accompanied by a strong injunction that the list was on no account to be used as a tariff. These were followed in March 1989 by 'starting points', including advice on measurement of seriousness, for over 20 other offences, an initiative which was headlined by the *Daily Mail* as 'a magistrates' guide to good sentencing, a new code that will make penalties firm and fair'. At first, some benches ignored the advice, and others (including some clerks) did not accept the guidelines at all. Later, they were extended beyond motoring offences, and published in partnership with the Justices' Clerks' Society under the title of *Magistrates' Court Sentencing Guidelines.* These were widely used until the creation of the national Sentencing Advisory Panel in 1998, which was followed by the Sentencing Guidelines Council (under the 2003 Criminal Justice Act), and finally by the Sentencing Council in 2010.

A further notable MA achievement, aimed at promoting public awareness of the magistracy and demystifying the justice system, is the Magistrates in the Community (MiC) scheme, incorporating the national mock trial competition. This was developed by the association from its Schools Project in the late-1980s, through which unpaid JPs give additional voluntary service, with the tacit support of the Ministry of Justice and the ancillary agencies, to promote and explain the work of the magistracy to schools, colleges, community groups, journalists and employers; nearly 250,000 adults and children are reached in this way each year. Talks and information are given on such subjects as the type of cases handled, how JPs are appointed, and how guilt, innocence and sentence are decided. This venture has been remarkably successful in achieving its original purpose: 'to raise community awareness of the magistracy and its work in the courts, thereby increasing respect and confidence in justices and the criminal justice system'. However, it is not unreasonable to question why the nation remains content to leave the magistracy as the sole champion of its own cause. Such self-promotion ought not to be necessary. One may ask: Do we rely on unpaid part-time doctors to run schemes during their free time to boost respect and confidence in themselves and the National Health Service? Of course not.

In the 1960s, the LC was responsible for the magistracy, but the courts were administered by the Home Office (HO) through the MCCs. The 1971 Courts Act paved the way for the creation of an enlarged Lord Chancellor's Department (LCD) with increased responsibilities, a development with which the magistracy felt more comfortable. Therefore, as chairman of the MA in 1990, I took the opportunity to ask Prime Minister Margaret Thatcher to transfer total responsibility for the magistrates' courts from the HO to the LCD, because we felt increasingly (not least because of the Le Vay *Scrutiny of the Magistrates' Courts*) that the HO showed less respect for our independence, and less sensitivity to the needs of the justice system as a whole. However, it is now clear that the LCD in the end was no more helpful to the future of the magistracy than the HO; true or not, it is usually believed that the Treasury has the last word anyway.

A 2012 article in *Criminal Law and Justice* Weekly touched on these events in describing the growth of the MA and its contribution to the development of training for magistrates. It said,

> 'From the late 1980s onwards, the officers of the Association adopted a more pro-active stance towards their role, and it was their skilful footwork that took the magistrates out of the somewhat hostile care of the Home Office to the much more welcoming shelter of the Lord Chancellor's Department—a move which made a good deal of sense. From then on, most of the work of the MA was positive. The lobbying skills of its officers were most apparent in the passing of the Courts Act 2003, whereby they ensured that the organization had representation on many of the new groups being set up by the Act. They also helped to change the wording of the legislation, to make it abundantly clear that justices' clerks and their teams of legal advisers were truly independent when offering counsel to JPs'.

Despite these careful moves, it has to be said that the years since the formation of the unified courts administration have not been easy for magistrates grappling with the reality of lost self-governance and the centralised bureaucracy of HM Courts and Tribunals Service.

Some observers have reckoned that the last 20 years of the twentieth century marked a high point for both the association and the magistracy as a whole. Within a few years after that, further changes in the newly-formed MoJ foreshadowed a decline. More out-of-court disposals, court closures and cost-cutting followed, and insult was added to injury by a largely unjustified increase of district judges, which undoubtedly contributed to a break-up in the cohesiveness of the magistracy, and to falls in the number of JPs and MA membership.

Although it was claimed that the MA and Central Council of Magistrates' Courts Committees were among those who had agreed to support more centralisation as early as the 1960s, my recollection is that what emerged by 2005 was far from the vision held by the association 50 years earlier. The MA saw little point in the continuance of the Central

Council itself; however, it is unlikely that either organization would have agreed to see it replaced by another centralised body composed of no JPs at all—at least, not without strong guarantees in regard to full participation in local management decisions and retention of links with the senior judiciary.

In 1990, the full implications of the Le Vay *Scrutiny of the Magistrates' Courts* had yet to become clear. Even though initially the MA expressed deep apprehension about some of the proposals, neither it nor Le Vay himself envisaged that the government would exploit them to such an extent as to nationalise the whole courts administration within six years, and bring to an end more than half a century of devolved, relatively successful, control. It would have been pleasing if the association had found it possible to save the lay magistracy from the thoughtless treatment it subsequently received at the hands of successive governments, but in reality—and without the wholehearted support of politicians, legal profession or media—it is unlikely that unilateral resistance could have made much difference to the final outcome. The total demise of the lay magistracy would indeed be a national calamity, but it is not JPs themselves nor the MA that can save the nation from the consequences of government folly.

A further major change affecting the MA almost abolished the ancient title of the politically-appointed LC. It took place following the 2005 Constitutional Reform Act, enshrining judicial independence in law for the first time. Eventually, the LC's title was retained (including shared responsibility with the LCJ for the appointment of magistrates), but he ceased to be speaker of the House of Lords and head of the judiciary, the upper house having ceded its judicial functions in the meantime to the newly-formed independent Supreme Court. All these innovations had the effect of binding the magistracy more closely to the judiciary under the LCJ, so it was logical that in 2005 the MA decided that he should replace the LC as its president *ex-officio*.

Almost invariably, LCJs and LCs, whether as president of the MA or not, have personally encouraged direct access to them by MA chairmen, and given generous support whenever needed. I recall how keen we and Deputy Lord Chief Justice Watkins were in 1989 to ensure that this link—between the country's highest officer of state, the head of the judiciary and the senior representative of the lay magistracy—was recognised and strengthened, so as to make it even easier to exchange views on matters of mutual concern. It was therefore agreed that a High Court judge should be designated to liaise with the association, but that he or she should not be regarded as a liaison judge for the magistracy as a whole, in case that might inhibit direct communication. Any other channel inserted between the most senior members of the judiciary, particularly the LCJ as MA president, and the chairman of the MA should be condemned.

Described by a former MA chairman as a 'disastrous decision', one such superfluous organization—a national bench chairmen's forum—was created by the government in 2004, and encouraged initially to work under the MA umbrella. 'Key tasks' were assigned to it by the LC, but these amounted in fact to little more than the classic ingredients of a 'talk shop'. Inevitably, marriage with the MA ended in divorce, leaving the forum to continue without purpose, other than as a puppet of the courts service and MoJ through which to 'divide and rule' the magistracy. Such a government-sponsored and financed consultee is not only costly and potentially divisive, it dilutes the voice of the magistracy as a whole, and the contribution of the MA in particular.

Following the constitutional reform, it is the LCJ rather than the LC who now carries the main responsibility of representing the judges to media and public, but it would be most unfortunate if the judiciary's embrace of the magistracy were ever to be so restrictive as to deny chairmen of the MA the right and freedom to speak separately on matters relating to the lay magistracy, without the prior approval of 'higher authority'. In this respect it needs to be accepted that there still exists a valid distinction between lawyers, bound by the rules and customs of their profession, and unconstricted lay JPs. Both are members of the judiciary, but the justices comprise a discrete constituency whose leaders must be trusted and responsible enough to be permitted freedom of speech.

Influence and reputation

The MA has sometimes been portrayed as 'a highly effective pressure group' which, although perhaps flattering, is not how it would wish to describe itself. It does, however, take its independence and image seriously; it is always wary of being bounced into making decisions on the hoof, and takes care to ensure 'that its expressed views are cautious, measured, balanced, reflective and responsible' (1998 MA Briefing Paper on policy principles). It is easy to over-state its influence on official policy, but it has earned consistent respect over the years for its advice to government on fundamental issues. A good example of this was the association's reaction to the 1990 Criminal Justice Bill, when *The Times* reported that 'In the face of strong opposition from the influential 27,000-member MA, ministers are expected to drop or modify plans to make parents pay their children's fines and attend court ... and to overhaul proposals that courts should ignore offenders' previous convictions when imposing sentence'. In this connection, a Home Office spokesman agreed that the MA is regarded as 'a very influential body ... anything it has said will be taken very seriously'.

Praise also came from the Minister of State at the Home Office, Sir Patrick Mayhew, in connection with the 1984 Police and Criminal Evidence Bill, when he said in Parliament, 'I always pay great attention to the Magistrates Association'. There were also warm words from a House of Commons Home Affairs Committee report which referred to 'the high quality of evidence submitted by the MA to parliamentary committees'. It is important that the association should be strong and intellectually well-equipped enough to raise issues in Parliament on its own account.

Governments constantly introduce plans and proposals for changes in the law, procedure and administration of the courts. The MA is usually consulted in the early stages; even then, the periods allowed for this are sometimes unreasonably short. A large amount of the association's time and resources are devoted to debating relevant sections of parliamentary Bills and other measures affecting JPs and their work. Not infrequently, the association finds itself having to express strong views on penal matters and other government policies, magistrates' courts and the administration of the law, and it is right that it should do so. But, unlike almost every other organization associated with the justice system (including some lawyers), it has never sought to behave like a trade union, trying to justify its members' existence or protect their jobs, nor to advance its opinions through crude threats of 'industrial action', however strongly provoked. Moreover, repeated objections to humdrum issues like re-organization and reduction in status can be counter-productive and open to a charge of self-interest which the magistracy is obviously keen to avoid. In the absence of numerous loyal followers, JPs can only rely for support on self-evident worth, integrity and the high reputation of the MA.

While 'professional' organizations in the health, education and legal sectors may try to obstruct government proposals and bring their respective services to a standstill by withdrawing their labour and bringing their members on to the streets, the MA would never contemplate using its influence in this way — not even over the closure of yet more courthouses. When it speaks, its views are based on principle, not on the imperative to protect the livelihood of its unpaid members. This virtually guaranteed devotion has sometimes led governments and administrators to take unfair advantage of JPs' commitment and to undervalue the importance of their services to the nation. The result, all too often, is not open disagreement and public demonstration, but the dignified and silent loss of experienced justices, driven to make the protest of last resort: resignation from the bench. The reluctance to behave in an irresponsible manner has also made it particularly difficult at times for the MA to react effectively against contentious changes which enable others to shape decisions to their own convenience rather than that of the magistracy.

The aim of the MA is always to retain a sense of responsibility, and to rely on the power of persuasion and good argument to encourage changes of mind. It is a regrettable fact, however, that while paying lip-service to so-called 'consultation' and 'careful consideration' of adverse views, governments still ignore logical opinions which conflict with their ambitions, pursue their original intentions regardless, and are not unwilling to side-line the MA if it suits them. When this happens, the magistracy, by the nature of its being, usually has no option in the end but to fall into line. This has occurred too often for comfort in the last 50 years, when ill-considered centralisation, amalgamation of benches, closure of courthouses, the dismantling of local summary justice, the insertion of unnecessary DJs, and the creation of quasi-independent bodies 'to represent the magistracy', have been among the most contentious issues. It is difficult to avoid the impression that things might have been ordered differently and better if the government had not been able to rely on the loyalty of the MA and the ultimate compliance of the magistracy. Moreover, it can reasonably be claimed that, far from attracting increased respect and consideration, this support is too often taken for granted.

The *Criminal Law and Justice Weekly* once described the MA as

> 'a somewhat genteel organization, very conscious of not being a trade union and inclined to shelter both behind its charitable status and the limitation imposed on it by Royal Charter ... That is not to say that from time-to-time there have not been formidable chairmen of the Association who provided skilful leadership in times of difficulty. Those who did so usually gained their ends by working behind the scenes'.

Certainly, the MA's charitable status has sometimes proved to be a frustrating handicap when more forthright lobbying was needed to combat the magistracy's adversaries. History may show that it could sometimes have been more robust in resisting the disempowerment and re-organization of the magistracy by successive governments; but, rightly or wrongly, it has always preferred to act responsibly and direct its activities primarily towards 'promotion of sound administration of the law and justice, the education and instruction of magistrates, the treatment of offenders and the prevention of crime'.

A further indication of how much the MA's contribution to discussions on proposed legislation is appreciated has been the noticeable increase over the years in requests from the government for its views. Other bodies were, and are, also keen to have its ear, but the extra work, some of which is not always strictly connected with its purposes, threatened at one time to become excessive; for instance, discussing Russian judicial reform, supporting a centre for women in Worcester, and becoming involved with 'co-ordination of government initiatives' were hardly relevant to its aims. In 1989, the editor of *Justice of the Peace* wrote,

'It remains something of a miracle that the officers, working with the council and various committees of the MA, and backed by a comparatively small headquarters staff, can discharge all these functions, as well as using their undoubted skills to promote the aims of the Association and the work of the magistracy through regular public appearances and the use of the sophisticated organs of the press, radio and TV … the organization appears to be as committed as ever in providing a strong national voice for this country's magistrates'.

Others have not always been so complimentary. One of the most iniquitous inventions of the modern age is 'blogging', whereby anonymous and mischievous users of the internet can write with impunity the most scurrilous things about all and sundry. Not surprisingly therefore, the MA was among several organizations in 2010 that attracted the attention of a sour, disenchanted blogger, who described the association as 'a top-heavy organization that has reached its sell-by date, (run by) a coterie at the top, exposed as a hard-working, self-opinionated group of aged JPs (who) do not represent the rank and file'.

Sometimes, the day-to-day experience of magistrates in England and Wales throws up anomalies in the law, problems in procedure or situations which oblige them to pass invidious sentences (e.g. unit fines and court charges). The association is an ideal channel through which these can quickly be brought to government attention, and is well-placed to initiate proposals for alterations to the law. In many ways, this is the MA at its best. At times, it makes specific suggestions for change or the introduction of new offences (e.g. use of hand-held phones while driving) and, it has to be admitted, a few members have occasionally been tempted to use it as a route for the advancement of personal views on road traffic issues, social problems or penal reform. A few motions proposed at MA annual meetings over the years reflect this, but the greatest care has to be exercised when deciding whether or not such matters should be taken further; however compelling the reasons, the association must not allow itself to look like, or be used as, a campaigning organization or lobby for good causes.

The 20-year period between 1970 and 1990 provided examples of subjects covered by the 130 motions proposed at MA annual meetings: 36 per cent were about sentencing, 22 per cent legal, 16 per cent juvenile (youth), 14 per cent executive (admin.), eight per cent road traffic, three per cent domestic (family) and one per cent licensing. Eighty-three per cent of the motions were carried (usually by a large majority), and 17 per cent rejected. Among the former were proposals that (a) the maximum prison sentence available to JPs on any one charge should be increased to twelve months, (b) the salaries and conditions of service for, and resources available to, probation officers should be improved, (c) minor indictable offences should be tried summarily unless the lower court decides otherwise, (d) co-ordinated action should be taken to reduce delays in magistrates' courts, and e) that the oath should be replaced by a simple promise to tell the truth, failure to do so being perjury. It is notable that, after more than 30 years, three of these requests have been ignored or not implemented, and two remain only partially realised.

The 'lost' resolutions during this period included suggestions that licensing should be retained by justices; that community service should be reserved for those at risk of receiving a prison sentence; that the serious nature of an offence should in itself be a sufficient ground for refusing bail; and that there should be substantial increases in the maximum penalties for insecure loads and over-loaded commercial vehicles. Again, it is clear from this small sample that many matters of high concern to magistrates up to 50 years ago are still with us. It is also interesting to note that in those days it was common for MA AGMs to debate up to eight resolutions at one meeting; in more recent years, far fewer have come forward, and the association has sometimes struggled to find any that are suitable. Is this a sign of declining MA influence, of futility or of apathy?

It is not unusual for public bodies, commercial organizations and charitable groups to seek meetings with the MA for reasons which can vary from hopes of persuading courts to be more lenient towards motorists and women, to requests for a more punitive attitude towards health and safety offenders, vandals and fly-tippers. Again, the MA has to be cautious in responding to obvious attempts to influence the judicial mind, and it always has to distinguish between approaches which may compromise its neutrality, and those that are offered with the genuine intention of assisting magistrates to make intelligent decisions. It is part of a JP's duty to keep himself well-informed; and one of the lay magistracy's great strengths is that, in spite of repeated claims to the contrary, most justices are closely in touch with everyday life. As a result, they not only possess an abundance of common sense, but are also wise enough to seek opportunities of increasing knowledge relevant to their work. Provided all parties appreciate from the start the importance of preserving magisterial impartiality, it is not improper (it may even add to achievement of better justice) to allow occasional discussion with selected organizations.

Appendix to Chapter 12: Chairmen of the Magistrates Association (1962–2020)

1962–1970	The Rt Hon. Lord Merthyr KBE PC
1970–1976	Sir William Addison DL
1976–1979	J B Edwards
1979–1981	Sir Thomas Skyrme KCVO CB CBE DL
1981–1984	Lady Ralphs CBE DL
1984–1987	Dr Douglas Acres CBE
1987–1990	John Hosking CBE DL
1990–1993	Joyce Rose CBE DL
1993–1996	Rosemary Thomson CBE
1996–1999	Anne Fuller OBE
1999–2002	Harry Mawdsley OBE DL
2002–2005	Rachel Lipscomb OBE
2005–2008	Cindy Barnett OBE
2008–2011	Dr John Thornhill OBE
2011–2013	John Fassenfelt OBE
2013–2015	Richard Monkhouse
2015–2017	Malcolm Richardson OBE
2017–2020	John Bache

Some Key Sources

Auld, Lord Justice Robin Ernest (2001), 'Review of the Criminal Courts of England and
    Wales', now in the Ministry of Justice archives.

Le Vay, Julian (1989), *Magistrates' Courts Service: Scrutiny Report,* HMSO.

HM Treasury/Casey, Louise (2010), 'Ending the Justice Waiting Game: A Plea
    for Common Sense', see: https://www.ourwatch.org.uk/uploads/pub_res/
    EndingTheJusticeWaitingGame_LouiseCaseyReport3Nov2010.pdf

Dickinson, Sally (ed.) (2012), *The Magistracy at the Crossroads,* Waterside Press.

Every Child Matters: see https://www.gov.uk/government/publications/every-child-matters

Falconer, Lord (2003), *Local Business, Local Justice,* Department of Constitutional Affairs.
    (2005), *Supporting Magistrates to Provide Justice,* Cm 6681, Department of
        Constitutional Affairs.

Hailsham, Lord (1973), 'Selecting Magistrates', Speech given at the AGM of the MA.

Hitchens, Peter (2003), *A Brief History of Crime,* Atlantic Books.

Home Office (1992), *A New Framework for Local Justice.*

Judicial Studies Board (now College) (2004), *Equal Treatment Bench Book.*

LCD (2003), *Local Business, Local Justice.*

Magistrates Association, *The Magistrate.*
    (1990), *Magistrates' Court Sentencing Guidelines.*

Morgan R and Russell N (commissioned 2000), *The Judiciary in the Magistrates' Courts,*
    A report for the Home Office and LCD. See https://webarchive.nationalarchives.
    gov.uk/20110218143303/http://rds.homeoffice.gov.uk/rds/pdfs/occ-judiciary.pdf

Runciman (1993), 'Report of the Royal Commission on Criminal Justice',
    Cm 2263, see https://www.gov.uk/government/publications/
    report-of-the-royal-commission-on-criminal-justice

Sentencing Council (before 2010 Sentencing Guidelines Council) (various years),
    Sentencing Guidelines issued for use in magistrates' courts.

Skyrme, Sir Thomas (1991), *History of the Justices of the Peace,* Barry Rose.

'Venne Report' (1996), Proceedings of the Lord Chancellor's Department 1995 Working
    Party on *The Role of the Stipendiary Magistrate,* written for the LCD by the Centre
    for Criminal Justice Studies, University of Leeds.

Index

The Magistracy at the Crossroads

Edited by David Faulkner, assisted by Sally Dickinson.
With a Foreword by Lord Dholakia.

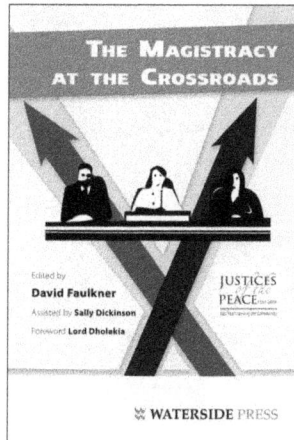

'A most impressive book to help shape the magistracy of the 21st century'—
John Fassenfelt, Chairman of The Magistrates Association (2011–2013)

'A highly readable collection and carries some radical ideas
about what the magistracy might have to offer in the seventh
century of its existence'— *The London Advocate*

Paperback & ebook | ISBN 978-1-904380-86-3 | 2012 | 176 pages

www.WatersidePress.co.uk

Essential Magistrates' Courts Law
Howard Riddle CBE and Judge Robert Zara

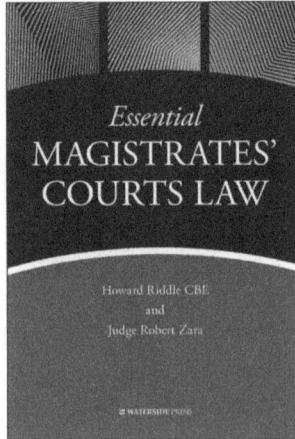

'Readable and blissfully concise... There are some nuggets for every reader, however much we might think we know... An excellent addition to the bookshelf at a modest price'— *The Law Society Gazette*

'A must-read for any judge, magistrate or lawyer practising in the magistrates' courts. This book will become the reference book to carry to court … We thoroughly recommend it to all new judges, deputies and magistrates'— *Emma Arbuthnot, Senior District Judge (Chief Magistrate) for England and Wales; John Bache, Chairman of the Magistrates Association; Duncan Webster, Chairman, Magistrates' Leadership Executive*

'A very clear, succinct and practical guide which would be of great value to a pupil or junior practitioner finding their feet'— *Anna Banfield, BPP*

'How useful your book is and how clear and well written I have found it. Undoubtedly an extremely useful resource'— *Tom Lees JP, Greater Manchester*

Paperback & ebook | ISBN 978-1-909976-68-9 | 2019 | 254 pages

www.WatersidePress.co.uk

www.ingramcontent.com/pod-product-compliance
Lightning Source LLC
Chambersburg PA
CBHW032347280326
41935CB00008B/481